REASSESSING
PEARL HARBOR

REASSESSING PEARL HARBOR

Scapegoats, a False Hero and the Myth of Surprise Attack

James Johns

To Melissa Globensky my very dear friend who actually makes it possible for me to hear what's going on in the world.

McFarland & Company, Inc., Publishers

Jefferson, North Carolina

All photographs are from the author's
collection unless noted otherwise.

LIBRARY OF CONGRESS CATALOGUING-IN-PUBLICATION DATA

Names: Johns, James, 1934– author.
Title: Reassessing Pearl Harbor : scapegoats, a false hero
and the myth of surprise attack / James Johns.
Description: Jefferson, North Carolina : McFarland & Company, Inc.,
Publishers, 2017. | Includes bibliographical references and index.
Identifiers: LCCN 2017002196 | ISBN 9781476668277
(softcover : acid free paper) ∞
Subjects: LCSH: Pearl Harbor (Hawaii), Attack on, 1941. | Kimmel,
Husband Edward, 1882–1968. | Short, Walter Campbell, 1880–1949. |
MacArthur, Douglas, 1880–1964.
Classification: LCC D767.92 .J627 2017 | DDC 940.54/26693—dc23
LC record available at https://lccn.loc.gov/2017002196

BRITISH LIBRARY CATALOGUING DATA ARE AVAILABLE

ISBN (print) 978-1-4766-6827-7
ISBN (ebook) 978-1-4766-2833-2

Front cover: insets, left to right Walter Short (U.S. Department of the Interior),
General Douglas Macarthur, 1945 (Library of Congress), Admiral
Husband E. Kimmel, Commander in Chief of the U.S. Pacific Fleet
(Office for Emergency Management, Office of War Information),
background burning and damaged ships at Pearl Harbor, December 7, 1941,
left to right: USS Arizona, USS Tennessee and USS West Virginia
(Department of the Navy, Naval Photographic Center)

Printed in the United States of America

McFarland & Company, Inc., Publishers
Box 611, Jefferson, North Carolina 28640
www.mcfarlandpub.com

For

Ensign E. Tom Child
Torpedo Officer, USS *Cassin* (DD 372)
Pearl Harbor
7 December 1941

Ensign Barron W. Chandler
Executive Officer, PT 34, Motor Torpedo Boat Squadron 3
Manila Bay
8 December 1941

and

First Lieutenant Lars C. Jensen
45th Infantry, Philippine Scouts
Ft. McKinley, Luzon
8 December 1941

Table of Contents

Preface

November 25, 1941, was the thirteenth day before the attack on Pearl Harbor. Several things happened on that day. The Kido Butai departed the Kurile Islands. A secret White House conference was convened to determine how the Japanese could be maneuvered into attacking first, hopefully without Americans suffering too much damage. And on that day, the Vacant Sea Order was issued, which cleared the way for the Japanese attack force.

On November 26, knowing that the Japanese were on their way, FDR ordered that the *modus vivendi*, which would have provided a diplomatic cooling-off period, be replaced with the Ten Point Note which, in essence, demanded war. And on November 27, 1941, the eleventh day before the Pearl Harbor attack, the weak and ambiguous war warnings were sent to Pacific commands which, compared to what Washington actually knew, didn't warn of a thing. Even by then, the American public had no conception of how drastically their lives would change in just ten more days.

As a young boy, I had no idea how these events would shape history, but I knew family members and close family friends who would become veterans of Pearl Harbor, Bataan, and Bulkeley's PT boats, some of whom did not return. After serving a career in the military, and with fifty years of aviation experience, my interest in the Pearl Harbor attack and the fall of the Philippines came naturally.

Throughout my career, I have aligned myself with numerous organizations whose exploits have held my interest. Those organizations include the Fourth Armored Division Association, the Philippine Scouts Heritage Society, the Army Aviation Association of America, the Eighth Air Force Historical Society of Minnesota, and the Minnesota Aviation Hall of Fame. My ten years of research for this book also includes countless interviews with World War II veterans, many of whom were Pearl Harbor and Bataan survivors; documentary research at the National Archives in Washington, D.C.; correspondence with the Japanese Fighter Pilots' Association in Tokyo; and base heritage records in Hawaii.

One cannot count the number of books that have been written about Pearl Harbor, as well as the fall of the Philippines in 1942. Many credible historians have specialized in various aspects of these events, but because the attacks on Pearl Harbor, the Philippines, Malaya, and the Indies were all timed to the minute by the Japanese, it is important to report all of these events simultaneously as part of Japan's major operation. What went wrong for them actually provided the Allies with a warning and time to prepare, an opportunity that was ignored by General MacArthur.

Given that the attacks on Pearl Harbor and the Philippines were so intertwined, through similarities, contradictions, and devastation, it is very disconcerting to consider the disparity in how the Hawaiian and Philippine commanders were treated after the fact.

Millions of Americans sacrificed much during the war. Two of those Americans, Admiral Husband Kimmel and General Walter Short, who had dedicated their lives in service to their country, were also *sacrificed* to meet the political motivations of the day, while General Douglas MacArthur was actually rewarded. I want readers to know that the real story is not always as it seems. While some will attempt to conceal the facts to suit the purposes of a few, those who open their minds to the underlying themes will discover a story that uncovers the power and politics at play—the power and politics that really opened the door to war.

Although I originally had no intentions of publishing this manuscript, I have been fascinated with Pearl Harbor since the age of seven. After transcribing my work, Marilyn Curski, a World War II enthusiast, convinced me that perhaps a reminder was due Americans of the actual events surrounding the Pearl Harbor disaster. Over the next several years, she helped me with countless additions, revisions, and editing, for which I am very grateful.

And to my wife, Dorothea, I owe my deepest gratitude for her patience and all the sacrifices she made on my behalf throughout this entire project. Without her support and understanding, it may have otherwise wound up buried in a closet.

Principal Characters

UNITED STATES

President Franklin D. Roosevelt
Secretary of State Cordell Hull
Secretary of War Henry Stimson
Secretary of the Navy Frank Knox

Rear Admiral Walter Anderson	Commander Battleships, Pacific Fleet
Colonel Rufus Bratton	Chief, Far Eastern Section, Military Intelligence Division
Brigadier General Lewis Brereton	Air Force Commander, Philippines
General Leonard Gerow	Assistant Chief of Staff, War Plans Division
Joseph Grew	United States Ambassador to Japan
Admiral Thomas Hart	Commander-in-Chief, Asiatic Fleet
Harry Hopkins	Advisor to President Franklin Roosevelt
Admiral Husband Kimmel	Commander-in-Chief, Pacific Fleet
Lieutenant Commander Alvin Kramer	Section Chief, Naval Intelligence
General Douglas MacArthur	Commanding General, Philippine Department
Lieutenant Commander Arthur McCollum	Head of Far Eastern Section, Naval Intelligence
General George C. Marshall	Chief of Staff, U.S. Army
Brigadier General Sherman Miles	Assistant Chief of Staff, Military Intelligence Division
Rear Admiral Leigh Noyes	Director, Naval Communications
Lieutenant William Outerbridge	Captain, USS *Ward*
Captain Laurence Safford	Head, Communications Security Division, Naval
Lieutenant General Walter Short	Commanding General, Hawaiian Department
Admiral Harold Stark	Chief of Naval Operations
Brigadier General Richard Sutherland	Chief of Staff to General MacArthur
Rear Admiral Richmond Turner	Director of War Plans
Rear Admiral Theodore Wilkinson	Director, Naval Intelligence

JAPAN
Emperor Hirohito
Prime Minister Fumimaro Konoye
Prime Minister Hideki Tojo

Lieutenant Commander Mitsuo Fuchida	Commander, Air Group, Kido Butai
Captain Minoru Genda	Mastermind, Pearl Harbor Attack
Kensuke Horinouchi	Japanese Ambassador to the United States
Saburo Kurusu	Japanese Ambassador to the United States
Yosuke Matsuoka	Minister of Foreign Affairs
Admiral Osami Nagano	Chief of General Naval Staff
Admiral Chuichi Nagumo	Commander-in-Chief, First Air Fleet, Kido Butai
Admiral Kichisaburo Nomura	Japanese Ambassador to the United States
Admiral Koshiro Oikawa	Naval Minister
Shigenori Togo	Minister of Foreign Affairs
Admiral Teijiro Toyoda	Minister of Foreign Affairs
Admiral Isoroku Yamamoto	Commander-in-Chief, Combined Fleet

Introduction

Where does the responsibility really lie for the disaster at Pearl Harbor on December 7, 1941? Were Admiral Kimmel and General Short, who were so readily relieved of their commands, actually at fault? Or were there underlying political motives and maneuverings at play? November 26, 1941, a day as catastrophic as December 7, would be the day that changed everything in Washington.

Those who question the highly publicized versions that Kimmel and Short were derelict in their duties find it ironic that General Douglas MacArthur allowed the Philippines to fall into the hands of the Japanese, an event that resulted in significantly higher casualties. How could two commanders be relieved for not acting on intelligence they didn't receive when a third commander was rewarded for not acting on the same intelligence he did receive? Washington's buy-in of MacArthur's grandiose plan to save the Philippines only hastened its early defeat, and essentially, the destruction of U.S. air power in the western Pacific. While Kimmel and Short were called to task in at least nine investigations following Pearl Harbor, MacArthur's inactions were never even questioned. Instead, he was given greater responsibility and eventually acclaimed a hero. How could two commanders live the balance of their lives in public shame while the third became a millionaire and was awarded the Medal of Honor?

In the following pages, the author sets the record straight, providing evidence of failed communications, ignored intelligence, and poor military planning that led to Americans' early defeats in World War II. This book addresses the parallel events in Europe, often overlooked in many accounts of Pearl Harbor, particularly on December 7 with Hitler at the gates of Moscow, and the speculations of and ramifications for Japan's Tripartite partner, Germany. The chapters also detail the decisions that forced Kimmel and Short into retirement; the dispersion of military armaments already in short supply; and the actions of a leader who ambiguously swayed the American people and contradicted international law.

Then there were the yachts, FDR's last-minute attempt to invite Japan to shoot first. And contrary to the specific orders not to shoot, it would be a commander at Pearl Harbor who would open the war with Japan.

Most Americans are under the impression that the United States entered World War II when the Japanese attacked Pearl Harbor. Pearl Harbor was attacked to no insignificant extent because President Roosevelt, aided by the Democratic majority in both Houses, passed the Lend-Lease Act. Lend-Lease, which was passed a full nine months prior to Pearl Harbor, gave unlimited military aid to any nation at war with any member of the Tripartite Pact, all at American taxpayer expense. It put weapons into the hands of Great Britain, Greece, and Russia in their wars with Germany. Using the Burma Road and planes, it delivered supplies and weapons through the back door of China to Chiang Kai-Shek in his defensive war with Japan. American military aid to these warring nations clearly breached international law, and the Japanese attack on Pearl Harbor was the natural response.

Contrary to the most commonly told story of Pearl Harbor, the president knew thirteen days before the "day of infamy" that the Japanese task force was coming. And as the congressional hearings would later reveal, the administration cleared the way for them with the issuance of the Vacant Sea Order. Presented here are the chronological events leading up to the Ten Point Note, the final ultimatum issued Japan. And although there were attempts by leaders of both sides to meet and settle differences, each one was ill-timed and turned down by the other side.

With over seventy years to examine the events of history, there remains absolutely no doubt that President Roosevelt and his cabinet did much to make the Japanese attack at Pearl Harbor inevitable. There is wide disagreement, however, on what the result of the alternatives would have been. This book does not venture into such speculation; rather it reports the events as they occurred, as well as the subsequent fending or parrying of each political action that resulted on both sides.

The argument has been made that, while serving as President Woodrow Wilson's assistant secretary of the navy during World War I, Franklin Roosevelt had developed such a great devotion to the U.S. Navy that the thought of allowing a surprise attack on it would have been personally irreconcilable. This opinion has prevailed among many, cementing the notion that there is no evidence that the Japanese attack at Pearl Harbor was not a complete surprise. Yet it is obvious that those who claim there is no such evidence have either refused to look for it, or to look at the American leadership during the years when the nation was emerging from the Depression and about to enter another world war.

The premise of this book is that the president and his cabinet, with the aid of the Democratic platform, had the ability to make the decision as to when the United States would enter World War II. Policies and dictates of the president, with the endorsement of his cabinet, may not both have had the power to prevent a Pearl Harbor, but they certainly had the ability to postpone the Japanese attack for at least several months. Those critical months would have allowed time to build up American forces in the Philippines and on U.S. Pacific outposts. With additional time provided the Americans, would Japan have risked such an attack?

Even members of the U.S. Joint Chiefs disagreed with the decisions made on Capitol Hill that made war a certainty. The Americans' ability to read Japanese Purple diplomatic intelligence provided the capacity, even in the eleventh hour, to alter the inevitable. By supplying war material, overhauling British warships, employing naval convoys in the Atlantic, and moving to occupy Iceland and Greenland, the Americans were as much an aggressor as any foreign power.

In late August 1941, Japanese Prime Minister Prince Konoye sent a personal message to the president, through Ambassador Kichisaburo Nomura, suggesting that the two of them sit down in a neutral environment to reach a settlement of their respective differences. FDR's conditions for such a meeting were so difficult that the Japanese government backed down. It was known in Washington that such a rejection of this meeting would topple the moderate Konoye government in favor of the militant Tojo cabinet.

OAHU

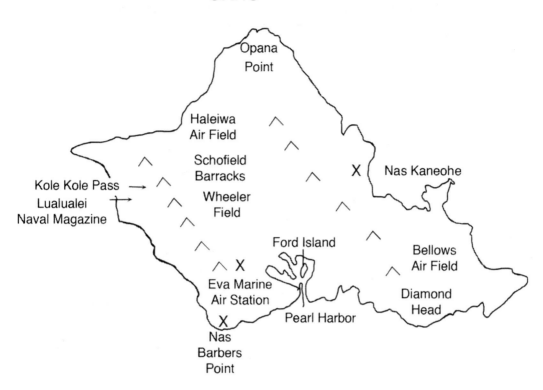

Island of Oahu

And that is exactly what happened in October 1941 when General Hideki Tojo became Japan's Prime Minister. There was no question that war was coming. But rather than blindly moving ahead with decisions that no longer addressed the problems or raised solutions, the administration could have modified hard and established dictates to meet each situation. Even up to two weeks before the Pearl Harbor attack, there was still a unique opportunity to stave off a war for another three months, an opportunity that was officially shunned; the *modus vivendi* to forestall an attack suddenly became the demanding Ten Point Note.

In November, Japan had sent a second ambassador, Saburo Kurusu, to Washington in the vain hope of assisting in a negotiated settlement of what were unthinkable alternatives. Even decisions made on the Japanese embargo in July 1941 were argued by the Joint Chiefs of Staff. To all of this, one might add dereliction of duty. There was absolutely no attempt to organize the Allies or establish unity of command, both duties that belonged to the president. The British and the Dutch in the Pacific were left in the dark as to what U.S. policy would be in the event of attack. After all, the aircraft carriers stationed at Pearl Harbor, Japan's main targets, had conveniently left port.

Even Admiral Nagumo's message of December 2, "Niitaka Yama Nobore, 1208," or "Climb Mount Niitaka, 1208 Repeat 1208,"[1] was an eleventh-hour instruction that nothing had changed in the American hard line that would cause the Japanese to cancel the Pearl Harbor attack. The American government had just let the last opportunity to gain valuable time slip away, and that lead to chaos. For a strike that had its origins twelve months earlier, the

Japanese had held out until the last minute. But in the end, it was America's friends and allies who closed the door to any final negotiations favorable to the United States.

Shifting to the Philippines, this book also chronicles General Douglas MacArthur's acceptance of the leadership role in defense of the Philippines. His complete disregard of the long-established strategy for the islands' defense led to his grandiose replacement plan, which fell apart as soon as the shooting started. MacArthur's micromanagement in the defense of Bataan, geared to keeping him in the limelight, came at the expense of military logic, sealing the fate of those left behind to defend the peninsula. Defying orders, he took key military leadership with him when he left the Philippines, which only added to some of the chaos he had created. There were no investigations following the initial attack on the Philippines.

Of the nine investigations into Pearl Harbor, and with most of them influenced by heavy political agendas, only the army and navy inquiries exonerated Admiral Kimmel and General Short of most charges, mainly because security information available to these boards had not been made available to the prior civilian investigation. Their findings blamed some in Washington that would cast a shadow on the administration. The army and navy boards concluded their hearings, making their decisions available shortly before the 1944 presidential election, when FDR was running for his fourth term. Stalling tactics were used, however, to delay publishing the reports until after the election, as such a release might have guaranteed Republican New York Governor Thomas E. Dewey the presidency. In Roosevelt's opinion, the reports and opinions should be "sealed up"[2] in the name of the public's interest.

This book also addresses the disparity in judgment, not only by the administration during the war, but also by the media and the American public. Why was crucial information shared with some leaders and not others? What made some military leaders scapegoats of disaster while another, caught in similar circumstances, was branded a hero? Who actually held the power to determine how many lives were expendable in the name of a perceived greater good?

And finally, the reader is provided an overview of world and political events, including those on Capitol Hill, that led to disaster. Illuminating the facts, many of which have been ignored or disputed for decades, the author makes it clear that Pearl Harbor elevated deceptive statesmanship to a new level.

Chapter 1

Dereliction of Duty

At 0600 on December 7, 1941, approximately two hundred thirty nautical miles north of Oahu,[1] the first wave of 183 aircraft[2] took off from the decks of six Japanese aircraft carriers. They orbited, and when all were in the air, they headed south.

At 0700, the second wave of 167 planes[3] started taking off, and when all were airborne, they, too, headed south approximately forty-five minutes behind the first wave. Their mission: to eliminate the American Pacific Fleet based at Pearl Harbor, which had the ability to retaliate or prevent future Japanese aggressive moves in the western Pacific.

The attack force itself consisted of six aircraft carriers, the *Akagi*, the *Hiryu*, the *Kaga*, the *Shokaku*, the *Soryu*, and the *Zuikaku*, accompanied by approximately fifty support vessels including battleships, cruisers, destroyers, oilers, and an umbrella of submarines.[4] Five of the submarines carried the new, two-man midget subs strapped to their decks. Their mission would be the most dangerous, to actually attempt to get into Pearl Harbor itself. Named the Kido Butai, it was the largest naval attack force that had been assembled to date. (By the end of the war, only one ship from the entire attack force, the *Ushio*, a destroyer, would survive.)

The primary objectives of the attack force were the three American aircraft carriers, the USS *Enterprise* (CV-6), the USS *Lexington* (CV-2), and the USS *Saratoga* (CV-3), giving the Japanese a two-to-one superiority, and the eight battleships in port which were of about equal strength to the Japanese. The U.S. battleships mounted fourteen-inch guns, with the exception of the USS *West Virginia* (BB-48) and the USS *Maryland* (BB-46), which employed heavier, sixteen-inch batteries. The Kido Butai also had the speed to outrun the American ships, but on their way to the attack, they were committed to only fourteen knots so the slower support ships could keep up.

The most important question was if the Americans were warned, at what point would the mission be scrubbed? To reduce such likelihood, it was decided that all ships' transmitter keys would be locked in such a way that no accidental signals could be sent to alert listening ears of their approach.

On December 3, Japanese intelligence indicated that the tensions with the United States had continued to mount. The *Enterprise* had left port with two battleships, two heavy cruisers, and twelve destroyers. The two battleships returned, but on December 5, the *Lexington* left port with five cruisers. Where were they? The *Saratoga* had already been gone for some time. Had they just casually left port so as not to arouse undue suspicions?

Three submarines that were part of the Japanese attack force each carried one float plane in a waterproof hangar on deck. Capable of patrolling up to two hundred miles ahead, the planes had seen nothing. Was that good or bad? Actually, the decision had been made before departing Japan that if they were spotted before December 7, the fleet would turn around. But what if the American carriers were spotted after takeoff en route to Pearl? Would the carriers be attacked? The answer was that the actual circumstances would have to dictate the decision and solution. Japanese agents in Honolulu would provide the U.S. alert status by way of Tokyo.

Protecting Pearl Harbor itself would be three army airfields: Hickam, which adjoined Pearl Harbor; Bellows, located on the east coast of the island just five miles south of Kaneohe; and Wheeler, located in the middle of the island. The Marines also had an airfield at Ewa, just west of Pearl Harbor. And the navy had two airfields: one at Pearl Harbor itself; and one on the east coast at Kaneohe. It was from these last two that they conducted their long-range reconnaissance.

The three hundred fifty aircraft employed by the Japanese strike force included three varieties of aircraft, all single-engine. The Nakajim B5N (*Kate*) would be employed in two roles. The first wave would include fifty Kates in the level-bombing role, and forty were armed with torpedoes. The second wave placed all fifty-four Kates in the level-bombing role.[5] At the time, the Kate was considered the most advanced torpedo bomber in the world. Much of its credit was due to its torpedo that could be released and dropped farther and faster than U.S. torpedoes, thus requiring less run-in time to the target.

The dive-bombing role would be fulfilled by the Aichi D3A (*Val*). The fighters, Mitsubishi A6M *Zeros*, would be responsible for the protection of the others, as well as for finding targets of opportunity. While the planes were still approaching Pearl Harbor, if it became evident that the Americans were not alerted, the message "Tora, Tora, Tora" ("Tiger, Tiger, Tiger")[6] would be transmitted back to the fleet.

At about 0645 on December 7, the destroyer USS *Ward* (DD-139), on patrol outside of the harbor entrance, identified, fired upon, and sank a submarine that appeared to be following the USS *Antares* (AKS-3), a general stores ship, into the harbor while the entrance net was open. This in itself was a very bold order for its new captain, to chance creating an international incident. But the target was definitely within the U.S. defensive zone and mostly submerged in an area where such was not authorized. The *Ward* passed a "fired upon" message ashore to the Bishop Point Relay Station where, somehow, all time advantage was lost because of a request for confirmation. The warning went unheeded.

At 0702 at the Opana Point mobile radar site at the northern most point on the island, two operator trainees identified a large formation of aircraft straight north, 132 miles out and closing in fast. They passed the sighting on to the information center at Fort Shafter, where the duty officer, himself a trainee in his job, told them not to worry about it because it was assumed to be a formation of twelve B-17 heavy bombers that had departed Hamilton Field, San Francisco.[7] They had left the States on Saturday night and were due in at Hickam Field by about 0800 Sunday. After all, that's why the Honolulu radio station had been on playing music all night to serve as a homing beacon. The Japanese were homing in on the same station, a second warning with no action.

The Japanese attack on Pearl Harbor commenced at 0755 with the first bomb falling on the parked PBYs on Ford Island. About half of the entire Pacific Fleet was in port, roughly one hundred forty-five vessels including yard craft.[8] In all, some twenty ships suffered various degrees of damage. Five of the eight battleships were sunk, three of which would eventually be refloated: the USS *California* (BB-44), the USS *Oklahoma* (BB-37), and the USS *West Virginia* (BB-48). Human loss of life and aircraft losses were appalling.

Of the navy personnel, 2,008 were killed, with 710 wounded. Of the army personnel, 218 were killed with 364 wounded. The Marines lost 109 men, with an additional 69 wounded. In addition to the military casualties, 68 civilians were killed with an additional 35 wounded. Nearly 200 aircraft had been destroyed. The navy lost 93 planes with an additional 31 damaged; the army lost 96 planes, while another 128 were damaged.[9]

By 1000, it was over. The Japanese had lost only twenty-nine aircraft and all five of the two-man midget subs. And essentially the Pacific Fleet was, at least temporarily, out of business as a fighting force.

How could an attack force the size of the Kido Butai avoid the American long-range patrols and get close enough to launch an attack that would neutralize the U.S. center of power in the entire Pacific? Could it have happened because the Americans' guard was down due to the peace talks going on in Washington, looking toward the maintenance of peace in the Pacific? Had the Hawaiian commanders not been on the alert for war? Or could the chain of command have broken down at the top in Washington? America and Congress wanted to know.

But now that the United States was at war, the Americans needed to exercise caution as to how much would be revealed to the enemy, especially the extent of damage done at Pearl Harbor. President Roosevelt immediately sent Secretary of the Navy Frank Knox to Hawaii to make a firsthand inspection and report back to him personally. Upon Knox's return, a brief statement was made to the public, minimizing losses for public morale with no hints being made to indicate responsibility.

By the evening of December 7, panic had already spread across the nation. In San Francisco, two squadrons of enemy planes were reported making reconnaissance flights from the navy yard at Mare Island south of San Jose. The Panama radio reported such flights over the Panama Canal, but no bombs were dropped. In Seattle, crowds of people smashed windows and looted stores during the enforcement of the city's first blackout. Bases on both coasts were put on full alert, and dependents were evacuated from some that were considered likely targets.

Representative John Dingell (D–MI) told the House that he would demand court-martials for Admiral Kimmel and General Short, those in command at Pearl Harbor. (Dingell had been a staunch Roosevelt supporter and had even suggested to the president in August of 1941 that the ten thousand Japanese-Americans on Hawaii be interned. In his opinion, this might get Japan to behave and come around to the Americans' way of thinking.) Along with the court-martials of Kimmel and Short, Dingell demanded that Major General Hap Arnold, Chief of Army Air Forces, and Major General George Brett, Assistant Chief of Army Air Corps in Washington, be included. How could this have happened? Had these commanders been asleep? When advised of dispatches that Japan had also bombed Philippine objectives heavily and hit gasoline stores, members of Congress demanded to know where American planes and patrols had been. On the evening of December 7, when FDR met with congressional leaders and cabinet members, Senator Tom Connally (D–TX), head of the Senate Foreign Relations Committee, "banged a table with his fist and exclaimed: 'How did they catch us with our pants down, Mr. President?'"[10] By December 8, the United States would declare war against Japan.

On Tuesday, December 17, Admiral Kimmel was informed that he would surrender his command to his second in command, Admiral William Pye. Admiral Pye, thought by many to be the navy's best strategist, would hold the position until Admiral Chester Nimitz arrived. Nimitz had just been appointed commander in chief of the Pacific Fleet, and he would take permanent command about December 31. (Nimitz would later change the tide of the war in the Pacific, commanding the Battle of the Coral Sea, the Battle of Midway, and the Solomon Islands Campaign.) On the same day, General Short received the news that he, too, would surrender his command. In Washington, Army Chief of Staff General George Marshall had always wanted an officer of the Air Corps in command, and soon, Lieutenant General Delos Emmons, who would head up the Hawaiian Department until September 1943, was on his way to Hawaii.

When relieved of their commands, both Kimmel and Short were returned to their previous ranks. Admiral Kimmel was reduced to rear admiral, and Lieutenant General Short was reduced to major general.

The following day, December 18, the president, by his Executive Order 8983, selected a commission of five men, two army officers and two navy officers, headed by Owen J. Roberts, a justice of the U.S. Supreme Court, to conduct a complete inquiry into the Pearl Harbor disaster. The official purpose of the investigation was to determine if "any derelictions of duty or errors of judgment on the part of United States Army or Navy personnel contributed to"[11] the success of the attack, and if so, who was responsible. By design, their mission was limited to the investigation of army and navy personnel only, which would exclude examination of any high-level civilian authorities in the chain of command. The order also pointed out that the investigative procedure to be used was up to the discretion of the commission. As a result, the initial interviews with senior military leadership in Washington were not recorded, nor were the participants sworn in. Congress, by executive order, granted additional power to the commission to gather witnesses and examine them under oath.

Referred to as the Roberts Commission, it consisted of Brigadier General Joseph McNarney, Major General Frank McCoy, Admiral William Standly, and Admiral Joseph Reeves. All but McNarney were retired from active service.

The committee held three meetings in Washington for three days and then spent three weeks in Hawaii gathering evidence and interviewing witnesses, operating out of the Royal Hawaiian Hotel, Fort Shafter, and the submarine base. They then returned to Washington for another week of wrapping up. The commission interviewed 127 witnesses[12] resulting in over eighteen hundred typewritten pages[13] and accumulated another three thousand pages of records and documents.[14] Anyone who thought that he might have evidence worth contributing was invited to testify. The report, titled *Attack Upon Pearl Harbor by Japanese Armed Forces*, was completed, dated January 23, 1942, was delivered to the president the same day, and then released to the public on the following day. All information contained in the report fell into three categories or parts of the report, "Finding of Fact," "Summary of the More Important Facts," and "Conclusions."

"Finding of Fact" detailed the meetings and investigative efforts of the Roberts Commission, as well as a list of circumstances on Oahu prior to the attack. This section closed with the military's response to the attack itself.

Referring to the fact-finding efforts of the Commission, the Hawaiian Department (the army) had three types of readiness alerts: Alert No. 1 warned of acts of sabotage and internal uprisings; Alert No. 2 involved additional security preparations to defend against attacks from submarines, surface ships, or aircraft; and Alert No. 3, the highest level of alert, required that all field positions, on Oahu as well as the rest of the islands, be manned and ready for immediate enemy attack. At the time of the attack, Oahu was at Alert No. 1 when it should have been at Alert No. 3.

The report also identified the responsibilities of the army involving the installation of the aircraft warning system that would detect incoming airborne and waterborne craft. All the required installations had not been completed by the time of the attack. But by November 27, some of the mobile equipment had been set up, and these temporary installations were operating intermittently, from 0400 to 0700, to allow for personnel training.

The temporary installation radar site on Opana Point would have been closed Sunday morning, December 7, by 0700. But a noncommissioned officer in training requested to remain open longer, and he was given permission to do so. At 0702, he identified a large formation of aircraft slightly east of north, approximately one hundred thirty miles out and closing in fast. He reported this to the information center at Fort Shafter, where an inexperienced duty officer, having information that a formation of U.S. planes was due, assumed this was that identification and took no action.

The Roberts Commission determined that after November 27, there were sufficient, although only partially trained, personnel to have manned the temporary locations, which would have provided nearly three hundred sixty degrees of coverage around Oahu.

Up until December 7, Kimmel was under the impression that the aircraft warning system was in full operation by the army, but he had not confirmed this.

The Joint Coastal Frontier Defense Plan included aerial surveillance of the entire island, extending about twenty miles out beyond the coast. Pilot training took place each weekday, starting at 0800 and continuing throughout the day. No flights were conducted on Sunday.

When the Joint Coastal Frontier Defense Plan was put into effect, the navy was responsible for air reconnaissance of the island, extending seven to eight hundred miles out. Before December 7, however, there had not been any distance reconnaissance except for practice drills and maneuvers. During fleet operations away from Oahu, the fleet would conduct reconnaissance flights, but these distances of operations were not sufficient to meet the requirement of the Joint Coastal Frontier Defense Plan. General Short was under the impression that the navy was conducting regular distance reconnaissance, but he did not confirm this with the navy.

When the Federal Bureau of Investigation was established in Hawaii, it was decided that the FBI would take over from army and navy intelligence operations in matters of the civil population regarding Japanese spies, with the agreement that the three services would cooperate. The FBI made efforts to uncover espionage activities in Hawaii, but because the United States was at peace with Japan, "restrictions imposed prevented resort to certain methods of obtaining the content of messages transmitted by telephone or radio telegraph over the commercial lines operating between Oahu and Japan."[15]

By the summer of 1941, it was known that there were over two hundred consular agents suspected of carrying on espionage activities, but they were operating under the protection of the Japanese Consul.

The Naval District Intelligence Office raised this concern with the FBI and with army intelligence, asking why these agents weren't being arrested for failing to register with the

U.S. government as foreign agents. In response, General Short of the Hawaiian Department indicated that prior to the arrest of any of the agents, they had to be given notice, allowing them time to register. Short did not want to undermine the army's attempts at creating good-will among the Japanese aliens residing in Hawaii. Consequently, no actions were taken against the agents.

The Roberts Commission recognized that had American agencies intercepted the Japanese agents, Japan's total picture of military activities in Hawaii, including the lack of inshore air patrols and long-range navy reconnaissance, along with the berthing positions of every ship at Pearl Harbor, would have been revealed.

The commission's report also detailed pass and liberty information for military personnel, indicating that it was normal for peacetime. And due to the emphasis placed on sabotage in the war warnings, army guard had been ramped up by nearly 100 percent. Antiaircraft gun crews were ordered to remain on their ships, and all other navy personnel were ordered to return to quarters by midnight. The report also noted that by midnight in Honolulu, all places of amusement and entertainment were closed.

The report also detailed the whereabouts of the military officers. While most of them had attended social functions on the night of December 6, all returned to their quarters at a reasonable hour.

The percentages of military personnel available for duty were also cited in the report: 90 percent of the Twenty-Fourth Infantry Division was available, as well as 85.6 percent of the Twenty-Fifth Infantry Division, 87.5 percent of the Coast Artillery, and 88.9 percent of the Air Force. Other departments, including ordnance, quartermaster, and medical personnel, were reported at 92 percent. So, overall, nearly 90 percent of military personnel were available for duty.[16]

Battleships and destroyers reported that 60 percent of the officers and 96 percent of the men were on board at the time of the attack. Of the seventy-five vessels in port, forty-nine of the commanders were actually aboard, and another twenty-two commanders were en route to their ships at the time of the attack.[17]

At 0630, the *Antares* sighted a suspicious object in the prohibited area off Pearl Harbor. The object was identified, fired upon, and sunk by the *Ward*. The naval base watch officer received the report of this action at 0712, and in turn, notified his chief of staff. Although a destroyer was dispatched to confirm the report, no alerts were sent out.

Another small submarine was sighted inside the harbor and sunk at approximately 0835. Still another sub was grounded at Bellows.

Although the entrance to Pearl Harbor was equipped with an anti-torpedo net which would have blocked torpedoes or submarines from entering the harbor, the net had been opened at 0458 to allow two mine sweepers to enter the harbor. Orders to close the net were given at 0840. Generally, the net was closed during hours of darkness, and it is estimated that the first enemy two-man submarine may have entered the harbor around 0700.

As soon as the attack started, the commanding general of the Hawaiian Department ordered Alert No. 3, which was promptly executed.

"Summary of More Important Facts" focused on the army and navy's respective functions in the event of attack; the perceived inadequate adaptability of the Hawaiian commanders; and the perceived lack of consultation and coordination between them that would have provided a more effective defense. Although the Roberts Commission recognized the shortages of personnel, weapons, and equipment, the commission determined that these shortages should not have affected the commanders as to the state of readiness required.

"Conclusions," of course, detailed the failures of the Hawaiian commanders and, in turn, left most in Washington out of any level of responsibility for the American losses at Pearl Harbor.

The first part of this section stated emphatically that no high officials in Washington were involved. In essence, the secretaries of state, war, and the navy, along with the chief of naval operations and the army chief of staff, had all fulfilled their duties and had closely cooperated with each other. Their warnings to the Hawaiian commanders had been deemed sufficient. They had cooperated in Hawaiian and national defense and had given the Hawaiian commanders free reign in reconnaissance and defense of the islands.

The second part of "Conclusions" dealt with the Hawaiian commanders themselves, charging them with "errors of judgment [that] were the effective causes for the success of the attack."[18] They were accused of failing to confer on the November 27 war warning and of failing to put into effect existing directives to meet the emergency. Had orders from the army chief of staff and the chief of naval operations been followed, the army's aircraft warning system would have been operational, and there would have been distant reconnaissance of the island by the navy, as well as inshore air patrol by the army. Inshore batteries and antiaircraft batteries would have been manned, supplied, and ready. The commission determined that the Pearl Harbor commanders should have been at the ready regardless of the December 7 warning message from Washington that arrived too late. The report also asserted that the commanders had a "lack of interest in, the measures undertaken by the other to carry out the responsibility assigned to each other"[19] concerning defensive logistics, and that the commanders simply did not take their role responsibilities seriously.

The third group of "Conclusions" did call some attention to the officers in the War Department in Washington. They had failed to interpret or correct the Pearl Harbor commanders' misinterpretation of Washington's November 27 war warning, and instead had placed too much emphasis on the Far East and sabotage.

Kemp Tolley, who would be sent on a fishing expedition by FDR just prior to the attack on the Philippines, referred to the Roberts Commission report as a "whitewash."[20] But readers of American newspapers, when the report was released in early 1942, immediately came to the conclusion that everyone in Washington, military and civilian, up to and including the president, had fulfilled his obligations. All responsibility was placed on Kimmel and Short, who had been found guilty of "dereliction of duty and errors of judgment," which were the causes of the disaster at Pearl.

Both commanders would live the balance of their lives in the shadow of Pearl Harbor. Early on, there were death threats, not only to themselves but to members of their families and even their pets. Many Americans felt that these men should have to pay for the loss of their loved ones. The commanders would end their lives with most Americans convinced that they alone, Admiral Kimmel and General Short, were personally responsible for the loss of 2,403 American lives at Pearl Harbor. Not only were Kimmel and Short relieved of their commands, each officer was demoted, and both officers were reduced to two stars. The Roberts Commission would follow the president's instructions to the letter and point all blame for the surprise attack to Hawaii with no shadow cast on Washington whatsoever.

Chapter 2

Japan's Targets

For years, the entire Hawaiian Islands had stood as an issue amongst Americans. The five mountainous islands, representing an area of about the size of Connecticut and Rhode Island combined, two thousand miles west of San Francisco, were the last bastion of defense or warning for an attack on the U.S. west coast. But even in the years leading up to World War II, a national poll found 25 percent of American citizens had voted for its abandonment in the case of its invasion.[1]

It was Captain Cook who discovered the islands in 1778 and named them the Sandwich Islands. (On his second visit, Captain Cook had a dispute with the natives, who killed him, cut out his heart, hung it on a tree, and then later ate it.) By the early nineteenth century, American sailors, traders, and missionaries began to visit and make their homes there. But it was the American Civil War that opened the door to Hawaii's prosperity. When the Union states were cut off from their supply of Southern sugar, they turned to Hawaii, which had the world's finest sugar. With the Civil War focusing on the economic advantage of the islands, the westward expansion to the coast brought them even closer. It was President Ulysses Grant who realized that the United States had become a Pacific power and saw Hawaii as the apex of a triangle of west coast defense. Japan at this time was still considered just a barbaric kingdom.

Pearl Harbor, also known to the Hawaiians as Pu'uloa or "long hill," was handed over by the Hawaiian monarchy in exchange for a treaty that gave Hawaiian produce the right to enter the United States duty free. The annexation of the islands by the United States was first proposed by the Hawaiian government as far back as 1853, but the offer was rejected. Americans were at peace. Hawaii was foreign, and the two oceans would keep the United States safe.

Minds changed in 1898 when the United States went to war with Spain. Having occupied the Philippine Islands for three centuries, Spain was a Pacific power. This was prior to the Panama Canal, and America as yet had no base in the entire Pacific. So by 1898, the annexation proposal suddenly had priority, and by 1900, Hawaii officially became a territory of the United States. But beyond grass skirts, palm trees, and Waikiki Beach, most Americans with no other facts started to consider Hawaii as a liability.

Between the wars, American enterprise had developed two giant industries in the islands, sugar and pineapples. In 1900 the pineapple industry was next to nothing, but it grew to 80 percent of the world's supply by 1940,[2] by which time Hawaii was also supplying the United States with one-sixth of its sugar needs.[3] Because all of this production required labor and the work was long and hard, most of it was done by Orientals. The native Hawaiian population itself had begun to dwindle soon after the discovery of the islands.

Because of centuries of isolation, they had no immunity to introduced diseases. Minor illnesses like measles and chicken pox killed them off like major plagues. Between 1800 and 1900, the native Hawaiian population was reduced by 90 percent.[4] American plantation owners felt the disappearance of labor and turned to Asia, and in 1850 began to import Chinese and Japanese laborers an influx that reached its peak in the 1890s. Few Chinese women came, but the Japanese brought their wives with them with the end result that the Chinese population started to fall while the Japanese population rose. Since the Americans spoke neither Japanese nor Chinese, English became the universal language. Of the one hundred fifty thousand people of Japanese origin living in the islands, 75 percent were American citizens. And of the twenty-eight thousand Chinese, 85 percent were American citizens. Whites totaled about one hundred seven thousand, and native or mixed Hawaiians represented sixty-two thousand.[5]

As the majority of Orientals had now been actually born and educated in the islands, their Oriental forebears seemed strange to them and trips to the Orient were awkward. So when Japan went to war with China, it meant nothing to them. Their allegiance was to the United States, even though, as of 1941, the Japanese had on file a protest against American possession of the Hawaiian Islands. The Japanese government had even suggested that the white race should evacuate all South Seas islands. Such demands had just compelled France to cede its Thailand territory long held by the French.

Following the annexation of Hawaii in 1898, the U.S. Navy continued to make improvements at Pearl Harbor to allow access for larger ships, and by 1908, the Pearl Harbor naval shipyard was firmly established. Later, Ford Island would be purchased in 1917, bringing in the U.S. Army to establish military aviation as well. By 1940, Pearl Harbor would become the home of the U.S. Pacific Fleet, a move that was not supported by Commander in Chief, U.S. Fleet (CINCUS), Admiral James O. Richardson.

Prior to his appointment to CINCUS, Richardson had served as assistant to Chief of Naval Operations Admiral William Leahy, and then as chief of the Bureau of Navigation, where he helped to revise War Plan Orange, the military's strategy for dealing with potential conflict with Japan. By the time he was appointed commander in chief of the U.S. Fleet in January 1940, Richardson was well known as the navy's expert on Japanese warfare strategy. If war was coming, he believed that Pearl Harbor would be the first point of Japanese attack, and the navy in the Pacific simply was not prepared to defend itself. His protest to President Roosevelt over moving the Pacific Fleet to Pearl Harbor would be his undoing.

Leading the army operations on Hawaii was Lieutenant General Charles D. Herron, who served as commander of the Hawaiian Department from 1938 to 1941. Herron, too, was concerned about the Americans' inability to defend Hawaii, and in his warnings to Washington, he correctly predicted that an air-carrier attack was the most likely to occur, emphasizing the need for long-range reconnaissance patrols, as well as an early warning communication system.

Next on Japan's agenda to conquer the western Pacific would be the Philippines. The seven thousand islands comprising the Philippines[6] were mostly Catholic from centuries of Spanish occupation. The islands had been in American possession since the turn of the century, when the United States captured them in the war with Spain in 1898. In 1934, the

Tydings-McDuffe Act created a system of government in the Philippines similar to that of the United States, with two levels of congress, providing for the election of their first president, and later granting independence to the Philippines in 1946, contingent upon their ability to defend themselves.

When Franklin Roosevelt became president in March 1933, he had inherited General Douglas MacArthur as his army chief of staff, who had been appointed by President Herbert Hoover in 1930. As one of World War I's most decorated heroes, MacArthur had become the army's youngest major general, achieving that rank at the age of forty-four, and upon being promoted to the rank of general he would serve as army chief of staff until 1935.

One of the more controversial incidents during his tenure as chief of staff involved MacArthur's participation in the Bonus March of 1932. About forty-three thousand people, of whom eighteen to twenty thousand were World War I veterans, marched on Washington to redeem their World War I service certificates.[7] Technically, the certificates were not due to be paid until 1945. But with nationwide hardships resulting from the Depression, the veterans were looking for their cash early. U.S. Attorney General William Mitchell had ordered the veterans to leave government property, but the veterans refused, and the army was called in. Against the advice of others, MacArthur accompanied then Major George S. Patton, infantry troops, and six tanks in their action to force the veterans out. The first effort proved successful, and President Hoover ordered the army to cease, but MacArthur took things a step further: he ordered a second action by crossing the Anacostia River against the president's orders, forcing the veterans to burn their camp. Later criticized for his participation, MacArthur defended himself, claiming that the march had been an attempt at overthrowing the government.

Franklin Roosevelt never did like MacArthur, and now as president, he liked him even less. He considered MacArthur to have an extraordinary ego in that MacArthur considered his own decisions to be flawless. After Roosevelt was elected, he had proposed a significant budget cut for the army, which incensed MacArthur. In a heated discussion with Roosevelt about the cuts, MacArthur offered to resign, but Roosevelt wasn't quite ready to accept his resignation. By 1935, however, Roosevelt wanted to retire him. MacArthur knew that his days were numbered and that his only future may be in a rocking chair, when out of the clear blue appeared Manuel Quezon, the newly elected first president of the Philippines.

MacArthur's relationship with Quezon went back thirty-five years to the days when MacArthur's father, General Arthur MacArthur, Jr., had served as the military governor-general of the Philippines in 1900. Douglas MacArthur himself had paid several subsequent visits to the Philippines since: in 1903 as a member of the Third Engineer Battalion to supervise wharf construction; in 1922–23 as commander of the Twenty-Third Infantry Brigade of the Philippine Division, involving the Philippine scout mutiny; and in 1929 as commander of the Philippine Department. In 1935, when Quezon asked MacArthur to come to the Philippines to build the defense force necessary for their independence in 1946, MacArthur was happy to oblige, and Roosevelt was happy to give MacArthur his blessing.

Heading back to the Philippines as the U.S. Army's military advisor to the Commonwealth Government of the Philippines, MacArthur made two demands of President Quezon: that he, MacArthur, be appointed field marshal, and that he be paid $33,000 annually, including a salary of $18,000 with allowances of $15,000, by the Philippine government.[8] President Quezon met both demands. So, in addition to the U.S. military salary he was collecting,

MacArthur enjoyed the distinction of being one of the highest-paid officers in the military. With him he took then Major Dwight Eisenhower and Lieutenant Colonel James Ord as his assistants. (In July of 1936, Eisenhower would be promoted to lieutenant colonel.) Considering MacArthur's former role of army chief of staff, Quezon thought he would have available to him a bottomless pit of military hardware, reasoning that MacArthur's connections in Washington would be well worth the investment.

In May 1937, after a short trip back to the United States to get married, MacArthur took up his official residence on the sixth floor of the Manila Hotel at $1,500 per month, also paid for by the Quezon government.[9] And to settle the issue with those who objected to the squandering of government funds, MacArthur accepted a hotel staff position in exchange for free rent.

MacArthur's team of assistants, Major Eisenhower and Colonel Ord, were both assigned to work out the details of building the Philippine Army. Unfortunately, Ord was later killed in a plane crash at Camp John Hay (Philippines) on January 30, 1938, and he was replaced by Major Richard Sutherland in March 1938, while Eisenhower was in the States on leave. Eisenhower would have to return all the way to the Philippines to learn that Major Sutherland had replaced Ord. Sutherland would be promoted to lieutenant colonel in July 1938, and due

General MacArthur's officers and wives dining in the Manila Hotel's Fiesta Pavilion, 1940.

The Manila Hotel (center left), site of General MacArthur's penthouse residence, 1940. The Spanish-walled old city is just beyond the hotel complex.

to what many believe to be philosophical differences between MacArthur and Eisenhower, MacArthur assigned Sutherland to squeeze out Eisenhower. Eisenhower would return to the States in 1939, holding various staff positions, including Chief of War Plans, until his appointment as Commanding General, ETO (European theater of operations) in June of 1942.

Through most of the 1930s, Washington had considered the Philippines as just an American possession, not even defensible and of little strategic importance. As a result, what little armament was sent there was obsolete at best. When the bottomless pit of military hardware failed to materialize, the relationship between Quezon and MacArthur started to cool. Specifically, Washington had nothing to send. MacArthur told Washington that in order to meet the growing Japanese threat he was building a Philippine army that could be ready for anything the Japanese could throw at them. In the eyes of the rest of the world, MacArthur estimated he would be able to change the entire picture of the western Pacific.

It was during 1940 that a bill was introduced into the Philippine Senate limiting the terms to eight years that a president and vice president could serve. The bill would require FDR's signature, who was himself in his eighth year and running for re-election. He let a sleeping dog lie. After twelve years in office, and upon his death in 1945, the Philippine Senate was still waiting for his signature. And because the defense budget that MacArthur required was far more than Manila could afford, the relationship between President Quezon and MacArthur would eventually cool even more.

Many in the State Department and even some on the General Staff were questioning why MacArthur was not pursuing alternatives to war rather than building for it. They even tried to pressure FDR to recall MacArthur to justify his actions. But again, there would be no rocking the boat as long as Roosevelt was running for his third term.

Now General MacArthur announced to Washington his grandiose plan not to defend just Luzon in a defense retreat to Bataan per WPO-3, but to also defend the entire Philippine archipelago. Because Washington had faith in his optimism, believing his inflated figures on the size of the Philippine Army and the depth of its training, it regrettably bought into his plan. The challenge of modernization started to appear. Compounding the shortage of equipment for the Philippines was the means to deliver it.

Over one million tons of supplies gathered on U.S. docks, waiting for the ships to deliver them.[10] To counter former President Hoover's warning that economic sanctions were roads to war, the prospect of FDR's alternative, to do nothing, would have allowed Japan at her leisure to gobble up the balance of the European possessions, including the Philippines. This would have placed the United States in the same position that Japan had landed in, being cut off from the same tin, oil, and rubber, when it was most needed.

On October 31, 1940, the U.S. Army transport, USS *U.S. Grant* (AP-29), docked in Manila. Aboard was Major General Jonathan Wainwright, arriving to proudly accept command of the Philippine Division, the largest army unit in the Philippines and praised by MacArthur as equal to anything.

As the commander of the Philippine Department, it was up to Wainwright to resist the impending Japanese invasion, and after General MacArthur's departure from the Philippines in March 1942, Wainwright would assume the role of Allied commander of the Philippines, a no-win situation. By early May of 1942, Wainwright would be forced to surrender and was interned in various POW camps until he was liberated in 1945. In 1942, he had been nominated for the Medal of Honor, but it was MacArthur who actually blocked the nomination because he didn't think that Corregidor should have surrendered. After Wainwright's release, however, MacArthur did not oppose the second nomination, and in September of 1945, Wainwright would receive his just recognition.

The division of an estimated thirteen thousand men that General Wainwright accepted actually consisted of only seventy-five hundred men. Most were Filipinos, many of whom spoke little or no English.[11] If American units in the States had little, the Philippines, where the action would probably start, had nothing. Artillery, tanks, communications, and vehicles were virtually nonexistent. Troops had never trained as a unit nor held any maneuvers, and with the different dialects in the islands, communications were a challenge. Yet it would be their responsibility to defend the United States' most Far Eastern possession, and eventually, according to MacArthur, one hundred twenty-five thousand men would complete six months of training.[12] Defensive aviation was, at best, dismal. American pilots arriving in the Philippines could not believe that their operational aircraft were actually museum pieces, all overdue for the boneyards.

Based in Manila, Admiral Thomas Hart, who had studied at the Army War College as well as the Navy's, commanded the American Asiatic Fleet. He and Major General George Grunert, who had been in command of the Philippine Department since May 1940, both recognized the inadequacies of the Philippine troops. The Philippine Department was responsible for the actual American defense of the island, and both said that this army was capable of defense operations only without maneuvering, and then only if supervised closely by the American officers. Half of the Philippine officers had no active duty experience and 15 percent had no training at all.

Navy defenses were also less than adequate. Admiral Hart's Asiatic Fleet consisted of two cruisers, thirteen destroyers, seventeen submarines, twenty-four PBY patrol bombers, four seaplane tenders,[13] and a mix of other support vessels. Hart considered that any aid to MacArthur's defense plan would wipe out his navy in the first days. He even doubted MacArthur's sanity. As an example, Hart suggested that in closely coordinated air missions, when navy aircraft were supporting army missions, they should be under the army's control, and when army aircraft were supporting navy missions, they should be under the navy's command. Not understanding that logic, MacArthur disagreed. But General Marshall in Washington laid it on the line for him: he would support naval missions.

General Grunert told Washington that important decisions for adequate air offense and defense, as well as the air warning service, should be made not by infantry officers but by an Air Corps general. This finally resulted in the arrival of General Henry Clagett and his assistant, Colonel Harold George, in May of 1941. Colonel George, an expert on bombing strategy, had been instrumental while working in the Air War Plans Division in the planning and production of aircraft before the war. Upon his arrival in the Philippines, he found that the combined American and Philippine Air Force consisted of only a few obsolete aircraft, left over from U.S. mainland inventory.

In July of 1941, Washington created a senior military headquarters for the Philippines, namely the U.S. Army Forces, Far East (USAFFE), commanded by MacArthur with the rank of lieutenant general. (Shortly after, MacArthur dissolved the Philippine Department, and several months later, General Grunert returned to the United States.) By August of 1941, the Philippine Army was inducted into the U.S. Army and full mobilization was underway. This reorganization could mean only one thing: the Philippines would be the front line. They would be defended, but with what? Even the morale of the average man on the street in Manila turned from that of dejection to optimism. Suddenly modernization was top priority.

Washington did detour the delivery of a contract of U.S. fighters, intended for Sweden, to the Philippines. At the time, the fighters were thought to be state of the art. But the deal resulted in as many problems as it resolved. It was in January 1941 when the Philippines started to receive what would total fifty-two Seversky P-35 fighter aircraft.[14] In the end, they would not be a match for what the Japanese would put up against them. However, these P-35s, as export models, were still far superior to the Army Air Corps' P-35s because American military planners were not convinced of the added value of wing guns in addition to cowl guns, both of which were incorporated into the Swedish contract.

But the immediate problem was that the manuals, instructions, and cockpit data plates were in Swedish and the instruments were in metric. Of equal concern, there were no spare engines or parts, so their numbers decreased as they wore themselves out, and this was still during peacetime. In addition, for aerial defense, there were three squadrons of Boeing P-26 Peashooters, one squadron of Martin B-10 bombers, and one squadron of Douglas 0-46 observation aircraft, all long overdue for retirement.[15] It was well known at the time that when

Obsolete P-26 fighters that were flown by the Filipino pilots.

aircraft were worn out in the United States, they were sent to Hawaii. And when they were worn out there, they were sent to the Philippines.

More pleading from Manila to Washington finally resulted in the arrival of eighteen Douglas B-18 bombers from Hawaii. The pilots commented that the only advantage of the B-18 over the ancient B-10 was that you could get up and walk around in the aircraft. Still, General MacArthur was boasting that by Philippine independence in 1946, the islands would

Top: An unidentified group of soldiers pose on a Republic P-35 of the type rerouted from the Swedish contract to the Philippines (1941). *Bottom:* The B-18, which turned out to be yesterday's bomber in today's war.

be in such a strong defensive position "that it would cost the Japanese 'at least half a million men as casualties and upwards of five billions of dollars in money'"[16] if the Japanese were to invade the Philippines "with any hope of success."[17]

In addition to the bombers, General Marshall had rounded up some modern P-40s from squadrons in the States. When these arrived in the Philippines, a new challenge presented itself. It was discovered that the sole access road to the U.S. main fighter base, Nichols Field, was too narrow to admit the trucks carrying the disassembled planes because the road was hardly wider than the flatbed trucks. And when the road was finally widened and the P-40s were assembled, it was now discovered that someone had forgotten to send the coolant for the engines.

If the Philippines had little, U.S. allies in the Pacific were desperate. British Malaya, which supplied nearly half of the world's rubber and over half of its tin, an obvious priority target of Japan, was in need of everything. England had just survived the Battle of Britain and was cleaned to the bone. All that could be spared were about one hundred fifty aircraft to defend all of Malaya and its huge naval base at Singapore.[18] Many of the aircraft were Brewster Buffalo Fighters shipped directly from the United States; these had performed poorly at high altitudes, but they were considered sufficient to meet anything that the Japanese could mount against them. The ground defense force would consist of a mixture of Malayans, Indians, New Zealanders, Australians, and British, all poorly trained for the event and ill equipped. Even so, they were considered more than sufficient at the time.

Another strategic target of Japan's was Singapore. The original work on the Singapore naval base had started in 1919, right after World War I, and in 1921, the British government made the big financial commitment. But the 1922 Washington Naval Treaty was signed, establishing the allowable naval ratios and forbidding naval bases or fortifications east of one hundred ten degrees east longitude. Singapore was just outside the boundary by six degrees, so there were more delays. Late in 1924, the final decision was made to commit to construction. Surprisingly, Britain supplied only a fraction of the cost because the Malaysian states, Hong Kong, and New Zealand also contributed.

Strategically, Singapore commanded one of the most important waterways in the world where the Indian and Pacific Oceans meet. In 1928, work on the naval base was speeded up. That same year, the British House of Commons announced a plan for the Americans to take over or lease the base in case of war since the United States had nothing west of Pearl Harbor, and the Americans would be leaving Manila in 1946.

Although Singapore was three thousand miles from Japan, the Japanese had already occupied the Chinese-owned island of Hainan, three hundred miles south of Hong Kong, as well as the Spratly Islands, some seven hundred miles northeast of Singapore. They used all of these as launching sites in their conquest of the Pacific.

Singapore Island itself measured twenty-seven by fourteen miles and was connected to the mainland by a causeway. The naval base was on the north end of the island, about twelve miles from Singapore City. The naval base prided itself on its two huge docks, one of them a floating dock nine hundred feet long by two hundred feet wide. This dock had been built in England and then floated the ten thousand miles to Singapore at a cost of two hundred fifty thousand pounds, still listed as one of the most remarkable marine feats.[19] It was said to be able to lift any ship afloat. Up to eighteen-inch guns were installed for defense. The base covered about four square miles and was fully equipped to repair, refit, and refuel ships. The docks were equipped with cranes for repair of the largest deck guns. All fuel tanks were underground, and the base itself was heavily protected by antiaircraft batteries with ample storage facilities in the backwater Strait of Jahore. There were several military airfields on the island and up and down the Malay Peninsula that were located to strategically support Borneo, Hong Kong, Port Darwin (Australia), or Ceylon. For these reasons, Singapore was considered the British Pearl Harbor of the Western Pacific that would have to be reckoned with by the Japanese.

By October 1941, Britain considered the work complete, and earlier that year, reinforcements from Australia and New Zealand had started to arrive at prepared facilities on the Malay Peninsula to cover any potential attack by the Japanese through Thailand to its north. Interestingly, there were even British mock attacks against Singapore proper. The British Asiatic Fleet represented an enemy, and the regular garrison the defense, which always won out because the defense weapons only pointed out to sea with no thought that the Japanese might arrive through the back door. Tactically, the defense of Singapore was almost identical to that of Gibraltar, with its back door exposed to the enemy.

Also under major threat of the Japanese was the Dutch East Indies for its oil. By comparison, if British defense for Malaya was dismal, the East Indies had nothing. With Mother Holland occupied by the Germans, the Indies, with little or no potential outside help, were in desperate straits.

As of 1939, the Dutch East Indies' navy (Royal Netherlands Navy East Indies) consisted of three cruisers, the *Java*, the *Tromp*, and the *Sumatra*. It had six or seven destroyers, about fifteen motor torpedo boats, eight submarines, and a mine layer.[20] Its aviation consisted of roughly fifty flying boats, mostly Dorniers, as well as some fighters and observation aircraft.[21] Their army would consist of whatever they could build with the time that they had.

Neither the Philippines or Malaya, nor the Dutch East Indies themselves, could offer much resistance to a strong-willed enemy. Nor were they organized. There was no strategy among them, no alternate plans, nor any unity of command. Each one was on its own with very limited strategic resources. It is unimaginable that Washington, specifically the president in collaboration with Churchill, would fail to make any such move to unify them or to coordinate their operations. The only redeeming factor was that just five thousand miles away, the U.S. Fleet was berthed at Pearl Harbor. Eventually, there would be such an attempt in December 1941 to organize the American, British, Dutch, Australian Command (ABDA), but it was too little and too late.

Heading up these field commands was British General Archibald Wavell. While the head of the Middle East Command, Wavell had enjoyed earlier success when he defeated the Italians in North Africa. But only a few months later with the fall of Greece, Winston Churchill transferred Wavell to India in July 1941 to serve as commander in chief. By early December, Wavell was also assigned to head the American, British, Dutch, and Australian Command (ABDACOM), which was short-lived. Within two months, and with so little remaining to offer resistance to the Japanese, the ABDACOM was dissolved. In many U.S. influential circles, the question was often raised that, with the United States and Japan on a collision course, should steps have been taken to check any Japanese aggressive moves while the Americans had the British, Dutch, and Free Chinese available to help?

Another concern for Japan, the last figure in the equation, was Vladivostok, located on the Sea of Japan and representing the most easterly advanced base of Joseph Stalin's Siberian forces. Russo-Japanese antagonism had dated back to the 1870s, with their only mutual interest being the desire for more Chinese territory. Vladivostok was virtually autonomous from Mother Russia with its own munitions factories as well as a strong military and naval zone fortified with airfields and a naval base. From this command, the Russian planes and submarines would not be easy pickings for the Japanese. A glance at the map would place Vladivostok almost in the middle of the Japanese Empire.

Because of their limited range, the U.S. B-17 heavy bombers would not be able to take off from Clark Field, Luzon, fly a mission to Japan, and return. But if Vladivostok were available to American pilots, they could continue on and fuel up for a return trip. But no arrangement using Vladivostok was ever concluded because Stalin was aware that any such agreement could activate an attack by Japan on her thinly guarded eastern borders. (This logic explains the impounding of the aircraft and incarceration of one of the Doolittle Raider crews that, with low fuel, opted for landing in Russia in April 1942.)

For her mastery of the Pacific, Japan would have to deal with her first three obstacles. There was the British naval base at Singapore, which would require Japan to attack through the back door, landing in Thailand, Kra Isthmus, and pushing through the length of Malaya. There was the American sea and now air (B-17) strength poised to strike in the Philippines. And finally, there was the great U.S. naval base at Pearl Harbor. The key to success was to strike all three at once, negating each one's ability to go to the aid of another.

Timing was the key. Singapore would be hit by an air strike, and ground forces would cross into the north end of the Malay frontier with Thailand. Manila and American airfields on Luzon would be attacked from Formosa, some five hundred miles to the north. But nothing must happen prematurely that could warn Hawaii before the strike force could hit Pearl Harbor. Everything was to start in Asia, timed to dawn in Hawaii. With Pearl Harbor being the greatest distance, timing was essential.

For the mission itself, the main objectives at Pearl Harbor would be the carriers and the battleships, and secondly, the airfields from which the Americans could retaliate in the air. There had been discussion of actually occupying the island, but that was ruled out because of the logistical problem of supporting it once it fell into Japanese hands. In addition, the slower speed of the transports and the larger fleet of Japan's attack force headed toward Hawaii would increase the likelihood of detection. The only guarantee of sinking the ships at Pearl Harbor would be aerial torpedoes as the British action at Taranto, Italy, in November 1940 had demonstrated. Pearl Harbor offered no long, low approaches from which to ensure hits. The shallow water, similar to the Taranto harbor, also posed the problem of the torpedoes hitting the bottom. So, the Japanese set out to resolve both problems.

First, the torpedoes were fitted with fins that would prevent them from passing under the ships, and then the torpedo bomber pilots set out to master short, low approaches. During training exercises, the pilots found that by getting as close to the target as possible, releasing the torpedoes virtually at water level, and then banking sharply to avoid hitting the target, they could score eight out of ten attempts. A potentially successful strategy if torpedo nets were not employed in the harbor.

The last decision for the Kido Butai attack force was its route across the Pacific. There were two main courses under consideration. The southerly, more direct route would place the attack force in the proximity of well-traveled sea lanes and would risk detection. The northerly course would be longer, but it would offer better security from detection. And although refueling at sea in the rough winter waters also offered a challenge, detection was the primary concern. So the northerly route was the final choice.

Japanese reviews of the potential success of the Pearl Harbor attack were mixed. The High Command, or General Staff, gave the attack at Pearl Harbor a 40 percent chance of success. And although Vice Admiral Chuichi Nagumo, who would command the air fleet, personally thought that an attack on Pearl Harbor would bring strong retaliation, he was not replaced because Admiral Yamamoto, commander of the combined fleet, considered that such an action could affect the morale of the whole operation.

Oddly enough, the Americans had already proven that a surprise attack could be accomplished. Ten years before the Japanese attack on Pearl Harbor, it was successfully attacked in a mock army-navy exercise in early February 1932. Dispatched from California, the *Saratoga* and the *Lexington* launched one hundred fifty-two aircraft, approximately one hundred miles north of Oahu, on a Sunday morning.[22] Although the attack was expected, low clouds covered the approaches to the airfields during the dawn attack that successfully took the defenders by surprise.

Commander Minoru Genda, one of the actual masterminds of the Pearl Harbor attack, had reasoned that if twenty-one British biplanes could put the three Italian capital ships out of commission at Taranto, then two hundred modern war planes should be able to dismantle the entire U.S. Fleet. Genda, known for his aerobatic flying talent, had previously headed up the team known as Genda's Flying Circus, one of Japan's public relations efforts to promote naval aviation.

Along with Commander Genda, another key planner of the attack on Pearl Harbor was Admiral Osami Nagano. Considered an expert on the United States, he had served as naval attaché in Washington during the early 1920s. He also represented Japan at various naval conferences, including the London Naval Conferences of 1930 and 1935–36, all aimed at disarmament. In the late 1930s, he served as naval minister and commander in chief of fleet, and by April 1941, he was appointed naval chief of staff. It was in this capacity that he gave the ultimate command to launch the attack on Pearl Harbor.

Admiral Isoroku Yamamoto, who would command the entire operation against Pearl Harbor, had been opposed to Japan's invasion of China in 1931 as well as the Tripartite Pact with Germany and Italy. As such, many believed his career would be over when General Tojo became prime minister of Japan in October 1941. Yamamoto was highly respected by his men, and due to his popularity within the fleet, as well as his close relationship with the imperial family, Yamamoto remained as commander in chief of Combined Fleet. Known for his direct approach, he understood the risks Japan was taking by waging war on the United States, admitting that any victory would be limited to the amount of time that their oil resources held out. And despite some disagreement on naval strategy, Yamamoto would successfully lead his fleet across the Pacific.

Commanding the air fleet of the Kido Butai would be Admiral Chuichi Nagumo. Having studied naval warfare both in Europe and in the United States, Nagumo would eventually be promoted to vice admiral in 1939, and in 1941, he was appointed commander in chief of the First Air Fleet, Japan's aircraft-carrier force. Some claimed that he was not up to the task, relying too much on old-school tactics and perhaps being physically unfit. After the attack on Pearl Harbor, he would be criticized for not launching a third attack to destroy the fuel storage and repair facilities at Pearl Harbor.

And finally, commanding the Japanese pilots would be Commander Mitsuo Fuchida, the naval bomber aviator responsible for coordinating the entire aerial attack itself. It is interesting to note the course Fuchida's life would take after the war. A true warrior, Fuchida had argued unsuccessfully with Nagumo to launch a third attack on Pearl Harbor. But even with his two successful attacks, he would become such a national hero that he was granted a meeting with Emperor Hirohito. Fuchida had even helped to plan the attack on Midway, and by 1945, he was promoted to air operations officer of the Imperial Navy.

But after the war, he became a farmer, and in 1950, Fuchida met Sergeant Jacob DeShazer. DeShazer, one of Doolittle's Raiders who had participated in the bombing of Nagoya, was subsequently captured and held prisoner in Japan for the next forty months. In 1948, DeShazer returned to Japan as a missionary, and a couple of years after that, he met Fuchida. The two became friends and shortly thereafter, Fuchida converted to Christianity. For the next twenty-five years, Fuchida, the famous warrior known for his effective leadership in the devastating attack on Pearl Harbor, would spread the message of peace and forgiveness throughout Japan and other Asian countries.

Another key player in the early December attacks against the United States and Great Britain was Vice Admiral Mineichi Koga, commander of the China Area Fleet. He would lead the attack on Hong Kong on December 8. And after Admiral Yamamoto's death in April 1943, he would be assigned commander in chief of Combined Fleet.

While Japanese naval commanders were putting together their attack plans for Pearl Harbor, the Hawaiian commanders were trying to decide how best to defend the islands with what little they had. Hawaii's defense depended largely on her early warning, which was dependent on her eighty-one long-range patrol aircraft, the PBYs, under the command of Rear Admiral Patrick Bellinger.[23] Bellinger had been promoted to rear admiral in 1940 when he was put in command of Patrol Wing 2 on Hawaii, and on December 7, he would be one of the officers to sound the alarm, "Air Raid, Pearl Harbor—This is no drill."

Bellinger's aircraft consisted of twenty-seven old PBYs and fifty-four new PBYs that had just arrived in November.[24] The new ones were experiencing the shakedown problems of new aircraft, which were accented by the maintenance problem of no spare parts. Bellinger and Kimmel spent many hours discussing how best to utilize the aircraft. They had two options. They could do a minimum of flying so they could keep some in the air at all times, or they could maintain 100 percent coverage of the island until all would break down. Critics of Kimmel believe he should have chosen the latter.

To alleviate the shortage of reconnaissance aircraft, General Short might have offered his six B-17s to the navy for their patrol. But with Hawaii's only intelligence from Washington advising that any attack would be on Malay, Kra, or the Philippines with Manila as the priority, it didn't seem logical to discontinue critical training of crews for the Philippines to add what little he could to distant patrol. And when Admiral Kimmel pleaded for as many long-range submarines as he could get, Washington met his request by informing him that he would now lose some of his best subs to Admiral Hart's Asiatic Fleet. Clearly, the Japanese would have the upper hand unless additional reinforcements were provided by Washington.

Chapter 3

The World Stage

At the close of World War I, world leaders met at the Paris Peace Conference to establish peace terms for those countries defeated in the war, and to establish the first international organization aimed at maintaining world peace. The conference concluded their meetings in January of 1920, at which time the League of Nations was born.

Another attempt at maintaining world peace, particularly focused on the Pacific and East Asia, resulted in the Washington Naval Conference of 1921–22, the first conference of its kind aimed at arms control. Initiated by President Warren Harding, the conference consisted of representatives from nine countries: the United States, Great Britain, France, Belgium, the Netherlands, Italy, Portugal, Japan, and China. While each country had her respective list of demands, restraining Japanese naval expansion in the western Pacific, where so many resources were at risk, was at the top of the agenda. A ten-year agreement was reached that placed naval tonnage restrictions on the conference members by addressing limitations on new manufacturing and by scrapping existing ships.

Japan had been one of the founding members of the League of Nations, and Germany was admitted to the League in 1926. The concept of banishing war altogether seemed a reality in 1928 when the League members met in Paris and signed the Kellogg-Briand Pact. Both Japan and Germany signed the Pact, and although the United States was not a member of the League of Nations, it did support the Pact.

The Kellogg-Briand Pact of 1928 was established as a nonaggression pact in which the signatories agreed to settle their international disputes by peaceful means. Eventually, over sixty countries would sign the agreement. But it did not bring about the intended effect because countries would simply wage war without declaring war.

By 1932, the League of Nations hosted fifty-seven members. Although Costa Rica would withdraw in 1925 and Brazil in 1926, it would not be until 1933 that others would follow. Japan and Germany would be next.

One of the events that precipitated Japan's exit from the League was the publication of the Lytton Report in 1932, commissioned by the League of Nations. Representatives from five countries, the United States, Great Britain, Germany, Italy, and France, had been sent to Manchuria to investigate the Mukden incident of 1931. Japan had bombed the railway at Mukden, which essentially opened up their invasion of Manchuria. One of the conclusions of the report was that Japan had not acted in self-defense. And anticipating the criticism of the report and condemnation by the League of Nations, Japan's representative, Yosuke Matsuoka, walked out in February 1933, later formalizing Japan's withdrawal from the League in March 1933.

By the mid–1930s, Japan was also becoming disillusioned with treaties established by the Washington Naval Treaty. Although her representatives attended the 1930 and 1936 follow-up conferences held in London, Japan, among other participants, was not happy with the limitations and withdrew from the London Conference of 1936, which defeated the initial purposes of the arms-control efforts. And by the 1939 outbreak of war in Europe, any treaties arising from the conferences were dissolved.

After the Japanese marched into Manchuria in 1931, Henry Stimson, then the secretary of state, had suggested that the most effective way to express the Americans' total abhorrence, and to perhaps discourage further Japanese moves into Asia, would be to impose economic sanctions on Japan. Stimson's boss, however, did not agree with him. President Herbert Hoover overtly countered the suggestion, advising his cabinet members that "economic and military sanctions are roads to war."[1] Eventually, Stimson would get his wish. Exactly ten years later, serving as secretary of war, he would find President Roosevelt eager to do just that, announcing the sanctions of Japanese exports to the public on July 25, 1941. After all, FDR's victory at the polls in 1932 had been largely in defiance of Hoover's breaking up the Bonus Marchers' encampment in Washington, D.C. Many of the adult voters at the time had been veterans of World War I and sympathetic to the cause.

But meanwhile, the Japanese were at that time unimpressed. When the League of Nations finally condemned Japan's occupation of China in the spring of 1933, the Japanese simply walked out and sent in their resignation. Adolf Hitler, now in power in Germany, sent in the German resignation a few months later, and the League of Nations started to fall apart.

After World War I, the strong feeling of isolationism in the United States prompted Congress to reject membership in the League of Nations. Perhaps to pacify the strong Republican isolationist Congress of the 1920s and '30s, FDR would comment that he personally was against American involvement in the League. Between 1935 and 1937, Congress forced on FDR's Democratic administration the Neutrality Acts, whereby trade or loans to belligerent nations were prohibited, and all exports to those nations had to be paid for in cash before leaving American docks. Opinion polls were solidly for noninvolvement in foreign affairs.

In 1936, Japan had joined with Germany to form the Anti-Comintern Pact, followed by Italy in 1937. Hitler, already alluding to the master race, justified Japan's membership by claiming that Japanese blood contained the same qualities as those of Nordic ethnicity. The actual pact was an interesting line-up for future events. The five-year pact was a political statement that recognized Communism as the world's chief enemy of peace, and it was designed to provide diplomatic and economic aid in any war with Russia or to nations wrestling with international Communist parties. Hungary and Spain joined in 1939 and the pact was renewed in November 1941. Japan's interest in this pact was twofold.

First, it strengthened Germany's position against Japan's traditional enemy, Russia. Second, Germany contemplated that it would distract Britain from Asian affairs that would affect her colonies.

Just a few months later, in the midst of Stalin's reorganization of Soviet army leadership in the summer of 1937, roughly thirty-five thousand officers were arrested or executed, and many simply disappeared.[2] This purge included three of the five marshals and thirteen of the fifteen army commanders.

Following Japan's start of war with China at the Marco Polo Bridge outside of Peiping in July 1937, the Japanese made some gestures toward settlement, but by August, Chiang Kai-shek had committed China to fight. In October of 1937, FDR made his famous "Quarantine Speech" concerning lawless and aggressor nations. After the Rape of Nanking in December 1937, public sentiment in the United States demanded tougher sanctions against the Japanese. And the following July, the State Department imposed its "moral embargo" of 1938 on the export of airplanes to Japan as a first step toward peaceful persuasion. But the war in China continued, and additional embargoes were imposed in 1939 that "extended to materials essential to airplane manufacture and to plans, plants, and technical information for the production of high-quality aviation gasoline."[3]

The point was well taken in newspapers and magazines, showing the body of a lifeless Chinese woman holding her dead baby still clutched in her arms. The accompanying statement reminded the reader that the bomb that helped make this aggression possible was paid for by the American purchase of Japanese goods. The media proclaimed that every pair of silk stockings was a clip of rifle bullets. If Americans abhorred Japan's brutality in China, they could no more buy Japanese goods than they could help load a Japanese plane with bombs to be dropped on a helpless Chinese village. Readers were reminded that in order to buy raw materials abroad, Japan had to sell goods abroad, and it was the Americans who were buying the lion's share of the most critical item in Japan's foreign trade, raw silk. Advertisements went so far as to admonish American women for their fondness of silk stockings. Wasn't the sentiment for the Chinese people more important? Certainly, American women did not want the blood of Chinese people on their stockings. As pro–Chinese organizations and grassroots movements pushed for the boycott of Japanese goods, women resorted to wearing stockings made of cotton and rayon.

President Roosevelt started testing the waters of the American people's sentiment in one of his "fireside chats" on the radio, suggesting that since Japan's unabated war in China was made possible at least in part by American exports to Japan, maybe now was the time to start exercising sanctions on Japan. That speech was met in the United States with riots, demonstrations, and protests on such a scale that FDR actually had to back down. Americans were still so entrenched in the post–World War I isolationism that they would have no part of the president provoking another nation. This did not go unnoticed in Japan. It only further convinced them that Americans had no taste for war.

Negotiations with Japan fell primarily on the shoulders of Secretary of State Cordell Hull. Hull, a Democrat from Tennessee, was no stranger to politics. After serving eleven terms in the House of Representatives, he was elected to the Senate as well, resigning from that office in 1933 when Roosevelt appointed him secretary of state. He would serve Roosevelt faithfully for eleven years, holding that office longer than anyone else, and he would eventually win the Nobel Peace Prize in 1945 for his efforts in establishing the United Nations. But he would also be forever linked to the Hull Note, the Americans' final proposal to the Japanese that closed the door to any further negotiations with the United States just prior to the Pearl Harbor attack.

Since all were living in the same world, the State Department was certainly aware that issues affecting Europe and Asia would eventually affect the United States. To that end, Secretary of State Hull, in July of 1939, posed the Americans' primary concern to the Japanese ambassador that the whole of China should not be *Manchurianized*, which would affect American rights and interests in the Far East. It was in that same month that the United States canceled their commercial treaty with Japan. In itself, it was freeing up the United States for future sanctions.

Throughout 1940 and early 1941, however, Japan was still importing 80 percent of the material she needed to wage war, and 88 percent of that was coming from the United States: coal, iron, steel, rubber, oil, and aviation fuel.[4]

Traditionally, the Japanese were no strangers to aggression. In 1910, they had annexed Korea. Then in 1914, while the nations of Europe were bogged down in World War I, Japan quietly occupied the Marshall, Marianna, and Caroline Islands. The Japanese occupation included names like Palau, Truk, and Saipan, which would virtually isolate the island of Guam, a U.S. territory.

To accuse Japan of following the lead of events in Europe would be shortsighted. Japan marched into Manchuria in 1931, six years before Hitler denounced the Treaty of Versailles in January 1937, and five years before Mussolini invaded Ethiopia. Japan walked out of the League of Nations in May of 1935, exactly four months before the Germans. She started her war with China in July 1937, over two years before Hitler invaded Poland. In this sense, Japan was the leader.

December 12, 1937, was perhaps the Americans' first exposure to the affairs of the Far East with the Japanese invasion of China and the attack on the American gunboat, the *Panay*, on the Yangtze River. During the siege of Nanking, the *Panay* was loaded with refugees, diplomats, and journalists attempting to flee the city. Once they got out on the river, the *Panay* was attacked by Japanese aircraft, but the aircraft crews would later claim that on that bright, sunny day they couldn't see the American flag. Apparently the aviators were reluctant to attack the ship, but eventually they followed orders. There were conflicting views as to the reason for the attack. Some thought that Japan was testing America's reaction, while others thought there had been conflicts within the Japanese high command.

Regardless, the *Panay* was sunk with two people killed and forty-eight wounded.[5] Among the survivors were two American newsreel cameramen who had caught the attack on film. One of the newsmen, Norman Alley from Universal, shot over five thousand feet of film of the attack. Universal had advertised the film as unedited and uncensored, but before it was shown in American theaters, under FDR's orders, approximately thirty feet of the most damaging scenes were cut, scenes in which the planes were attacking low across the water, where the U.S. flag would be so obviously visible.[6] After all, the flag had been painted on the decks and awnings. So the scenes were certainly damaging to the Japanese government and were ordered extracted from the film. Then the U.S. government proceeded to sue the Japanese government for damages. Apparently, the waters had to be muddied for a quick financial and diplomatic resolve of mistaken identity. The administration was not quite ready for war with Japan at that point and needed to cover up any signs that the attack had been deliberate. In the end, Japan paid the United States $2 million in reparations for sinking the *Panay*.[7]

In July 1938, the Japanese Army in Manchuria bulged out to the east, occupying Russian territory around Vladivostok. Later, they were beaten back by eastern Russian forces. Seesawing back and forth with heavy casualties eventually led to a Russo-Japanese Neutrality Pact signed in Moscow on April 13, 1941.

After the German attack on Russia in June of 1941, this pact would release forty Soviet divisions that had been held to guard against any Japanese aggressive move. Those divisions were transferred to the west, where they arrived in the Moscow area in November in time to meet the German drive to take Moscow.

By mid–1939, however, Europe had become center stage, and the United States started shifting its attention from the Pacific to across the Atlantic. It would be remiss not to review the intrigue and logic of the various pacts being signed by Germany, Japan and Russia.

For Adolf Hitler, it would be in Germany's interest to be assured of noninterference from Russia in Germany's planned invasion of Poland. Because of the assumed incompatibility of Nazism and Communism, Britain and France had just assumed that Russia would be in the western camp against Germany should hostilities ever develop. Although Stalin was not sure he could trust Hitler, after observing events at Munich with the French and British sellout of the Sudetenland, he felt that he could trust them even less.

The leaders of Germany, the United Kingdom, Italy, and France signed an agreement known as the Munich Agreement at the end of September 1938 that both Great Britain and France believed would appease Germany and forestall future military aggression on Germany's part. It allowed Germany to annex a strategic portion of Czechoslovakia where border defenses and heavy industries were located. Heavily populated by Germans, this territorial designation was known as the Sudetenland. Prime Minister Neville Chamberlain of Great Britain tried to assure the British people that the agreement would lead to settlement of other European border disputes and would keep the peace between Great Britain and Germany. Nevertheless, by the middle of the following March, the agreement became meaningless when Hitler moved his troops in and took over the remainder of Czechoslovakia.

On August 24, 1939, in the time frame of less than one day, another agreement, known as the German-Soviet Non-Aggression Pact, was signed in Moscow that essentially divided Poland into two halves. Germany would also trade industrial machinery in exchange for foodstuffs and strategic minerals, an exchange that would continue until Hitler turned on Russia. And finally, the pact established a mutual agreement that Germany would not interfere with Soviet aims in Finland, Latvia, and Estonia, but the southernmost Baltic state of Lithuania would be at the mercy of Germany.

By the summer of 1940, the isolationist posture in Congress was weakening somewhat, which was illustrated at a hefty cost to American taxpayers. With congressional approval of one navy expansion bill after another, Americans witnessed for the first time events that would shape things to come. The expansion bills provided for not only hundreds of thousands of increased tonnage of combatant and auxiliary ships, but also the manufacture of 15,000 aircraft for the navy.[8]

Where only twelve private companies had been manufacturing for the navy as of June 30, 1940, this number would increase to over 100 companies by the end of June 1941. And by that same time, nearly 700 new navy vessels would be under construction. Frank Knox reported in his navy budget that unpaid obligations had, by June 30, 1941, reached over $10 billion and that over $7 billion in obligations were estimated for 1942.[9]

Amidst all the military expansion of 1940, the Republicans held their national convention in Philadelphia during the last week of June. Wendell Willkie was nominated as the Republican presidential candidate. While he did not start out as the strongest contender, he beat out Robert Taft, son of President William Howard Taft, and the party voted solidly for noninvolvement in the war in Europe.

The British Purchasing Mission, which had been established in Washington in November

1939, reached an agreement with the U.S. government allowing Britain to purchase 40 percent of U.S. aircraft production. To help finance this huge rearmament, Americans' taxes were increased, and 2.2 million people who previously did not pay taxes were brought into the fold.

By this time, it was obvious that in the interest of the Americans' own rearmament program, the export of strategic materials could not continue, and it was announced that as of August 1940, the president would no longer export to Japan aviation fuel and a variety of machine tools. The commanding general of IX Corps in San Francisco, John L. DeWitt, reported that if Japanese aircraft fuel purchases continued, the United States would run short within six to nine months. From this time on, Japan's fuel reserves started to dwindle. This event would redirect Japan's interest to the Dutch East Indies and British Malaya for their oil and rubber.

Congress was on a roll. With the recent passage of the military-expansion bills, the next logical step would be the Selective Service Act. Well into 1940, American mobilization had been set to U.S. military requirements on a World War I dimension. The U.S. Army appropriation of $6 billion in 1940 alone equaled appropriations spent over the previous sixteen years.[10] But World War II would require twice the call of World War I. The new equation was the fact that the Americans' future enemies were increasing at a far greater rate than their own new appropriations were. By the fall of 1941, the United States could still list only thirty-three infantry divisions, which included only four armored divisions.[11] By September, the War Department had plans for an army of over one and a half million.[12] By comparison, Japan alone at this time was calling up another two million. Another two million![13]

To meet the American manpower shortage, Congress had passed the Selective Training and Service Act of September 16, 1940, the first peacetime draft in American history. All men between the ages of twenty-one and thirty-five were required to register with their local draft boards.[14] Everyone who registered on October 16, 1940, received a draft number. Similar to the process used in 1917, all numbers were placed in a huge glass bowl, and in a ceremony two weeks later in Washington, a number was drawn and handed to the president. This number represented the order in which registrants would be drafted. Presenting the number to President Roosevelt was none other than Secretary of War Henry Stimson.

In addition to serving as President Hoover's secretary of state from 1929 to 1933, Stimson had previously served as secretary of war from 1911 to 1913 under President William Howard Taft. Although Stimson was a Republican, Roosevelt was counting on him to generate the bipartisan support he needed when he reappointed Stimson secretary of war in 1940. Roosevelt had made the perfect choice. By the time Stimson had left the Hoover cabinet in 1933, he had already become very outspoken in opposing Japan's aggression in China, and he would eventually assume personal control over the development of the atomic bomb. Described by some as a leading influence in declaring war against Germany, Stimson gave Roosevelt his full support, and throughout World War II, he would oversee armed forces of over sixteen million Americans who served.

Leading military operations at the beginning of World War II were Army Chief of Staff General George Marshall and Chief of Naval Operations Admiral Harold Stark. General Marshall had been heavily involved in planning and training during World War I, and between the wars, he was one of the key planners in the War Department, eventually being named Deputy Chief of Staff of that department. Generally, those who disagreed with President

Roosevelt would be shown the door, but that was not the case with Marshall. Even after he openly disagreed with Roosevelt about providing Britain with aircraft, Roosevelt actually nominated Marshall for the position of army chief of staff, and he was sworn in on September 1, 1939, the same day that Germany invaded Poland.

The relationship between Franklin Roosevelt and Admiral Stark dated all the way back to 1914, when Roosevelt was assistant secretary of the navy, and although they were friends, it was not the friendship that earned Stark the CNO appointment. Stark had served extensive duty on torpedo boats and destroyers during World War I, developing his expertise in anti-submarine warfare. During the 1930s, he served as aide to the secretary of the navy, as well as the chief of the Bureau of Ordnance, and it was in these roles that Stark was able to hone his diplomatic skills. He was taken by surprise when Roosevelt appointed him chief of naval operations, thinking that the role should have gone to Admiral Ernest King. But other top naval officials agreed with Roosevelt, and Stark was sworn in during August of 1939. (Stark would later be replaced by Admiral King in March of 1942.)

By late summer of 1940, as Congress was voting in the military expansion bills and the Selective Service Act, Roosevelt took another step in building up U.S. forces. He exercised his executive power to call up the National Guard, and on August 31, 1940, he signed the order that would bring three hundred thousand men into active federal service.[15]

But this still didn't solve the manpower shortage because all draftees would serve only twelve months of active duty and then be released at about the time that they were fully trained. Those drafted would only serve their twelve months in the Western Hemisphere, which eliminated them from manning the one hundred twenty American overseas thousand-man garrisons from Iceland, Panama, Alaska, and Hawaii, to the Philippines.[16] The American press, however, built a very impressive picture of American invincibility. Unfortunately, the Americans' perception of the Japanese was exactly the opposite. Americans considered the Japanese to have poor eyesight and to be incapable of flying. They also had the impression that the Japanese military possessed obsolete military hardware and were totally uninformed on the state of American defenses in the Far East. Soon they would learn differently.

Another manpower resource for the military came out of the CCC. In 1933, Congress had formed the Civilian Conservation Corps with the mission to put thousands of unemployed young men to work in many government-sponsored programs. FDR ordered that it be managed by the army. This had its advantages and disadvantages. Within two months, more than three hundred thousand men were mobilized into about fifteen hundred camps, a record for the army.[17] And because the army was in charge, about three thousand regular officers, as well as noncommissioned officers, were needed to operate and manage the program. In turn, it also required the War Department to call to active duty a number of reserve officers to replace the regulars. And by 1935, ninety-three hundred reserve officers were serving in the CCC.[18] Although no actual military training was involved in running the CCC, the associated disciplined exposure to hundreds of thousands, as well as the valuable tutoring by thousands of reserve officers, would offer a head start for World War II.

By September of 1940, the noninvolvement sentiment in the United States had mushroomed into a political movement by the name of the America First Committee (AFC). Roosevelt had just announced his conclusion to the Destroyers for Bases Agreement with Britain, and with each step taking the country closer to war, the group announced their formal organization on September 4.

Founded by a group of Yale law students, the AFC's ultimate focus was to keep Americans out of the European conflict, and they fought Roosevelt every step of the way in their opposition to Lend-Lease, U.S. Navy convoying, and repealing the Neutrality Acts of the 1930s. AFC's primary policy was, instead of aiding the Allies with armaments, to build up American defenses at home first. In their strategic viewpoint, a stronger defense at home was the only way to preserve American democracy. Although the organization banned Nazis, Fascists, and Communists, the mere fact that they opposed Roosevelt's interventionist policy put them at odds with the president and his cronies, who labeled AFC's members as disloyal and unpatriotic. Roosevelt went so far as to deem AFC's efforts as subversive, appointing John Franklin Carter, a journalist, to head up an investigation of AFC's leadership. To Roosevelt's dismay, Carter wasn't able to come up with any Nazi leanings among its leadership or within AFC's policies.

With backers like the powerful publishing magnate William Randolph Hearst, and Joseph Kennedy, ambassador to Great Britain, its membership eventually grew to nearly one million.[19] Other prominent businessmen included General Robert E. Wood of Sears Roebuck, H. Smith Richardson of the Vick Chemical Company, and Sterling Morton of the Morton Salt Company, along with Robert R. McCormick of the *Chicago Tribune*, Joseph M. Patterson of the *New York Daily News*, and other publishers. Congressional representation would include two of Roosevelt's most outspoken critics, Senator Burton Wheeler (D–MT) and Senator Gerald Nye (R–ND). Just a few of the many celebrities who joined up included Sinclair Lewis, Gore Vidal, Walt Disney, and Alice Roosevelt Longworth. Even former president Hoover became an AFC member, and by April of 1941, America's favorite hero who had made the first transatlantic solo flight, Colonel Charles Lindbergh, also joined the ranks of AFC membership.

At the other end of the spectrum, another committee promoting peace evolved from the revision of the neutrality laws after war broke out in Europe in 1939. This organization also consisted of membership from both parties, including Henry Stimson and Frank Knox. Formed in May 1940, and chaired by newspaper editor William Allen White, this organization's conviction that a war involving Britain and France would eventually involve the United States led to the revision of their title to the Committee to Defend America by Aiding the Allies. With the ultimate goal of keeping Americans out of the war by aiding the Allies, the group supported Roosevelt's Destroyers for Bases Agreement, Lend-Lease, and naval convoying, and sought support to have the Neutrality Acts revised. The views of the committee were shared by the president and Secretary of State Hull, who was largely responsible for the repeal of that portion of the Neutrality Act that prohibited the sale of arms to the belligerents. This concept in itself put thousands of Depression Americans back to work, assuming, of course, that the British and French cash would hold out.

On September 27, 1940, the representatives of Germany, Japan, and Italy met in Berlin to conclude the signing of the Tripartite Pact. Representing Germany was Foreign Minister Joachim von Ribbentrop, and for Japan, Ambassador Saburo Kurusu, who would in November 1941 be sent to Washington to aid Ambassador Nomura in the negotiations with the United States. Italy was represented by Count Galeazzo Ciano, the son-in-law of Mussolini, who was later able to read between the lines. Count Ciano came to the unfortunate realization that for Italy's survival, it must make a separate peace with the Allies, a position for which Mussolini would have him executed.

The Tripartite Pact in itself recognized Germany's leadership in economic, political, and military affairs in a new order in Europe. It offered the same for Italy in the Mediterranean and for Japan in the greater East Asia. Further, the three governments agreed to assist each other with the same economic, political, and military means when and if one of the three powers was attacked. Support would also be provided if one of the pact members declared war on a power at present not involved in the war in Europe or the Japanese war in China. Since Germany had already signed a nonaggression pact with the Soviet Union in 1939, this measure was aimed specifically at keeping the United States out of the war in Europe or out of any potential involvement in the Pacific.

Although the ceremony itself was brief, Hitler appeared at the end of the ceremony long enough to give it his blessing. The immediate goal of the Tripartite Pact was to keep the United States out of Germany's war with Great Britain. But Washington was worried about a sudden German takeover of the Suez Canal that would give Germany access to the raw materials in the Pacific, thereby cutting off Britain. And in the end, the pact achieved exactly the opposite of its intended purpose. Germany would later expect Japan to attack Russia from the east when Germany broke her pact with the Soviet Union in June 1941.

Tension between Japan and Russia had been traditional, and Japan's invasion of China's northern province of Manchuria bordering Russia didn't help. Russia considered this a threat to her eastern territory. Added to this were the Communist and Nationalist Chinese maneuvering for more territory in the 1930s. Tensions between the two countries would eventually be reduced with the Russo-Japanese Non-Aggression Pact, which was signed in April 1941. (In an interesting side note to history, it was President Theodore Roosevelt who brought Japan and Russia together to negotiate a settlement in 1905. This was the end of all Japanese naval engagements until Pearl Harbor.)

With the Japanese attack at Pearl Harbor, however, Germany would finally find herself in a war with the United States that she had tried to avoid. The existence of the Tripartite Pact involving both Germany and Japan provided mutual support if either were attacked by a third power. Because war between Russia and Germany seemed unlikely when the pact was drawn up in 1940, it secured Japanese fears from Russia while Japan concentrated on expansion in the Pacific. The subsequent Russo-Japanese Pact of 1941 carried a term of five years, but with the collapse of Germany in 1945, Russia denounced the pact in order to grab up space under Japanese control before the war would end.

Even before Germany, Japan, and Italy signed the Tripartite Pact, the U.S. ambassador to Japan, Joseph Grew, warned Washington against economic embargoes. America should not be deceived by Japan's limited progress in China. To impose sanctions on scrap iron and petroleum may have the reverse effect rather than the intended effect, and could force Japan to quicken aggression in order to maintain stockpiles of reserves.

Grew had served in several ambassadorships (Denmark, Switzerland, and Turkey) before being posted in Tokyo in 1932. Developing an intimate knowledge of the Japanese culture, he understood their unwillingness to back down, regardless of the cost. After the attack on Pearl Harbor, he was interned by the Japanese for nine months, before returning to the United States in August 1942.

By October of 1940, Japanese Ambassador Kensuke Horinouchi, who served in that role for just a short time, presented himself to Secretary Hull at the State Department and advised that the U.S. embargo was a very unfriendly act, and if it were continued, future relations could be unpredictable. Hull, who to this point felt that he had been exceptionally patient, unloaded. He could not understand how Japan could consider it an unfriendly act not to support Japan's war in China with the necessary war materials. To strengthen the Americans' message, FDR now demanded that the Japanese get out of French Indochina, get out of China itself, and drop out of the Tripartite Pact, or he would see to it that the Americans would arrange a total cut-off of exports to Japan.

To the Japanese, this was ill-timed while their military machine was in high gear. They had occupied the Marshall, Mariannas, and Caroline Islands, as well as Manchuria, Formosa, Korea, and French Indochina, and were fighting in China itself when their chief source of supply suddenly threatened to cut them off. As previously mentioned, Japan was importing 80 percent of the war materials she needed, and the majority of the coal, iron, steel, rubber, oil, and aviation fuel was coming from the United States. Since Japan was so dependent on the Americans, it was obvious that one of two things would have to occur: either the Americans would have to make a drastic change in their foreign policy, which didn't seem very likely, or Japan would have to step up her calendar for occupation to the south: to British Malaya for its tin and rubber, and to the Dutch East Indies, Java, and Sumatra for their oil. But such a move would bring upon it the wrath of the American fleet based at Pearl Harbor, and within a couple of months, the U.S. long-range bomber force based out of the Philippines.

In addition to the increasing embargoes, Roosevelt had made yet another political statement to Japan, and in April 1940, the Pacific Fleet based at San Diego was ordered to the Hawaiian area for fleet maneuvers. In May, the order came that Pearl Harbor would be their new home. Ostensibly, this decision was a political one to remind Japan that to enforce Washington's decision, the United States Navy was a force to be reckoned with. This decision did not sit well with the commander in chief of the U.S. Pacific Fleet, Admiral James Richardson, and his arguments were difficult to refute. He was of the conviction that political decision should not interfere with military logic. He flew to Washington in July to meet with Chief of Naval Operations Harold Stark, who politely informed him that there would be no change.

On October 8, shortly after the Tripartite Pact was signed, Richardson returned to Washington and was invited to a lunch with his former boss, Admiral William Leahy, and the president. FDR first asked Leahy's opinion on strengthening the U.S. Asiatic Fleet based in Manila. The consensus was that any ships sent would probably be lost in a shooting war.

Admiral Richardson now brought up the subject of returning the Pacific Fleet based at Pearl Harbor to San Diego. The president replied that the fleet was there to exercise a restraining influence on Japan and to return the fleet would show a sign of weakness. Again Richardson insisted that that may be true with a civilian government, but Japan had a military government that knew the American fleet, being unprepared, undermanned, and without auxiliary ships, could not possibly take on distant operations. The base itself lacked adequate repair and refueling facilities, and as a result, it would offer no restraining influence on Japan. The last words on the subject were that if the president could convince the American people and the Japanese government that such a move would not be backing down, he would consider it. In just a few months, however, Richardson would no longer command the U.S. Pacific Fleet.

Since May of 1940, Winston Churchill had been looking to the Americans for help. It was well known that British shipping was desperate for protection from German submarines, especially after the fall of France. This offered the instigation of FDR's deal to exchange fifty

U.S. destroyers for bases held by the British. Churchill himself had suggested the loan of forty or fifty destroyers, but FDR's hands were tied in the disposal of weapons that could weaken U.S. defenses. So he consulted with Attorney General Robert Jackson to determine if he could fall back on his executive power to make the deal with Britain.

Robert Jackson had held the position of U.S. solicitor general since 1938, before being appointed U.S. attorney general in January of 1940. He would only serve in this capacity until June of 1941, being nominated by Roosevelt to serve on the Supreme Court and taking that oath the following month.

Similar to the heated debates that would come with Roosevelt's Lend-Lease program in 1941, there were those who were equally concerned about Roosevelt abusing his executive powers. Some compared him to Hitler, Stalin, and Mussolini, but his critics in Congress were of the minority, and they were not successful in raising the votes that would have been required to kill the destroyers-for-bases deal. Jackson, in his written opinion of August 27, 1940, asserted that based on Roosevelt's role as commander in chief of the armed forces, it was within his power "to dispose of vessels of the Navy and unneeded naval material"[20] as he saw fit, and that his commander-in-chief responsibilities included providing "adequate bases and stations for the utilization of the naval and air weapons of the United States at their highest efficiency in our defense."[21] Jackson also relied on the absence of any international treaty, which would have required congressional approval, and in the end, he deemed Roosevelt within his power to make the deal with Britain. On September 2, 1940, Americans became the new lessees of seven naval bases, and the navy's inventory was reduced by fifty destroyers.

For those who may have questioned the bold move on Roosevelt's part, the trade was considered legal because it strengthened American defenses, and the bases absorbed were in Newfoundland, Bermuda, the Bahamas, Jamaica, St. Lucia, Trinidad, and British Guiana. It was a good deal for the Americans, but not that good of a deal for the British because of the destroyer vintage.

The destroyers, nevertheless, were updated to include the installation of sonar. They were then commissioned into the Royal Navy and immediately transferred to the Atlantic, where their only advantage was in having a greater range than their British correlates. Upon hearing of the proposed deal, the U.S. Joint Chiefs of Staff objected that if Britain fell, as many thought it would, the Americans would have assumed those bases anyway. The deal represented fifty fewer destroyers that the United States would have to fight with, and without a doubt, the trade would represent a step closer to the Americans' undeclared war.

As Congress was gearing the country up for war, American intelligence teams were also making breakthroughs. For years, Japan had used a number of military and diplomatic codes in their communications with their military forces in Asia and her diplomatic embassies around the world. The most secret of the diplomatic codes was an exceedingly complicated cipher system, used for her most secret, most sensitive communications with her embassies, code-named *Purple* by American intelligence personnel.

In 1930, the Army Signal Intelligence Service had been created in Washington, and heading up the SIS was a genius named Lieutenant Colonel William Friedman. For the better part of two years, Friedman and a small, select staff had been working feverishly to break the Purple code.

Naval intelligence operations, on the other hand, dated back to 1922 with then Lieutenant Laurence Safford heading what was now called OP-20-G, the navy's cryptanalysis and intelligence group. (Safford would later prove to be one of the most steadfast of all those brought into the ensuing Pearl Harbor investigations.) He had helped establish naval cryptography operations after World War I and worked closely with Agnes Meyer Driscoll, who not only held a degree in mathematics, but also was fluent in French, German, and Japanese. Given her many talents, she became one of the navy's leading cryptanalysts and made a significant contribution toward breaking JN-25, the Japanese naval operational code.

So dedicated and accomplished was Lieutenant Safford in breaking codes and mechanizing the cryptology operations, some compared him to Friedman of the Army Signal Intelligence Service, and many referred to him as the "Friedman of the Navy." By January of 1942, Safford was promoted to the rank of captain, only to be "demoted" in responsibilities a couple of weeks later. Being edged out of his role in OP-20-G, he was advised by his commanding officer, Admiral Leigh Noyes, that he would be relegated to Admiral King's staff to handle cryptographic research, work he had done nearly twenty years earlier. But his time would be well spent. By 1941, he uncovered the fact that the Germans were reading Naval Cipher 3, the code that the Americans were using to communicate with the British, which cost many lives and a great deal of shipping losses. He tried to warn the senior military staff in Washington, but he was not taken seriously. Out of frustration, he developed an electronic adapter that would allow the American and British cipher machines to communicate with one another, and at the same time, disable German access to decipher their communications. And again, the Joint Chiefs of Staff turned their heads. Not until December of 1943, after countless more lives and millions of tons of supplies were lost, did his superiors finally pay attention to him: his Combined Cipher Machine was finally put to use, and the German submarines were no longer victorious.

Although the Army Signal Intelligence Service and the Office of Naval Intelligence were neighbors in Washington, there was no cooperation or sharing of intelligence that each jealously guarded. They had collaborated on Japanese diplomatic code systems, but not a speck more. No one outside of intelligence circles was aware of this, least of all the president. In the near future, this non-sharing would be to the Japanese advantage at Pearl Harbor.

Breaking the Japanese code Purple involved building a copy of the Japanese code machine with the help of the naval cryptanalysts of OP-20-G. On September 25, they broke the code by being able to read a Japanese message. However, the Japanese then had to be translated into English. Ideally, a machine that would do it all was needed, and such a machine was invented. Because of the countless hours that it saved, this technology was named *Magic*. How much equipment was needed and who would get it also had to be decided.

Eight machines were decided upon. The SIS (army intelligence) would receive two, and two would go to the OP-20-G (navy intelligence). One would also go to General MacArthur in the Philippines for the Station CAST intelligence operations located on Corregidor. Chief of Staff General Marshall was of the opinion that because the Army SIS had broken the Purple code, they should make the decision as to whom the recipients should be. An agreement had already been made that Great Britain and the United States would share intelligence information, so it was decided that Britain would receive two Magic machines.

When it was announced that two would go to Bletchley Park Naval Intelligence, Britain's main decryption center and cypher school, some in naval intelligence operations were not happy. Admiral Walter Anderson, director of Office of Naval Intelligence, and Rear Admiral Leigh Noyes, Naval Communications Director, were foaming at the mouth. The British, it appeared, were in no hurry to share with Washington their breakthrough with Germany's *Enigma*, the encryption and decryption code machine the Germans used for their diplomatic and military communications.

Later, it was also decided that Bletchley Park would receive a third machine, one that had originally been destined for Station Hypo at Pearl Harbor. Station Hypo, also known as Fleet Radio Unit Pacific, was responsible for cryptographic intelligence on Hawaii, and diverting a third machine to Bletchley Park left Pearl Harbor totally dependent on Washington for their diplomatic intelligence. The third machine promised to Bletchley Park would be in exchange for Britain's sharing information about *Ultra*, the code name they had designated to the Enigma decryptions. But the two intelligence officers delivering the Magic machines to Britain came back empty-handed, while the British made headway with Ultra.

The question would later be raised as to why Pearl Harbor was not given priority in receiving a Magic machine, and the response was there was no need for military leaders to have access to diplomatic information. If this is a legitimate argument, why was one provided General MacArthur in the Philippines? American intelligence operations eventually learned to decode Purple faster than the Japanese Embassy could manually decode it themselves.

The end of 1940 also brought about a successful British operation that would later influence the Japanese attack on Pearl Harbor. In the late fall, the British gave the world a tactical lesson in such an operation. On the night of November 11, the carrier HMS *Illustrious*, in what would be the world's first carrier-based air attack, launched twenty-one slow but tough Fairey Swordfish biplane torpedo bombers that flew one hundred fifty miles at low level to attack the Italian fleet moored in port at Taranto, Italy. The full-moon nighttime operation was meant to minimize losses from Italian fighters. The Swordfish bombers attacked at thirty-five feet above the waves with twelve aircraft carrying torpedoes and nine of them carrying bombs and flares. All but two returned after successfully crippling three Italian battleships, the *Littorio*, the *Conte di Cavour*, and the *Caio Dullio*, with eleven torpedoes, in addition sinking two supply ships and damaging two destroyers, leaving only one battleship still operational. This mission contributed to the reluctance of the Italian fleet to challenge the Royal Navy's supply lines to troops in Greece. The success of this mission was observed by the Japanese Navy in studying offensive tactics. There is evidence that this operation convinced Admiral Yamamoto, as commander in chief of their combined fleet, that the Hawaiian operation could be achieved. For the Taranto operation, the British had used those special, shallow-running torpedoes the Japanese were studying.

On the same day of the Taranto attack, however, Germany would even the score with Britain. The defense of Britain's Far East possessions, Malaya, Singapore, New Zealand, and Australia, were of paramount concern to the British war cabinet. In the event of war with Japan, the 1937 defense plan would send a large battle fleet sailing around the Cape of Good Hope to arrive at Singapore within seventy days. This assumed that the fleet would be available. But by 1940, war with Germany had altered the situation. It would now be ninety days, and with a considerably reduced fleet because the main fleet was required in England to protect the supply routes from the United States. Could Singapore hold out that long?

Australia and New Zealand preferred a fleet permanently based at Singapore to discourage Japanese aggression. London didn't consider this to be within the realm of possibility, while both Australia and New Zealand had sent troops to support the British cause in North Africa. Consequently, their own strength to defend their Far East home territory was reduced.

They had hoped for some reciprocal agreement in terms of a permanent naval force to protect their interest in the Far East. It would not happen.

In August 1940, at the height of the Battle of Britain, the British war cabinet concluded a long, detailed study of Singapore and its defenses. The conclusion was that Malaya and Singapore would have to do with what they had. No aid could be spared. This was information that would be incalculably valuable to Japan. Known as the COS (Chiefs of Staff) Far Eastern Appreciation, the study also included Britain's intentions should Japan invade French Indochina, Thailand, or Hong Kong. The report confirmed that Britain, which was stretched so thinly in Europe, couldn't support these colonies either, which would give Japan free reign to move into French Indochina. Much emphasis was put on keeping secret the conclusion that no help could be spared, and the decision was made that only one person in all the Far East should receive the report: Air Chief Marshal Sir Robert Brooke-Popham, who was the commander in chief of Far East operations based in Singapore. And in the interest of communications security, the decision was made to send the COS report by the merchant ship, the SS *Automedon*, a British passenger and cargo steamer. The *Automedon* set sail from Liverpool on September 24, 1940, destined for Singapore, Hong Kong, and Shanghai.

There is a great deal of speculation as to why the green top-secret pouch was sent via the *Automedon*. After all, Shenton Thomas, the governor of Singapore, had left Britain on a seaplane before the *Automedon* set sail. Further, Brooke-Popham, for whom the information was intended, did not leave Britain until October 27. And he was scheduled to arrive in Singapore several days before the *Automedon* was scheduled to arrive. The COS report had come out of the British war cabinet meetings of August 15, and had been available for over a month before it was dispatched on the *Automedon*, which would not reach Singapore until mid-November. To some, sailing through the Indian Ocean infested with German raiders hardly seemed like a safe method for transporting such sensitive information.

During its voyage through the Indian Ocean off the Nicobar Islands, the *Automedon* was sighted and boarded by crew members of a disguised German surface raider, the *Atlantis*. Although the secret information was packed in a weighted pouch with instructions to be thrown overboard so it would not be vulnerable to capture, its courier had been knocked unconscious, and the pouch was found after passengers and crew were taken prisoner. The *Automedon* was sunk and the contents of the secret pouch, confiscated by *Atlantis* crew members, were delivered to the German naval attaché in Tokyo. After the Tokyo attaché reviewed the documents, he sent them over to the Berlin naval staff who, in turn, presented them to the Japanese naval attaché in Berlin.

The Germans had seized a treasure trove of intelligence. Not only did the one pouch contain the military details of Britain's inability to defend its colonies, new naval cipher tables, maps, charts, minefield information, and British Secret Service reports were found in the other top secret bags that were confiscated. Considering this "intelligence bonanza,"[22] the Germans expressed surprise at Britain's choice of transportation of such crucial and top-secret information. They could not understand why they would have risked sending such sensitive material on such a slow and aging vessel. But to risk sending the pouches along with high-profile government officials such as Thomas or Brooke-Popham, who may be targeted by the Germans, was out of the question.

When the British first heard of the sinking, they were confident that their secrets had gone to the bottom of the ocean. But two months later, word reached London that the mail and documents had, in fact, been seized by the Germans before they sunk the vessel. As far as this author knows, no further attempt was ever made to inform Singapore of the war cabinet's decisions. Quite obviously, the colonies would never have sent troops to beef up Malaya for a one-way trip with no help coming from Mother Britain.

Secondly, one of Admiral Yamamoto's chief concerns was not to have the Pearl Harbor attack fleet top-heavy, which would leave an insufficient battle force behind to meet any British reinforcements for Singapore. The capture of the *Automedon*, which sank on the same day, November 11, 1940, that the British attacked Taranto, had resolved that problem.

Chapter 4
_____

Change of Command

January and February of 1941 introduced the new commands at Pearl Harbor. On February 1, 1941, Admiral Richardson was relieved of his command with the underlining reason that the fleet commander could not be at odds with the president. It may have been deeper than that. October 1940 had put the president in the middle of his re-election campaign for his third term. It had been necessary to defend all his actions and fend off the charges of the isolationists, and his patience or tolerance on many issues of which he had already made decisions were probably reaching their limit. Initially, Richardson had been personally convinced that he had perhaps influenced the president, so his firing came as a total surprise. Political decision versus military logic would always keep the country at a disadvantage during a shooting conflict. (It should be noted that Richardson had also maintained a three-hundred-mile air reconnaissance from Oahu that was discontinued at the direction of Admiral Stark, shortly before Richardson was fired.)

Another thorn in Richardson's side was Admiral Walter Stratton Anderson, who may have been the one who would dispel any hope of Richardson's rapport with the president. Anderson had held several senior commands, including a battleship and a division of cruisers, before being appointed the director of naval intelligence by the president in June 1939. After about a year and a half in that role, "Roosevelt personally promoted the director of naval intelligence, Captain Walter Anderson, to rear admiral."[1] With his new rank, Anderson was appointed commander of battleships, Pacific Fleet, assuming his new role at the end of January 1941, just before Admiral Richardson was replaced by Admiral Kimmel.

Meeting with Roosevelt several times a week in Roosevelt's private office, Anderson felt he had had a special relationship with the president. However, he was not a favorite amongst his peers. One officer reported that the Office of Naval Intelligence (ONI) had been "a haven for the ignorant and well connected"[2] while under the leadership of Anderson. Even Admiral Stark, whose hands were tied, would later apologize to Kimmel for Anderson's appointment to Hawaii. In a letter to Kimmel, Stark explained, "The appointment was forced on us by the White House."[3]

Anderson and the president were in full accord on the policy whereby Japan would be provoked into firing the first shot. He was now where he could best influence things in Hawaii in the way the president wanted them done.

Upon arrival in Hawaii, Admiral Anderson was offered quarters at Pearl Harbor, where most senior officers lived. But being aware that Japan would probably attack Pearl Harbor, he rented property many miles away, east of Diamond Head, where the sky above Pearl wasn't even visible. He was at this remote location through the morning of December 7 while the battleships under his command were bearing the brunt of the attack.

Anderson attended the naval change of command in February, from Admiral Richardson to Admiral Kimmel, and over the next ten months, as the former chief of naval intelligence, he had at least the moral responsibility to inform Kimmel that Washington had been reading Japan's Purple diplomatic code since the previous September. As Pacific theater veteran and writer Robert Stinnett pointed out, Anderson had been sent to Hawaii to act as "intelligence gatekeeper."[4] So he was apparently committed to the president to leave Kimmel in the dark.

Another incident in Hawaii found Admiral Anderson stepping out of his assignment as battleship commander and back into his previous role in intelligence. In early 1941, one of the most notorious Japanese spies arrived in Honolulu. It was known that he would arrive by ship on March 24. His name was Ensign Takeo Yoshikawa, a young man in his twenties, and his undercover name was Tadashi Morimura. His ship, the *Nitta Maru*, arrived as expected and was met by undercover agents of the FBI and naval intelligence. In Honolulu, the FBI agent in charge, Robert Shivers, and his sixteen special agents would normally have observed

Left to right, front: **General Short, Lord Louis Mountbatten, commander of Britain's aircraft carrier HMS** *Illustrious,* **and Admiral Kimmel;** *rear:* **General Martin and Admiral Bellinger (Arizona Memorial).**

Morimura's activities. But on the first night of his arrival, Anderson told the FBI to stay away, stating that "the Navy would conduct the espionage investigation, not the FBI."[5] This directive carried the approval of FBI Director J. Edgar Hoover, with whom Anderson had cultivated a relationship during his naval intelligence days in Washington.

With this directive, Anderson arranged Morimura's complete freedom to do his work. Anderson was aware of the spy's daily activities, including his communications with Tokyo, and in no way limited his endeavors. (Anderson would retire from the navy in 1946. By the time of his death in 1981 at the age of 100, he was the oldest living Naval Academy graduate.)

And why was Admiral Husband Kimmel chosen to take over for Admiral Richardson? Roosevelt had chosen him over many others who outranked Kimmel. And when he was temporarily promoted to full admiral and assigned to take command of the Pacific Fleet in early 1941, Kimmel had become one of the few four-star admirals at that time.

Certainly Kimmel had the credentials for the job. Having graduated from the Naval Academy in 1904, he had commanded several ships and staffs, and by 1937, was promoted to rear admiral. At this rank, he had served as commander of Cruiser Division 7 in 1938 and as commander of Cruisers, Battle Force in 1939. Described as "brilliant, energetic ... a work horse"[6] who expected as much of himself as he demanded from his men, Kimmel was highly respected by those who served under him. It is interesting to note that earlier in his career, Kimmel had served as an aide to Franklin Roosevelt while Roosevelt was the assistant secretary of the navy (1913–1920). Considering the outcome of Pearl Harbor and FDR's subsequent treatment of Kimmel, one might question how that previous association had ended.

By February 1941, other changes in the top chain of naval command were also made. Besides Richardson's being replaced by Kimmel, his counterpart commanding the Atlantic Fleet would be Rear Admiral Ernest King. King, in 1939, had been assigned to the General Board, the naval advisory board that consisted primarily of senior officers nearing the end of their careers. It was Admiral Stark who believed King's abilities were being wasted on the board, and he appointed King as commander in chief of the Atlantic Fleet.

And on Oahu, the army was also getting a new commander. General Walter Short was being sent to take over the army garrison from General Herron, who was nearing retirement. Herron retired in 1941, but would be recalled in 1942 to serve on the Personnel Board.

During World War I, Short had served as a training officer with the First Infantry Division in France, and later during the war, he served in the training section of the Army General Staff. By 1920, he was promoted to major, worked in military intelligence for several years, as well as other training roles, and was promoted to brigadier general in 1936. After serving as commander of the First Infantry Division in 1939, Short was promoted to major general in 1940. Through his progressive roles, he became known as a very diplomatic and efficient leader who could work with other leaders to get the job done. It seems he was a highly suitable candidate when General Marshall called upon him to command the army's Hawaiian Department. With this appointment, he was promoted to lieutenant general.

Considering the larger picture, the chain of command in Hawaii would not be a simple one. Because of later adverse publicity given to Kimmel and Short after the successful Japanese attack, the American public was left with the impression that they, and only they, made all the decisions. Yes and no. Kimmel was commander in chief of the Pacific Fleet (CINCPAC) berthed at Pearl Harbor. But Pearl Harbor itself was under the command of Rear Admiral

Claude C. Bloch. Bloch, who had previously been commander of the Pacific Fleet, was now commander of the Fourteenth Naval District.

Prior to 1920, regional naval districts had been established to handle the administrative functions of coastal and shore activities of the navy, and the Fourteenth Naval District, among other Pacific islands, included Hawaii, Midway, and Wake Island. Bloch's chain of command now included Kimmel and the Navy Department. In essence, Admiral Bloch was the landlord and Admiral Kimmel was the renter.

Nor did General Short hold any authority over Admiral Bloch. Naval aviation at Pearl Harbor, from combat planes to long-range patrol, all came under the command of Rear Admiral Patrick Bellinger. And Bellinger wore many hats. He was commander of Patrol Wings (PATWING) One and Two, responsible for the long-range air patrols from Oahu. But he was also commander of the Naval Base Defense Air Force, which was just on paper and only existed if and when the need arose. But in both of these positions, Bloch controlled at least part of his authority. In addition, Bellinger was Kimmel's fleet air wing commander, but in this capacity, he also reported to San Diego. So Kimmel had to share this authority with the mainland. Now it gets complicated.

The actual air defense of the island was the responsibility of the army under the command of Short's air commander, Major General Frederick L. Martin. Martin had taken over as commander of the Hawaiian Air Force in October 1940, and he worked closely with Admiral Bellinger to juggle the limited resources they had to work with. Although his responsibility was the defense of Hawaii itself, the long-range PBY (patrol bomber) protection was under the command of Bellinger. Martin and Bellinger would be the two to draft the Joint Coastal Frontier Defense Plan that would be finalized in early 1941.

Jumping ahead to 1944, the Army Pearl Harbor Board would point out that Bellinger was subordinate to at least five different authorities, not including the army, and was the commander of the Navy Base Defense Air Force, which was actually the army's responsibility. In the board's opinion, Short's command could only cooperate once they determined who it was that they were supposed to cooperate with. On this note, the Army Board concluded, "In this [naval] organization, in which there were two governing heads, Admirals Kimmel and Bloch, with whom General Short had to do business, and their respective staffs with whom Short's staff had to deal, as well as the many-titled Admiral Bellinger with whom General Martin dealt, the problem of cooperation was made somewhat difficult."[7]

It was now quite obvious that meeting an air attack was the most critical mission of the combined defense forces, with neither branch possessing nearly the hardware necessary for the job until the critical reinforcements would arrive. It would mean that both services would have to have a cooperation of unimaginable detail with only limited resources to work with.

By March of 1941, the army and navy would develop a plan that recognized the necessity to defeat an enemy force before it could reach the island, a task that the navy was ill equipped to perform with its PBYs. For this mission, the navy would borrow from the army whatever long-range bombers were available to be loaned, and those bombers would come under temporary command of the navy. Conversely, if the enemy should reach the island, the defense of which was an army responsibility (although it was insufficient to meet the requirement), the army would borrow fighters from the navy. This document or agreement was basically the result of the Bellinger-Martin collaboration.

The inauguration of the plan was April 11, 1941, with the official signing by Admiral

Bloch as Pearl Harbor base commander and General Short as army garrison commander, with credit given to Rear Admiral Bellinger and Major General Martin as the authors. Its official title was the Joint Coastal Frontier Defense Plan. A copy was forwarded to Washington at the end of March, and a lack of response would tend to indicate official approval. But in meeting the solution, they first had to recognize the problem.

The situation as envisioned by Martin and Bellinger was that, because "[i]n the past Orange [Japan] has never preceded hostile actions by a declaration of war ... an Orange fast raiding force might arrive in Hawaiian waters with no prior warning from our Intelligence Service,"[8] which would most likely be accomplished with an air attack on Oahu. Bellinger and Martin also predicted that the attack would be launched from air carriers situated within three hundred miles of Hawaii. And they further predicted, "In a dawn air attack there is a high probability that it could be delivered as a complete surprise ... and that it might find us in a condition of readiness under which pursuit would be slow to start."[9] This additional assessment was sent to Washington along with the Joint Coastal Frontier Defense Plan.

But there were still many holes to be filled in, considering that at the time, neither branch really had anything of value to loan to the other. The army did have thirty-three obsolete Douglas B-18 Bolo short-range bombers that were of little value.[10] They were worn out when they came to Hawaii, and at best, they had less than half the range of the navy PBYs.

More meetings, discussions, and refinements. Bloch had referred to the whole concept as a sort of "volunteer fire department."[11] All the aircraft and personnel would be involved in their daily training, but when the whistle blew, they were to drop everything and respond to the alarm. As one of Admiral Bloch's officers explained, "You sounded an air-raid alarm, and all these planes, coming off these various forces, with their own duties, their own tasks, their own missions, they came over to Bellinger's, and all the fighters went to Martin; and ... all of Martin's bombers came over for search and attack."[12]

A number of experimental drills using this concept were conducted, and surprisingly, they all worked, possibly because there was prior notice of the exercises, and there was so little to work with. But what would happen with no advance notice, which was the purpose of the whole plan to handle an actual attack?

With such a shortage of planes, General Martin made another plea to Washington on August 20, 1941. This highly detailed report to support his request included an analysis of a potential Japanese attack. His analysis, reiterating an early-morning attack, pointed out: "Our most likely enemy, ORANGE, can probably employ a maximum of 6 carriers against Oahu ... it will be necessary for the carrier to approach within 233 nautical miles of Oahu before it can launch its aircraft."[13] Martin also communicated that Japan's approach would probably come from the north, possibly from the west or south, and most unlikely from the east. What could have been more precise?

The bright spot of the Joint Coastal Frontier Defense Plan was that it would or could work with advance warning. So everything depended upon Kimmel's being fed the latest intelligence from Admiral Stark, which would allow Kimmel to make any changes necessary to meet the changing situation.

There had also been a plan suggested to create a joint services center, similar to what the British had created, in a huge cave near Fort Shafter, but Bloch recommended against it because of dissimilarity of missions. But within two weeks after December 7, 1941, there would be one.

With both the army and navy being so inadequately equipped, the thought of having to go to war in the next year or so was certainly a sobering one. Most sobering was the line-up of the world armies.

By the end of 1940, Germany had eighty-nine infantry divisions, plus nine armored divisions with twenty-five hundred tanks, including satellite armies. Troops totaled about 2.5 million men, armies that had been combat tested in Poland and Western Europe.[14] Italy's army had seventy-three divisions, which included fifty-nine infantry and three armored divisions, combat tested in North Africa.[15] Japan had forty-one divisions and growing, combat tested in China, with about 1.7 million troops in uniform.[16] The Axis then totaled, conservatively, over two hundred combat-tested divisions, against which the United States on paper could muster only thirty-some divisions that were neither operational nor fully equipped. Training was insufficient, and there had been no combined maneuvers.

Also by 1940, Germany's Luftwaffe was the most powerful air force in the world with thirty-eight hundred modern combat aircraft.[17] Japan's army and naval planes totaled about four thousand each.[18] Italy's Regia Aeronautic rounded out at twenty-five hundred combat planes,[19] giving the Axis over fourteen thousand combat aircraft. The United States had some catching up to do.

Most of the aircraft that the United States would fight World War II with were still on the drawing boards, which was of little consolation to those pilots who would meanwhile have to engage America's enemies on one-way trips. Standardization was still in the future, as was mass production. But thanks to a superb advertising campaign, the American public was convinced that the United States had the best air force in the world. For all the publicity given at the time to the Boeing B-17, a four-engine strategic bomber known as the Flying Fortress, there were no more than fifty-six of these in service as of June 1940. And defensively, these were helpless when compared with much later variants.

The man who would get the Army Air Corps *off the ground* would be General Henry "Hap" Arnold. A true aviation pioneer, Arnold was taught to fly by the Wright Brothers and was among the first thirteen aviators to fly for the U.S. Army. After graduating from West Point in 1907, Arnold rose through the ranks, and by 1935 had attained the rank of brigadier general. In 1936, he was appointed Assistant to the Chief of Air Corps, and only two years later, was appointed Chief of Air Corps with the rank of major general.

Known for his impatience, Arnold struggled to convince Roosevelt of the dire state of the Air Corps, and once that was accomplished, getting the needed funding was the next step. Determined to make the United States the number one air force in the world, Arnold was not at all hesitant to directly lobby members of Congress on his own, and he often used Charles Lindbergh's celebrity to help get the job done. Working with Hap Arnold, Lindbergh had become the point person for the Air Corps, "involving himself in countless discussions with members of Congress, bureaucrats, diplomats, business executives, scientists, and engineers about what needed to be done—and spent—to make America No. 1 in airpower."[20]

Britain's success at Taranto the previous fall had raised the eyebrows of the United States Navy, and it provided the inspiration both in Washington and Hawaii to re-think Pearl Harbor's defenses. The concerns were in the form of attack that Japan might employ: bombing, torpedo attack by air, submarine mining of waters, or off-shore naval bombardment, with any of these accompanied by sabotage. These concerns were all embodied in a communication from Secretary of the Navy Frank Knox to his counterpart on the army side, Secretary of War

Henry Stimson. The emphasis was that these possibilities could become realities. In Knox's opinion, fighters, a radar warning system, antiaircraft guns, and joint army-navy exercises were of the highest priorities with which to defend Oahu.

Stimson was in total agreement. An air attack without warning would put the burden of repelling it in the army's lap, which was totally incapable of meeting it. Fighter strength on Oahu was a joke. There were a few Boeing P-12 biplanes with a top speed of less than 200 miles per hour. An improvement on those was the fourteen Boeing P-26s which, designed in 1933, had open cockpits and fixed landing gear. Known as Peashooters, these only had a top speed of 230 miles per hour. The modern fighters consisted of thirty-nine Curtiss P-36 Hawks, which, with a top speed of 290 miles per hour, were considered state of the art, but only until the shooting actually started.

The only warning systems on Oahu were the sound detectors, whose maximum range of five miles made them useless. And if the detectors did warn in time, there was a shortage of antiaircraft artillery and ammunition, so proper or adequate defense was virtually impossible. There wasn't even one barrage balloon on the entire island. And at this point in 1941, proper radar for the ships was still in the future.

Fifty P-40B fighters had been promised the army. By March of 1941, General Marshall had finally accepted the fact that the only way to get the fighters that Short needed for the defense of Oahu was to not wait for assembly-line production but to strip existing fighter squadrons in the States. A number of units were thinned out of their modern P-40B aircraft so that Marshall could muster fifty of the fighters for Hawaii. These were transported from the west coast aboard the *Lexington*, along with other vitally needed supplies.[21]

Both the barrage balloons and radar were assured by summer. It was the radar that had saved England in the Battle of Britain the previous summer, but the system had been in place years before the shooting started.

The only bright spot in Short's defenses was the manpower of his two infantry divisions, the Twenty-Fourth and the Twenty-Fifth. The former was considered trained, but the newly formed Twenty-Fifth was created by robbing a regiment of the Twenty-Fourth, adding a regiment of reservists, and creating a regiment of draftees. But the mentality of prewar concepts considered the two sufficient to defend the island against invasion.

The increased tensions in the Pacific did, however, bring a greater number of B-17s to Hawaii than to any other garrison. The first flight of twenty-one B-17Ds departed Hamilton Field in San Francisco on May 13 for the thirteen-hour flight. The Hawaiian air force would now transition into the heavy bombers. But by late summer, the focus shifted to sending reinforcements to the Philippines, which changed the picture somewhat at Hickam Field in Hawaii.

The B-17s from the States destined for the Philippines had to be stripped of full crews, weapons, and ammunition for the two-thousand-mile leg to Hawaii. And with more B17s to come, new crew members had to be trained to fill the vacancies. In addition, the aircraft had to be serviced or repaired to continue on to the Philippines. This meant stripping General Short's B-17s of parts. Soon he would be reduced to just six flyable aircraft to provide the crew training.

The navy was experiencing the same supply problems. The lessons of Taranto had provided the impetus for Washington to lean on the Bureau of Ordnance to develop additional torpedo nets to place within Pearl Harbor, which would have provided additional protection

B-18s, P-26s, and P-12s at Hickam Field, 1940.

for the ships in harbor. Almost a year of prioritizing would fail to produce one net, and on December 7, none had materialized. Admiral Stark, in a letter written shortly before Kimmel assumed command in early 1941, said it all: "In my humble opinion we may wake up any day … and find ourselves in another undeclared war…. I have told the gang here for months past that in my opinion we are heading straight for this war, that we could not assume anything else and personally I do not see how we can avoid [it] … many months longer. And of course it may be a matter of weeks or days…. I have been moving Heaven and Earth trying to meet such a situation, and am terribly impatient at the slowness with which things move here."[22]

Of historical significance was a communication in February 1941 from General Marshall to General Short in Hawaii, wherein he stated, "The real perils of the situation lay in sabotage,"[23] as well as in an attack by air or sea. He even admitted that it would be difficult to protect the fleet with the current shortage of both fighter planes and antiaircraft guns. It was Marshall's opinion that if the Hawaiian forces could survive the first six hours of an enemy attack without suffering serious damage, then the armaments they currently had on hand should be sufficient to ward off further aggression. To explain the shortage of planes and artillery, he went on to say:

> What Kimmel does not realize is that we are tragically lacking in this materiel throughout the Army and that Hawaii is on a far better basis than any other command in the Army.
> The fullest protection for the Fleet is a major consideration for us, there can be little question about

that; but the Navy itself makes demands on us for commands other than Hawaii, which make it difficult for us to meet the requirements of Hawaii.... You should make clear to Admiral Kimmel that we are doing everything that is humanly possible to build up the Army defenses of the Naval overseas installations, but we cannot perform a miracle.[24]

And amidst the discussions of armament shortfalls and potential threats to Hawaii, the U.S. ambassador in Japan, Joseph Grew, would confirm for them what was to come.

Peru's ambassador to Japan, Ricardo Rivera-Schreiber, had passed the information on to Max Bishop, the American embassy's third secretary, indicating that the information had come from a conversation overheard by a cook. And on January 27, 1941, Ambassador Grew sent a coded message to Washington which included, "A member of the Embassy was told by my ... colleague that from many quarters, including a Japanese one, he had heard that a surprise mass attack on Pearl Harbor was planned by the Japanese military forces, in case of 'trouble' between Japan and the United States; that the attack would involve the use of all the Japanese military facilities. My colleague said that he was prompted to pass this on because it had come to him from many sources, although the plan seemed fantastic."[25]

Grew was the relay to Japan of Americans' concern with Japan's war in China, and now there was a new twist: a hint of war with the United States. The message was passed from naval intelligence to CNO Admiral Stark, and then onto Admiral Kimmel in Hawaii, who was just starting to settle into his new command. But Washington had put little military value into the message, and diplomatically speaking, who would give the Peruvian Embassy privileged information that the Americans couldn't get themselves? As a result, it was soon forgotten. When the information was passed on to Kimmel, a note was added to it emphasizing that naval intelligence only considered the information a rumor. "Furthermore, based on known data regarding the present disposition and employment of Japanese naval and army forces, no move against Pearl Harbor appears imminent or planned in the foreseeable future."[26] Not in the foreseeable future.

But the message did have what should have been an alarm because it was at this precise time in late January that Admiral Yamamoto was ordered to make a plan for the Pearl Harbor attack. In retrospect, U.S. naval intelligence had been trying to figure out how to launch a successful attack on Pearl Harbor for twenty years, and it just seemed too far from home and too big a risk for what Japan would have to employ to chance it. Yamamoto was convinced, however, that Japan would have no hope of winning a war with the United States unless the American fleet at Pearl Harbor was destroyed.

In responding to another reminder from Marshall for an "early review"[27] of Hawaii's defenses, General Short replied that he was cognizant of the entire situation and reiterated the most pressing need for an aircraft warning service, a radar system that would detect an enemy farther than the five-mile sound detectors. Protection of the island was "so dependent upon the early completion of this Aircraft Warning Service that I believe all quibbling over details should be stopped at once."[28] Marshall concurred and wrote back on March 15:

It will be necessary to comply with certain fixed regulations in those cases where [radar] facilities are to be established on lands pertaining to the Secretary of the Interior. The National Park Service officials are willing to give us the temporary use of their lands when other lands are not suitable for the purpose, but they will not waive the requirements as to submission of preliminary building plans showing the architecture and general appearance. They are also very definitely opposed to permitting structures of any type to be erected at such places as will be open to view and materially alter the natural appearance of the reservation.[29]

Secretary of War Stimson had promised the radar by June. The radar sets were of two varieties, fixed and mobile. Then there was the issue of the trained personnel necessary to install, operate, and maintain them. By December 7, the fixed sets had still not been installed, but a few of the shorter-range mobile sets were operative, and crew training had begun. Short's further concerns emanated from the fact that U.S. airfields offered perfect targets. Where aircraft were parked in precision rows, they were invitations to disaster. In no case had any funds been allocated for dispersion or bunkers to offer the survival of some.

Because of the United States' precarious position in the Pacific, the major question was still: when do the Americans fight, short of being attacked themselves, or if the British and the Dutch are attacked? Assuming an affirmative decision was made, what would they do, and what would they fight with? They would have a difficult time to just defend what they currently had.

One of the obstacles in fortifying the Pacific commands was inefficient and poorly managed wartime production. The business of transitioning the American economy into a military-oriented economy was exacting a toll because no one knew with absolute certainty how to achieve it in the best business sense. The country wasn't really at war, yet it was.

Management of the new wartime economy justified the creation of the National Defense Advisory Commission (NDAC) which surrendered to the Office of Production Management, and finally the War Production Board (WPB). In 1941, Donald M. Nelson, executive vice-president of merchandising at Sears and Roebuck, was appointed director of the Office of Production Management, and in 1942, he became the chairman of the War Production Board. Known to some for his inability to make decisions, he was highly criticized by Secretary Stimson, who tried to have him replaced. For whatever reason, Harry Hopkins, who was by then Roosevelt's most trusted adviser, talked Roosevelt out of it, and Nelson remained in the role for the duration of the war.

Millions were being spent, but the finished wartime products were slow in coming off the assembly lines, which hit a low of production during the summer of 1941. But the corporations were booming, manufacturing for the civilian economy while building plant additions to produce for the military economy. New car sales were reportedly at record levels. The military demands for raw materials were such that they were starting to crimp the civilian market. With the civilian economy becoming a seller's market, how long could the nation continue to support both?

The new Ford Motor Company plant at Willow Run, Michigan, was a case in point. As the largest aircraft production plant in the country, designed to turn out one B-24 heavy bomber per hour, it found its production stressed to the point that it was turning out only one aircraft per day.[30] With thousands of parts per aircraft and hundreds of design changes, each required the major retooling of machines that Ford was equipped to deal with.

The plant was about an hour's driving distance from Detroit, and with the eventual rationing of gasoline and tires, as well as a lack of local housing, the daily absentee rate at the plant was just under 20 percent. At times, just as many workers were leaving as were being hired. Added to this was Henry Ford's policy of not hiring women for factory jobs. The employment dilemma was finally resolved by scaling down the workforce, made possible by farming parts out to subcontractors and to other plants. But it would still take until 1944 to fine-tune the operation to the point that it could actually produce one aircraft per hour. Meanwhile, with skepticism running high, the employees of Willow Run jokingly asked the question, "Will it run?" Detroit was just one example. Other varieties of aircraft, plus artillery barrage balloons and radar, were coming off the assembly lines in dangerously low quantities.

Senator Harry Byrd (D–VA) announced that he considered it "an act of utter folly for the nation to become a voluntary shooting participant in the war."[31] Byrd reported glaring examples of production inefficiency. As examples, he explained that only sixty, four-engine bombers were coming off the assembly lines each month, adding that only a dozen 90mm antiaircraft artillery had actually been delivered.[32] He cited that tank and naval ship production was a disgrace for the money spent. He then suggested a total reorganization of the U.S. war production system to be redesigned "along sound lines of business efficiency."[33]

Byrd had been asked to run for the presidency back in 1932, but instead, he chose to endorse Roosevelt and served on Roosevelt's first presidential campaign. Known for his pay-as-you-go policy from his early days, Senator Byrd held a much more conservative view when it came to government spending. He was opposed to Roosevelt's New Deal, so their relationship changed, and it was only fitting that he became the chairman of the Joint Committee on Reduction of Non-Essential Federal Expenditures in September 1941.

The president, of course, denied all of these charges made by Byrd and attempted to assure the nation that the senator was presenting a distorted description. But FDR was in a corner and had to admit that the figures referring to aircraft production were correct.

In his April 3, 1941, radio broadcast, House Minority Leader Joseph Martin, Jr. (R–MA) warned Americans of the necessity to police those who were charged with overseeing the nation's budget, particularly in a time of impending war. Referring to the New Deal, which could result in "financial, political and social bankruptcy,"[34] he also compared the current debt of $47 billion to that of $1.25 billion at the beginning of World War I,[35] emphasizing, "We cannot tolerate extravagance or dishonesty. Racketeering must have no place in our national defense."[36] Alluding to "political henchmen with juicy contracts or luscious loans,"[37] he cautioned that internal forces could be as destructive as external forces. "Events abroad must not be permitted to distract us from the vigilance required at home. Our greatest danger is still from insidious inside forces. That fact will be apparent to every American as we proceed with the defense program."[38] The man who would eventually oversee the investigation of mismanagement of government materials and funds was the man who would be the next president, Senator Harry Truman (D–MO).

In early 1941, following rumors of mismanagement in his home state of Missouri, Truman had reported back to Washington on apparent corruption at Fort Leonard Wood. He followed up with inspections of many other forts and defense plants. His report recommended what became the Senate Special Committee to Investigate the National Defense Program also known as the Truman Committee, headed by Truman himself. He held the lead role until he became vice-president in 1944. The end result of these investigations would save the U.S. taxpayer roughly $15 billion on everything from faulty hardware to improvements in methods of construction.[39]

In the competition for raw materials, big industry was getting the lion's share, which left small industry desperately competing for what was left. In these so-called prosperous times, with the Depression seemingly far behind, it was still almost impossible for a company to stay in business unless there was a government contract involved. In addition, Donald Nelson had banned production of almost three hundred items not considered essential to the war effort. Included were items such as refrigerators, bicycles, and beer cans.

Americans had come to the realization that they had to see the emergency through, but were totally ignorant of the required sacrifices necessary to achieve it, which involved doing without things such as gasoline, coal, metal, and plastics. Wool, nylon, and dyes were just around the corner. At a press conference, FDR told reporters that Abraham Lincoln had faced the same situation in 1862 with his statement, "The fact is that the people have not yet made up their minds that we are at war with the South. They have not yet buckled down to a determination to fight this war through."[40]

The increasing demands of war production provided the perfect opportunity for the labor unions, and by the spring of 1941, strikes were on the rise. The president's demands to halt the strikes were of no avail. Hitler, having abolished the German unions years before, must have chuckled at the ability of one man to tie up the entire defense industry.

In August, the shipbuilders had struck the Federal Shipbuilding and Dry Dock Company in Kearney, New Jersey. In the end, the president had to seize the shipyard to get everyone back to work. The five major rail unions that moved the raw materials were threatening a strike for December 7.

In the race for raw materials, the unions continued to take advantage and organized strikes under the guise of fair wages for all. John L. Lewis, head of the United Mine Workers and other unions, seemed to have a hand on the pulse of the nation. Already branded as an isolationist, he knew when, amid other national distractions, to call strikes. In the midst of this national demand for raw materials, Lewis called yet another strike of fifty-three thousand mine workers in November who were supplying the steel industry.[41] This strike was called off a week later when union members accepted an arbitration proposal made by the White House. Americans wanted to know who was running the country. Was it John Lewis or Franklin Roosevelt?

During the Depression, Lewis had supported President Herbert Hoover, but the longer the Depression went on, Lewis's loyalties started to shift to Roosevelt. Through his influence with the CIO (Congress of Industrial Organizations), over $500,000 would be contributed to Roosevelt's election campaign in 1936, which helped him win the presidential election by a landslide. Having Lewis at his side was a good thing for Roosevelt.[42]

John Lewis was the icon of organized labor. Getting involved in the coal mining industry after the turn of the century, he was the leading influence in establishing the CIO, and in turn, the United Steel Workers of America. As president of the CIO in 1937, Lewis and his affiliates convinced both General Motors and United States Steel, both nonunion organizations at the time, to sign collective-bargaining agreements. The agreements would establish the CIO's strong competitive position against the American Federation of Labor (AFL). With 85 percent of the CIO, however, in favor of Roosevelt's upcoming war, Lewis resigned from the CIO, taking his mine workers, the United Mine Workers of America, with him.

The downside for Roosevelt was that Lewis was also an isolationist. And by 1940, Lewis had no doubt Roosevelt was taking the country to war, making himself a major thorn in Roosevelt's side. Violating the no-strike pledge by repeatedly calling his miners to strike, Lewis would continue to challenge Roosevelt throughout World War II, forcing the government to seize the mines to bring the workers back in. With all the production delays this caused, having John Lewis on the other side was not a good thing for Roosevelt.

The resulting trickle-down effect in weapons of war felt in the overseas commands forced the Hawaiian commanders to exert even more pressure on Washington. Kimmel complained that his entire complement of fighters representing three aircraft carriers, plus his shore-based navy and marine squadrons, amounted to but fifty-two aircraft, mainly Grumman F4Fs, with the balance obsolete. He also complained of a shortage of patrol vessels.

Most of what did arrive in Hawaii was just using the island as a stopping-off point for war machinery destined for the western Pacific. And Hawaii's combat efficiency would actually be reduced because 25 percent of Kimmel's overall strength was being transferred to the Atlantic in support of Lend-Lease. Training was being conducted by raw, green replacements from the States. And the shortage of equipment was complicating this training process.

Finally, by November 1941, the navy did receive the fifty-four new, much-needed PBY Catalina patrol bombers.[43] These aircraft had a phenomenal four-thousand-mile range and were designated to Admiral Kimmel for protecting the fleet at sea because the fleet could not go to sea without this overhead and scouting protection. So the PBYs would only be available to Admiral Bellinger for island long-range patrol during the activation of the Joint Coastal Frontier Defense Plan.

By comparison, the army was operating those thirty-three obsolete B-18 Bolo bombers with a range of only 690 miles. This meant that with pinpoint navigation and shallow turns on the return trip, the bomb-loaded B-18 could wander out, perhaps, 350 miles before turning back.[44]

General Short also had twelve B-17s of his own, but now he was faced with a new problem.[45] The B-17s flying from the States and destined for the Philippines would take some of his flight crews with them, and the B-17s he did have would be stripped of parts to equip those going to the Philippines. It wasn't long before he was left with just the six B-17s for crew training. It will be recalled that the PBY's main advantage was its long-range reconnaissance ability. The long-range bombing superiority fell on the twelve B-17s that would be loaned to the navy to implement the Joint Coastal Frontier Defense Plan, but now that capacity was cut in half.

Meanwhile, General Short would fall victim to a later charge that history would heap on him for which he held only partial responsibility. It was on November 5 that he issued the new alert system within his command, the new SOP (Standard Operating Procedure) that created three stages of alert. Until now, the army had traditionally had only one stage of alert. Even during the tenure of his predecessor, General Herron, an alert created a battle-stations atmosphere in which everyone dropped what he was doing and assumed a combat readiness posture. During the pre–1941 days, one category of alert fit the bill. But under the watch of Short, the island was caught in military expansion, material and equipment shortages, and urgent training required in preparation of war.

With espionage being a primary concern, it seemed like a reckless and ruinous squandering of valuable time to send the troops into the pineapple fields to guard against mythical dangers. And with one hundred fifty thousand first-, second-, and third-generation Japanese living in the islands, whose allegiance was questionable, and with the topography of the island leaving the military installations accessible to curious eyes, the idea of sabotage was not that of General Short's alone.

Shortly before being relieved of his command, Admiral Richardson, in a January 24, 1941, study of the defenses of Pearl Harbor, had cautioned that sabotage was a greater threat than the likelihood of a submarine attack. And on at least two occasions, General Marshall had advised that sabotage would be Short's "real peril." The fear of sabotage in the United

States was growing. For General Short, the answer seemed obvious: establish the three stages of alert as opposed to using just one.

Alert No. 1 called for posting sentries at likely targets of saboteurs: bridges, airfields, certain buildings, and the like. Alert No. 2 added air attack, manning the antiaircraft installations, issuing ammunition, and dispersing aircraft. Alert No. 3 was the main, all-out alert that anticipated an airborne or seaborne attack or an invasion that put the men at their battle stations and kept them there. The alert numbers would scale up, not down. History has wrongly criticized Short for being overly sabotage-conscious.

Now, with three different alerts, the army was more alert conscious, and there were increased numbers of alerts. But it doesn't take long before too many alerts don't alert to anything.

Late 1941 also brought a new commander to the Philippines. November 4 was a banner day when the arrival of Major General Lewis Brereton as Chief Far Eastern Air Force, replacing General Henry Clagett, was announced. Clagett, who had been ailing for some months from a combination of arthritis and malaria, was sent to Australia to temporarily command the U.S. forces there, and by 1943, he would return to the United States. Brereton's arrival on a Pan American clipper was met by squadrons of P-35 and P-40 fighter aircraft flying in V formations. The clipper was almost two weeks late due to weather delays in Hawaii, Wake, and Guam.

General Brereton had been handpicked by General MacArthur, and similar to Hap Arnold, he, too, was one of the first military pilots of the U.S. Army. His flying days had started back in 1912 with Aeronautical Division, U.S. Signal Corps, the earliest predecessor to the Army Air Corps, as it was known in 1941.

Summoned to Washington in early October, Brereton had met with the air corps chief, General Hap Arnold, and his assistant chief of staff, Brigadier General Carl Spaatz, who filled Brereton in on his new role in the Philippines. During the preliminary meetings, Brereton learned that it was the intention of those in Washington to begin dispatching bombardment squadrons to the Philippines, in advance of the other, very badly needed defense armaments such as reconnaissance squadrons, fighter squadrons, and air warning systems. Considering it very risky, Brereton made it known to all he met with, including General Gerow, who headed up War Plans Division, and Chief of Staff General Marshall, that the bombardment squadrons should be held back until the other squadrons and air warning systems could be provided. In his October 5, 1941, diary entry, he confirmed, "After learning these facts, I told General Arnold I considered it extremely hazardous to place bomber forces in any sensitive area without first having provided the necessary fighter cover and air warning service. I strongly urged the necessity for providing air warning services and fighters before sending bombers to a location that was exceedingly vulnerable to surprise attack, as were the Philippines."[46] The risks were understood by all, but the plans would move ahead as they were. After all, per the opinion of MacArthur and many others in Washington, nothing was going to happen in the Philippines until at least April of the following year.

On his way to the Philippines, Brereton stopped off in Hawaii for a couple of days, where he met with the commanders and toured the facilities. He quickly picked up on the tension that was mounting due to lack of armaments. As he noted on October 22, "Apprehension was evident, not so much because anyone felt we were on the eve of war with Japan, as because insufficient attention had been given to provide even the minimum requirements for

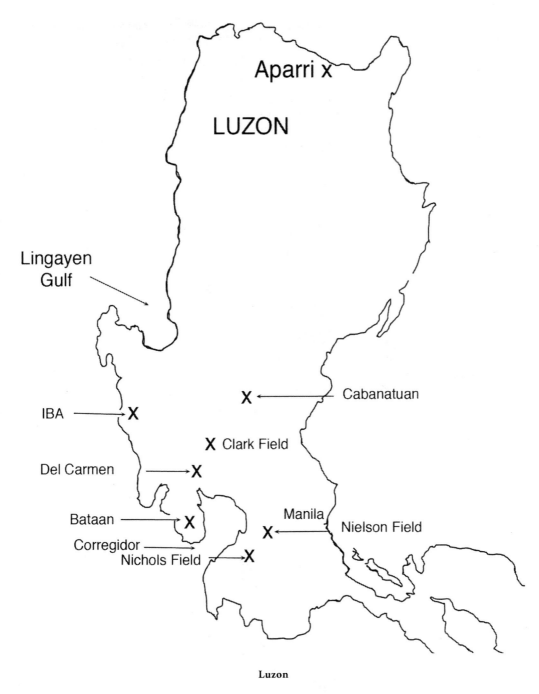

Aparri x

LUZON

Lingayen
Gulf

IBA

X Cabanatuan

X Clark Field

Del Carmen

Bataan

Manila

Nielson Field

Corregidor

Nichols Field

Luzon

defense."[47] Similar to the concerns he had expressed in Washington, Brereton was "surprised and somewhat disappointed to note the incomplete preparations against air attacks, particularly the lack of adequate air warning equipment."[48] The consensus of the discussions he had with General Martin, Admiral Bellinger, and others, was that Japan's initial attacks would likely involve Hawaii, the Panama Canal, or even the west coast of the United States, but that Hawaii was "the most probable."[49]

Upon landing in Manila Bay, Brereton called on MacArthur, who was ecstatic to hear that reinforcements (bombers) were on the way. In the wake of Brereton's pessimistic briefings in Washington, he wondered if reinforcements would even get there in time. However, Brereton was equally delighted to hear from his new frontline commander that nothing would happen until at least next April. MacArthur assured his new air chief, "The mobilization and training schedule of the Philippine Department and of the Philippine Army was based on that assumption."[50] The Philippine Army had been inducted into U.S. service on August 15.

In November 1941, the army had established the Far East Air Force, predecessor of the Fifth Air Force. Brereton's hand-carried orders to MacArthur stated that the FEAF would transition from a defensive posture to an offensive one, and that in the event of war, MacArthur would activate Rainbow 5, the basis of America's war-plan strategy during World War II. Both elicited a smile.

Shortly after his arrival, General Brereton conducted a week-long inspection tour of the airfields in his command. Similar to the situation on Hawaii, what he saw was completely inadequate in so many aspects, from duty hours maintained, training schedules, lack of spare parts, and a borderline air warning service, to insufficient or undependable communications, most of which were commercial and all based on the "good old days."[51] The obvious result was a shake-up of command with many of General Clagett's staff now becoming assistants in their former jobs. All fighter aircraft henceforth would be considered on alert and always gassed and armed, and 40 percent of all flight training would be at night.

Taking inventory of the aircraft available, Brereton found that the Far East Air Force consisted of only thirty-five B-17s, two squadrons of B-18s (medium bombers), seventy-two P-40 fighters, twenty-eight P-35 fighters, and two squadrons of fighters of the Philippine Air Force.[52] Half the fighters were stationed at Nichols Field, and half were stationed at Clark Field. There were no spare parts for the P-40s and none whatsoever for the bombers. Overall, it was quite a dismal situation.

The P-35s fired thirty-caliber ammunition, as did the P-40Bs, while the newer P-40Ds and P-40Es fired fifty-caliber ammunition, but this was all incidental because most pilots had never fired any of the guns. Not only was ammunition in short supply, but many aircraft had never been bore-sighted to align the guns to the pilots' gun sights. This process required test ammunition, of which there was little or none allocated. All the USAFFE (U.S. Army Forces Far East) had on hand were 3.5 million rounds of fifty-caliber ammunition, as opposed to their estimated requirement of sixteen million rounds.[53] The difference was promised to leave the States by March 1, 1942. For the bombers, it was the same. While some bombs were in short supply, others were nonexistent.

While many were unhappy with the changes made with Brereton's arrival, others felt they were long overdue. The overall situation concerned Brereton even more than Washington's decision to send the B-17s to the Philippines, where they would not have adequate fighter protection, and still more were on the way. The only airfield in all the Philippines capable of handling the heavy bombers was Clark Field, sixty miles north of Manila. The only other field was Del Monte, about six hundred miles to the south on the island of Mindanao, but that airfield was still under construction. The one highlight was that Del Monte's existence was still unknown to the Japanese.

What would be Luzon's only operable radar site was nearing completion at the Iba Airfield on the coast, some distance west of Clark Field. Few had any high hopes for the air warning service. It depended solely on local native volunteers who were inexperienced and poorly trained, and to collect their reports, an information center was established in Manila. This entire schedule was based on MacArthur's assurances that nothing would happen until April of 1942.

As the Pacific commanders struggled throughout 1941 to build up their defensive resources, the navy would lose some of what they already had. Another obstacle in building up in the Pacific came with the historic foreign aid bill, Lend-Lease. Early in the spring of 1941, Kimmel had lost over forty of his ships to the Atlantic Fleet, unofficially, to support the delivery of Lend-Lease to Great Britain. His contribution to Lend-Lease included one aircraft carrier, the USS *Yorktown* (CV-5); three battleships, the USS *New Mexico* (BB-40), the USS *Mississippi* (BB-41), and the USS *Idaho* (BB-42); four light cruisers and eighteen destroyers.[54] Many of his experienced officers and seamen were transferred back to the States as well, to man new ships just being launched. These personnel were replaced with inexperienced crews that would take time to train. With the replacement of competent officers and enlisted men by new officers and recruits, more than half of the Pacific Fleet was manned by new personnel, and at times, three-quarters of them had never heard a gun fired. With the loss of ships and experienced personnel, Kimmel's fighting strength was reduced by roughly 25 percent.[55] It has been observed by many that Japan's final decision to attack Pearl Harbor was made after these transfers, leaving just eight old battleships and three carriers at Pearl Harbor.

And by December 7, the analyses of Admiral Bellinger and General Martin would hold true. Their predictions that Japan would likely employ up to six carriers and would strike from either the north, south, or the west at a distance of 233 miles out, was virtually a blueprint of what was to come.

Chapter 5

Lend-Lease and Its Delivery

The big debate in Congress in January and February of 1941 was: would Lend-Lease actually keep the country out of war or take the country into war? How had FDR's assurances and the people's protestations come to this? Lend-Lease was a foreign aid bill for which no author could be found that virtually gave dictatorial powers to the president to decide who, when, and how much recipient nations would receive. With the president's insistence on passage of H.R. 1776, so called to give it a patriotic flavor, and with the Democrats in control of both houses of Congress, it nevertheless stirred bitter arguments like none in recorded history, with many in Roosevelt's own party taking issue. FDR had just won his third term as president on the assertion that he and he alone knew how to keep America out of war. His Republican counterpart, Wendell Willkie, had also campaigned to keep the country out of war, but his credentials lacked the experience of the presidency.

In 1940, both the Democratic National Convention held in Chicago and the Republican National Convention held in Philadelphia were solidly antiwar. And even though both FDR and Willkie made solemn promises to keep the Americans out of war, events in Europe continued to heat up. It was also in 1940 that Norway, Belgium, Holland, and France fell to Germany, leaving Britain to stand alone.

Though England had just barely survived the Battle of Britain, German U-boats had since surrounded the British Isles and were tightening the noose. Britain was starting to starve. British war production could not compete with German war manufacturing, and now it looked like just a matter of time, measured in months, before Britain would fall.

It had been a scant twenty years since the conclusion of the Great War, and now it seemed that the clock had turned back to 1917. President Woodrow Wilson had told Americans that they were fighting for lasting peace in the world. World War I had been the war to end all wars. By 1939, one who wanted to remind Americans of the "agony and devastation"[1] suffered in the preceding war was Republican Senator Gerald Nye. Roosevelt was pushing to get his cash-and-carry amendment to the Neutrality Act passed, and Nye told the American people that Americans should mind their own business this time around, a concern he expressed to Congress on July 18: "With that experience still fresh in our minds, it is amazing that so many persons, in high and low places, should forget the lesson of 1914 and 1917,"[2] adding that the country was already on its way into another conflict. "Steps are being taken, policies are being inaugurated, precedents established today that in large degree parallel the 'road to war' which American[s] trod only a little more than 20 years ago."[3]

In early 1918, President Wilson had composed his *fourteen points* that would guarantee the Great War to be the final world conflict. But the Treaty of Versailles, which was aimed at bringing peace between Germany and the Allies of World War I, had only incorporated a few of them. The U.S. Congress had voted not to join the League of Nations and wanted no further involvement in European affairs. In 1932, while seeking the Democratic nomination for president, Franklin Roosevelt had stated that he personally was against the United States' getting involved in the League or any other European affairs. After his election in 1932, the 1935 Neutrality Laws were the next logical step. Trade or loans to belligerent nations had become forbidden, and all exports had to be paid for before leaving the American ports. The effort to prevent a shooting war on the high seas, however, was exactly what would get the Americans into the next war.

The Japanese invasion of China in July 1937 and the German occupation of Poland in September 1939 resulted in the repeal of various sections of the Neutrality Laws, to the point that, on November 3, 1939, the American government allowed cash-and-carry arms sales to China and Britain.

Now that Great Britain was the last democratic fortress in a Nazi-occupied Europe, FDR became convinced that if Britain fell, sooner or later, the Americans would have to fight Hitler alone. But the United States would not be fighting only Hitler, since in September 1940, Germany had joined with Japan and Italy to form the Tripartite Pact. To fight one would be to fight them all. As long as Britain survived, the United States would be safe. In looking ahead, had Britain fallen, from where would U.S. strategic bombing of Europe have been conducted? From where would an invasion have been launched? Neither would have occurred, and the world would be far different today. There is evidence that Churchill had provided the initial idea for Lend-Lease by suggesting a type of aid that would be free of the dollar sign. But he would later insist that the idea was FDR's.

But involvement of any sort was bound to incite the American public that, up to this point, was so bent on isolation from European affairs that they had even objected to the arms industry having profited during the last war. It would require a selling job to the nation, after years of promising to keep Americans out of war, that would be risky. Roosevelt now had the delicate task to risk his popularity with his change of direction that was bound to embitter Americans. He had to choose his words carefully.

Starting with his regular fireside chat of December 29, 1940, FDR warned Americans that Hitler and his Axis partners could dominate the rest of the world if Britain fell. Rather than live "at the point of the gun,"[4] he suggested that the United States should become the "arsenal of democracy"[5] and give full aid to Britain, regardless of threats from other countries. He then stated, "You can, therefore, nail any talk about sending armies to Europe as deliberate untruth."[6] Over the next few months, Americans were hearing what the president was saying when they should have been listening to the nonchalant undertones. As he emphasized the need to defend the nation, Americans could not consider such defense a foreign war, and "Of course, we'll fight if we are attacked. If somebody attacks us, then it isn't a foreign war, is it?"[7] "We cannot escape danger, or the fear of danger, by crawling into bed and pulling the covers over our heads,"[8] followed by, "A nation can have peace with the Nazis only at the price of total surrender."[9]

The president and his Democratic platform had promised to keep the United States out of war with statements like, "We will not send our Army, naval, or air forces to fight in foreign lands outside of the Americas, except in case of attack.... The direction and aim of our foreign policy has been, and will continue to be, the security and defense of our own land and the maintenance of its peace."[10]

But since the November election, the president was making some alarming retreats. After the New Year of 1941, he was making promises to aid peace-loving peoples around the world, "consistent with law and not inconsistent with the interests of our own national self-defense."[11] At the same time, FDR offered the solution of how to aid American allies and still remain neutral on a casual basis. His solution came in the form of Lend-Lease.

On January 3, FDR announced to members of the Senate that he would propose to Congress "a comprehensive plan for all out-aid to Great Britain 'short of war.'"[12] The plan would involve establishing a government corporation to manage the program. The big question in FDR's mind and the crux of the whole problem was how to satisfy the American people on how the Lend-Lease would be repaid. Britain could be solvent one day and broke the next. In his December 17 press conference, reporters had pushed Roosevelt, asking how the aid to Britain would be financed. Avoiding questions pertaining to the legal technicalities, he used the analogy that if his neighbor's house caught on fire, he would be perfectly willing to loan his neighbor his garden hose. After the fire was extinguished, he expected his neighbor to either return the hose or replace it. In essence, Americans were morally committed to loaning armaments to Britain, and one way or another, things would work themselves out. Whether it was through actual payment, trade, or return of the goods loaned, Americans would eventually be repaid. But how would Britain return war goods that had been expended?

To aid the Allies, FDR was sure that a way could be found, and then added that he was sending his personal friend, confidant, and advisor Harry Hopkins to Great Britain to hopefully smooth things out. When the news media inquired as to a specific mission or government compensation for the trip, the president responded that although they might cover some expenses, Hopkins was "just going over to say 'How do you do?' to a lot of my friends."[13] Based on Hopkins's direct approach in getting to the bottom of things, Roosevelt was confident that Hopkins would return to the United States with a clear picture of Britain's situation, details with which to sell his Lend-Lease program to Congress. Without going into detail, Hopkins himself expressed his role in going to London as simply acting as the catalyst "between 'two prima donnas.'"[14]

At his State of the Union Address on January 6, 1941, FDR told Congress and the nation of his plan to supply huge quantities of weapons, munitions, tools of war, and other commodities to be supplied on loan or lease by the U.S. government. Although these goods would not be paid for by the American taxpayers, the up-front money must be borne by American citizens and businesses and not by the governments that receive them. "For what we send abroad, we shall be repaid within a reasonable time following the close of hostilities, in similar materials, or, at our option, in other goods of many kinds, which they can produce and which we need."[15] But in the meantime, the taxpayers would foot the bill.

Harry Hopkins, after resigning from his secretary of commerce post in September of 1940, now assumed what could be a delicate mission. At issue was FDR's request for the British gold reserve in South Africa to be transferred to Washington, which was deemed by Winston Churchill as "a sheriff collecting the last assets of the helpless debtor,"[16] to support the cash-and-carry rule until the commencement of Lend-Lease. This assumed, of course, that FDR could sell his plan to Congress. As far as the legality of this scheme, international law was quite specific. Any neutral government that supplied weapons of war to a belligerent nation at war does itself commit an act of war. However, FDR insisted, "Such aid is not an act of war, even if a dictator should unilaterally proclaim it so to be,"[17] inviting an attack on the United States.

Congress was about to have a field day. This would not be a party-versus-party issue. On the day following the president's announcement, Democratic Senator Burton Wheeler, speaking for many of his colleagues, called the plan "idiotic."[18] "If it is our war, we ought to have the courage to go over and fight it, but it is not our war."[19] In a subsequent radio broadcast, Wheeler went on to say, "Never before has the Congress of the United States been asked by any President to violate international law…. Never before has the United States given to one man the power to strip this Nation of its defenses. Never before has a Congress coldly and flatly been asked to abdicate…. The lend-lease-give program is the New Deal's triple A foreign policy; it will plow under every fourth American boy. Approval … 'means war, open and complete warfare.'"[20]

Similar to Democratic Senator Byrd's previous support of FDR, Burton Wheeler's relationship with Roosevelt went back to 1932, when he ardently campaigned throughout the west for Roosevelt's election. While he supported Roosevelt's New Deal, their break would come when Roosevelt tried to pack the Supreme Court in early 1937. Of the opinion that Roosevelt's lust for power was getting out of control, Wheeler was quoted as saying, "Once he was only one of us who made him. Now he means to make himself the boss of us all."[21] As a noninterventionist, Wheeler opposed any aid to Britain, and became the Senate's lead of the opposition to Roosevelt's Lend-Lease program. When asked about the Lend-Lease being a blank-check bill, FDR responded:

> Write me another that you would not put that label on, but which would accomplish the same objective. That is a perfectly good answer to all these people. That is not an answer at all, however, to those who talk about plowing under every fourth American child, which I regard as the most untruthful, as the most dastardly, unpatriotic thing that has ever been said. Quote me on that. That really is the rottenest thing that has been said in public in my generation.[22]

But when a correspondent inquired as to who had made the original statement, it would have been difficult to admit that it had come from his own party. The best that Roosevelt could recall was that he had read it someplace.

In deliberating the pros and cons of the proposed Lend-Lease Bill, members of Congress questioned the matter of delivery of this arsenal. It made little sense for Americans to manufacture these war goods, load them onto British ships in U.S. ports, only to have them sunk by German U-boats on the high seas. To use American ships to convoy would not only be a breach of international law, but it would also invite Americans into a shooting war.

Representative Hamilton Fish (R–NY) pushed this point in his March 30, 1941, speech in Washington with, "The signal bell ringing in the engine room of an American naval vessel to start the first convoy would be the equivalent to a declaration of an undeclared war by the President."[23] Fish did grant some leeway to Roosevelt, stating that he didn't believe the rumors that the administration had already decided to convoy. Nonetheless, he added that if the rumors turned out to be true, and if "the Pied Piper of Pennsylvania Avenue leads the American youth to war in spite of his promises and pledges for peace, I know of no language strong enough to denounce such a betrayal of trust."[24]

Unless there was a guarantee of delivery to at least Iceland, Lend-Lease would achieve nothing. When questioned, FDR assured the public that he had never considered the use of American ships. Certainly those in favor of Lend-Lease did not want to see the shipments go to the bottom of the ocean, but more importantly, they didn't want to see American men and boys winding up there either. In their view, seeing to it that the goods got to Britain was up to the British Royal Navy.

The Lend-Lease Bill as presented to Congress was a means of helping Britain to survive Germany's siege without direct U.S. involvement. It authorized the president to lend, lease, sell, exchange, or transfer title of any military equipment, planes, guns, munitions, ships or any military goods deemed essential to the survival of any government on whom the Americans would depend for their own survival. Who would be the recipients, what goods would be involved, and the conditions of transfer were all at the discretion of the president. U.S. shipyards would be prepared to receive, overhaul, or recondition British ships with the repayment conditions also at the discretion of the president. Nor was Roosevelt required to report any of this to Congress. His decision would prevail.

The congressional deliberations immediately brought a number of questions to light. Who authored the bill? If it were to become law, would this material get overseas with the help of the U.S. Navy, or would the shipments be left to the fortunes of the German U-boats? If the United States Navy convoyed, was that not an act of war? Finally, was this bill designed to maintain U.S. neutrality or was it fulfilling what many perceived as FDR's underlying wish to bring the Americans into the conflict?

The authorship of the bill would certainly betray its motives. An extensive search was made but no originator could be found. Many in the FDR inner circle could conceive his craftiness, his deviousness to create such a bill, giving him such unprecedented power. It was for that very reason that nobody would admit to being author of the bill. At long last, Senator Alben Barkley (D–KY) admitted only to being its sponsor in the Senate, as did Majority Leader John McCormack (D–MA) of the House. (In addition to his Lend-Lease support, it would be McCormack's vote that would carry the House in extending the Selective Service Act just prior to Pearl Harbor.)

On the second point concerning opposition to the bill, it was argued that it would be sheer nonsense for the United States to manufacture war materials from ordnance to aircraft, then ship it all to Great Britain only to be sunk on the high seas by German U-boats or surface raiders determined to make sure it never reached its destination. On the other hand, if the United States protected those ships with U.S. naval convoys, wasn't that an international act of aggression that would bring the Americans to war?

When Secretary of the Navy Frank Knox, a new Republican appointee and former publisher of the *Chicago Daily News*, was questioned, he stated that he was personally against naval convoying because it was risky. But Knox continued by commenting that if the president ordered him to do it, he would commit that act of war in obedience.

Frank Knox had been Republican Alf Landon's vice-presidential candidate in 1936. Landon would suffer a humiliating defeat, carrying only 8 electoral votes to Roosevelt's 523.[25] While he was no New Dealer, Knox did believe in military preparedness, as well as providing aid to the Allies. In another attempt to generate bipartisan support, Roosevelt appointed him secretary of the navy in July 1940. Knox fully supported Roosevelt's navy expansion but would not see the end of the war, dying of heart failure in May 1944.

In testimony to the Senate Foreign Relations Committee's hearings concerning the

Lend-Lease Bill, Secretary of War Stimson was of the opposite opinion. Nothing in the Lend-Lease Bill, he told the Senate committee, concerning manufacturing nor shipping would violate law nor constitute an act of war.

For almost three months, Congress argued the merits and demerits to the point where the only remaining arguable issue was that of delivery. To address this, Congress amended specific provisions of the bill to make it more palatable to those fearing its aggressive interpretation.

Included in the amendments to the bill were the stipulations: "Nothing in this Act shall be construed to authorize or to permit the authorization of convoying by naval vessels of the United States. (e) Nothing in this Act shall be construed to authorize or to permit the authorization of the entry of any American vessel into a combat area in violation of section 3 of the Neutrality Act of 1939."[26]

And for those who still did not trust the president, another provision was added, stating, "Nothing in this Act shall be construed to change existing law relating to the use of the land and naval forces of the United States, except in so far as such use relates to the manufacture, procurement, and repair of defense articles."[27]

Even by enacting the Lend-Lease law, Congress would not authorize the president to use American armed forces for combat purposes, nor would it authorize him to order them to commit acts of war. This would prevent him from ordering undeclared war. Those united in both Houses against the bill were convinced that it would grant to the president dictatorial powers over Americans' human and material resources to wage declared or undeclared war where and when he so chose, with the end result of leading the country into another war.

Probably no one was more outspoken against Lend-Lease and the president's abuse of power than Colonel Charles Lindbergh. As far back as September of 1939, Lindbergh had vocalized his opposition to intervention with radio broadcasts, appealing to Americans for neutrality and the need to build up American defenses. Roosevelt had attempted to quiet Lindbergh by offering him a cabinet position as secretary of the air, but Lindbergh declined. By April 1941, Lindbergh would officially join the America First Committee and become one of the organization's key spokesmen, delivering thirteen speeches around the country.

Lindbergh's isolationist posture would not be the first time he butted heads with Roosevelt. Even before his famous transatlantic flight of 1927, Lindbergh had established himself as a highly competent airmail pilot. After the organization of the U.S. Air Mail Service in 1918, the army had been designated the job of carrying the mail. When so many pilots were losing their lives in the effort, Congress opened the bidding process in 1925 for private companies to take over. Employed by Robertson Aircraft, Lindbergh would join the mail service in 1926.

During Roosevelt's first term in office, rumblings began to stir of fraud and corruption between the Post Office and the airlines. Senator Hugo Black (D–AL), who was hungry for publicity, headed up the initial investigation to raise the issue to Roosevelt's attention, and by January of 1934, the Air Mail Scandal was born. Without due process, Roosevelt used his executive power to cancel the existing mail contracts and forced the airmail delivery back onto the Army Air Corps. The chief of the Army Air Corps at that time, General Benjamin Foulois, advised Roosevelt of the unsuitability of the army for carrying the mail, but in spite of this and numerous other protests, Roosevelt insisted. And of course, the leading opposition of Roosevelt's action came from Charles Lindbergh, who by now was on the payroll of both Transcontinental Air Transport (later known as TWA) and Pan American Airways, serving as a technical consultant in their route selections, flight testing, and equipment manufacturing.

Having served as an airmail pilot himself, Lindbergh was in a far better position to judge who should carry the mail, and he was vehement that Roosevelt's actions were not warranted, pointing out that the contract cancellations "condemns the largest portion of our commercial aviation without just trial."[28] He went on to emphasize that actual guilt of the airlines that were supposedly corrupt had not even been established. In conclusion to his February 1934 message to Roosevelt, Lindbergh asserted that any illegal practices on the part if the airlines needed to be established and proven, and that "the condemnation of commercial aviation by cancellation of all air mail contracts and the use of the army on commercial air lines will unnecessarily and greatly damage all American aviation."[29] In Lindbergh's opinion, Roosevelt was putting the cart before the horse, judgment without due process, not too different from Roosevelt's actions after the attack on Pearl Harbor.

After several months, twelve army pilots had lost their lives trying to deliver the mail, and the public outcry over these deaths could not be ignored. Roosevelt was forced to go back to Congress, requesting that a bill be passed to return the airmail service to civilian companies. Bidding reopened, and by early May, the airlines resumed their control of the airmail. It was obvious that Lindbergh had been right, and Roosevelt had been wrong. And Roosevelt would not forget Lindbergh's willingness to publicly denounce his earlier decision, which Roosevelt clearly considered as politically damaging. As the president had previously mentioned to his press secretary, Stephen Early, "Don't worry about Lindbergh. We will get that fair-haired boy."[30]

Since September 1940, membership in the America First Committee was growing significantly. Their ranks were swelled with prominence, and their arguments were tough to refute, using the assurance of President Wilson that the last war had been "the war to end [all] wars."[31] John Flynn, who headed up the publicity efforts for the America First Committee, took things a step further by promoting advertisements that reminded Americans of what the last war had done for the world. Hadn't it only brought Communism to Russia, Fascism to Italy, and Nazism to Germany? What did Americans think another war would bring to America?

By December 1941, the AFC had grown to over four hundred chapters to support its (nearly) one-million-strong membership.[32] Its principles were clear: to build a strong defensive posture, and to not allow foreign aid to weaken that strength and draw Americans into a foreign war.

Even before his direct involvement with the America First Committee, Colonel Lindbergh testified before the House Foreign Affairs Committee on January 23, 1941, and a couple of weeks later, before the Senate Foreign Relations Committee on February 6. Lindbergh stood firm on the belief that the United States should not "police the world,"[33] that Americans should promote a negotiated peace between Britain and Germany, and that by sending military armaments to Britain, Americans were only weakening their defense at home. When asked by a congressman in one of the hearings which side he would like to see win the war, he responded with, "I want neither side to win,"[34] which only furthered the notion that he was pro–German.

On April 23, Lindbergh made his first speech for the America First Committee, reiterating that no amount of American aid could create a victory or even survivability for Britain.

"I have said before, and I will say again, that I believe it will be a tragedy to the entire world if the British Empire collapses. That is one of the main reasons why I opposed this war before it was declared, and why I have constantly advocated a negotiated peace."[35]

In Lindbergh's opinion, Britain was only looking out for herself, and Americans needed to do the same. He stressed that Americans needed to view the European conflicts objectively, and that in his attempts to do so, he concluded that "we cannot win this war for England, regardless of how much assistance we extend."[36] At the base of Lindbergh's opposition to Lend-Lease, he tried to impress upon his supporters that the passage of Lend-Lease would be a "major step in getting us into war."[37]

Commentator Norman Thomas, the Presbyterian minister who became one of the most outspoken pacifists against Roosevelt, was even more emphatic that Lend-Lease would result in "total war on two oceans and five continents; a war likely to result in stalemate; perhaps in such a breakup of western civilization, that Stalin, with his vast armies and loyal Communist followers, will be the victor."[38] He further declared that FDR would "put us in war gradually, knowing that we would refuse to go into it all at once."[39] Secretary of State Cordell Hull, in testimony to the Senate Foreign Relations Committee, stated that for years he was of the opinion that neutrality or simply not getting involved was the best way to keep Americans out of war. But he had become gradually convinced that "the surest way to keep out of trouble [is] to prevent an invasion of this hemisphere…. I want you to know that in my view there is danger in any direction."[40] He was carefully steering down the middle of the road.

Secretary of War Stimson suggested to the Senate committee that he was locked into blind obedience. "As Secretary of War, I became a subordinate of the President and was directed to follow out his policies…. Now, so long as I remain his Secretary of War I shall endeavor loyally to follow out his policies."[41]

In his attempts to solicit support, Congressman McCormack referred to the bill as a peace measure:

> The real warmongers are those who oppose action, and in their blind opposition are attempting to divide our people. This is no time for division…. Suppose, in the papers of tomorrow or later on, the people of America should read of the defeat of Britain, what do you suppose will be their feeling? Will it be one of calmness, of safety and security, or will it be one of alarm, one with the feeling of fear, or impending danger? Would not their feelings be properly summed up in the words, "are we next?" That is the reason why this is a defense measure and a peace measure so that "we will not be next."[42]

But similar to Democratic Senator Wheeler's concerns of Roosevelt's abuse of power, some of the Republicans in Congress were more concerned with the powers being transferred to the president than the merits of Lend-Lease being a war bill. One such congressman was Representative Usher Burdick (R–ND). Although Burdick supported the war after the attack on Pearl Harbor, he had been a confirmed isolationist, supporting Senator Nye's neutrality legislation, opposing the build-up of arms, the Selective Service Act, and in turn, Roosevelt's Lend-Lease. Expressing his concern about the powers this bill would transfer to the president, Congressman Burdick also stressed that "if we grant these dictatorial powers to the President, war is inevitable. A war for what? The last war was fought 'to make the world safe for democracy.' Did it make it safe? Is democracy safe now anywhere in the world, even including our own country? What will we enter this war for?"[43]

Congressman Hugh Peterson (D–GA) was another one of Roosevelt's party who opposed intervention of European affairs, viewing Lend-Lease as a war bill as opposed to a peace bill.

In his opinion, "This is no defense measure. It is a measure of aggressive warfare. If it is enacted into law and its provisions are really made effective the inevitable result will be the sending of the armed forces of this nation—the sons of this Republic—to stand guard or do battle even unto the uttermost parts of the earth. Only a miracle could save us from such a sad fate. And no one can predict what the final outcome would be."[44]

The question of who drafted the bill had been overshadowed by the rest of the debates, but it was not forgotten. And Representative Thomas Jenkins (R–OH), one of Ohio's longest-serving congressmen (1925–1959), still wanted to know who had actually authored the bill:

> At first we were given to understand that this bill was drafted as a free handiwork of Congress. That is not true. This bill has been cautiously and clandestinely put together. Ostensibly the physical drafting of it was done by a group of Congressmen, but its genius was in the heart and mind of someone aside from the active membership of Congress. Its genius comes from those who want the United States of America involved in this world conflict. There are powerful influences in the United States of America that would not stop in their determination to involve us in war, regardless of how dire the consequences might be. The cry of American mothers against another war that would rob them of their sons is not heard by this group. The prospect of the loss of lives and the loss of property and the bankruptcy of the Nation do not deter this group. They want Hitler destroyed for a different reason than what most of us have for his destruction. That this bill had all been thought out is proven by the president's message to Congress delivered on the sixth of January.... In this message he said that he would be compelled to ask Congress for money and materials that he might transfer them to the belligerents in this war. Through all these debates and through all these hearings I have been seeking to locate the real genius of this bill. Can it be the insatiable ambition of the President to want to have a hand in the domination of the world? Can it be in moneyed influences against whom Hitler has committed some special act which they resent? Or can it be as the result of fear of world domination from Hitler and his followers? I must confess that I do not know the answer, but I have a strong conviction that, as I have already stated, this bill has behind it and back of it some motives the purposes of which have not yet been disclosed.... There are some who think that the President wants this bill so that he may then be able to take from Great Britain, or at least to share with Great Britain, the active management of the war. If the President could, under threat of withholding money and supplies, demand that the war be carried on along certain lines, he would be in a position to have his demands recognized. If he assumes a position of collaboration and co-generalship with the war leaders of Great Britain, we are then actively in the war.[45]

Underlining this was the fact that Americans could manufacture all the planes, tanks, and guns that they wanted, but as soon as the government started transferring those weapons, either on American or British ships, Americans became an ally of Britain, and according to international law, subject to attack by her enemies. Senator Wheeler cautioned the Senate:

> Everyone in his right sense will grant that power must reside in someone to take the necessary immediate measures to meet and beat back such assaults. But everyone else knows that such cases have nothing to do with the underlining premise of H.R. 1776, namely the fantastic claim that our frontiers are no longer our seacoasts; that they are no longer even in the Western Hemisphere, but lie along the Rhine, or on the English Channel, or at Salonika, or at Singapore. The people have a right to pause and think and choose for themselves before they plunge into war on any such theory.[46]

But after three months of debates and several amendments, both Houses by large majorities passed the Lend-Lease bill. In the House, the vote was 260 for and 165 against, and in the Senate, it was 60 for and 31 against.[47] Titled "An Act to Promote the Defense of the United States," it was signed by President Roosevelt and became law on March 11, 1941. Technically, Roosevelt's signature immediately put the United States at war with members of the Tripartite Pact. March 11, 1941, was the day Americans entered World War II, not December 7, 1941.

Almost immediately after signing, FDR asked Navy Secretary Frank Knox to transfer twenty-eight motor torpedo boats and sub chasers to the British, as well as guns and infantry equipment to the Greeks to also defend against the Germans. At this point, the Germans were planning to use Greece as a southern launching area for the upcoming invasion of Russia.

With the onset of Lend-Lease and continuing until Pearl Harbor, and in spite of massive orders to get the nation transitioned to a military economy, Great Britain would still outproduce the United States in weaponry.

Although one of the Lend-Lease amendments prohibited U.S. naval involvement, Congress continued to debate the means of delivery. Opponents had feared that once passed, the next step would be an executive order from the president ordering the formation of U.S. naval forces to initiate convoys to Great Britain. The original bill had no provision for delivery, but as a means of resolving the issue, it will be recalled that Congress amended the bill with the provision that nothing should be construed as authorizing convoying.

In March of 1941, with the ink drying on Lend-Lease, the delivery question still needed an answer. At the same time, rumors abounded that British merchant ships were already being protected by the United States Navy. If just supplying Britain was an act of war, it didn't involve shooting at that point. If the U.S. Navy participated in any way to get Lend-Lease to Britain, it would involve shooting. But anyone in authority denied that it was happening. Navy Secretary Frank Knox had openly stated to Congress that he was opposed to convoying and considered it as "an act of war."[48] The president himself had reiterated, "Convoying means shooting, and shooting means war."[49] FDR had assured Congress and the nation that Lend-Lease would not be administered as a war policy. But now, he was changing his wording. The word *convoy* now became *patrols*, which developed into *neutrality patrols*. So if and when the shooting started, the word *neutrality* would stand out to Americans. Would those neutrality patrols established back in 1939 now become convoys?

It was during the first week of the European war that FDR had established what he called the Neutrality Patrol. The German Army invaded Poland on September 1, 1939, and shortly after Admiral Stark assumed his new role as chief of naval operations, he organized a task force of thirty battleships, destroyers, cruisers, and aircraft carriers to patrol the U.S. Atlantic coast and the Caribbean. Appointed to head up the Neutrality Patrol was Rear Admiral A.W. Johnson.

With the patrol area initially broken down into seven zones, Johnson would lead the effort to, for outward appearances, protect American neutrality and report on any ship movements of belligerent nations. In reality, the Neutrality Patrols served, first, to help Great Britain in a limited way because of her access to the Atlantic, and second, to harass Germany to the point of declaring war on the United States. FDR regularly created situations using the Neutrality Patrols that he hoped would anger the Germans into declaring war. The patrol area would later be expanded to include the northeastern coast of South America.

Perhaps the best, yet least known, example of patrol activity was that of the North German Lloyd Line passenger ship SS *Columbus*, the thirteenth largest steamship in the world at that time. In late August 1939, just days before the war started in Europe, the *Columbus* departed New York City for a tourist cruise. When the shooting started in Poland at the beginning of September, Captain Wilhelm Daehne entered Havana Harbor, discharged all passengers, and headed for the neutral port of Veracruz, Mexico. By December 14, Captain Daehne was ordered back to Germany, and he made a break for the open sea. He felt he had a good chance with the *Columbus* because her cruise speed was faster than that of most British ships.

Soon Daehne discovered an American destroyer on his trail. There was no apprehension, however, because President Roosevelt had announced that the United States would remain neutral. Shortly after he discovered the destroyer, it was replaced by a second destroyer, the USS *Benham* (DD-397).

The British were now notified of the location of the *Columbus*. Suspiciously, the *Columbus* was now being followed by a number of American ships, the destroyers USS *Cole* (DD-155), USS *Ellis* (DD-254), USS *Schenk* (DD-159), USS *Jouett* (DD-396), USS *Philip* (DD-76), USS *Lea* (DD-118), USS *Greer* (DD-145), USS *Upshur* (DD-144), and the cruiser USS *Tuscaloosa* (CA-37). Captain Daehne was careful to navigate well within the International Neutrality Zone along the U.S. East Coast until he made a break for the open sea off the Delaware Capes, heading east.

Now the Canadian destroyer HCMS *Hyperion* appeared in time to witness the reported scuttling of the *Columbus*. Her crew was put aboard the *Tuscaloosa*, whose captain was briefed as to what to report to the media upon his arrival in New York. Basically, while on their neutrality patrol, they just happened to be in the area of the *Columbus* and were happy to rescue the nearly six hundred who had survived the sinking.

Other examples of the Neutrality Patrols' efforts included the American destroyer *Broome* (DD-210), which identified, reported, and tracked a German freighter and monitored its position until a British ship arrived and sunk the freighter while the *Broome* observed. And the American destroyer USS *Niblack* (DD-424), was rescuing Dutch survivors from a freighter south of Iceland when she detected a U-boat and attempted to sink it with depth charges.

Everyone in Congress who had voted for or against Lend-Lease had done so with the sincere opinion that his vote was the best means to keep the country out of war. And now there were rumors that each month, American naval yards would refit ten Royal Navy destroyers, another breach of international law inciting another act of war.

Another outspoken senator who had opposed Roosevelt's Lend-Lease bill was Senator Charles Tobey (R–NH). An isolationist who allied himself with the America First Committee, Tobey was also concerned about what many believed to be Roosevelt's abuse of executive power. With convoying becoming such a hot debate, Tobey confronted Senator Barkley for his opinions.

Barkley had been another fervent Roosevelt supporter, giving the keynote address at both the 1932 and 1936 Democratic National Conventions. Supporting the New Deal, as well as Roosevelt's attempt to pack the Supreme Court in 1937, he served as House Majority Leader from 1937 to 1947 and would later become President Harry Truman's vice-president. Although he was the Senate's sponsor for the Lend-Lease bill, he still could not provide Senator Tobey with any straight answers. And during congressional debate at the end of March, Tobey questioned Barkley as to whether or not he would defend convoying. Barkley responded, "And I am answering the Senator in good faith; if we have violated international law in such a way as could result in a declaration of war against us by Germany, we have already done that, and the convoying of ships would only be an incident."[50] Barkley continued, "If Germany wants an excuse to declare war against us, she already had it, and we know from her history with other nations that if it was to her interest, she would have done it without any excuse."[51]

When Senator Tobey inquired as to whether convoys were not a greater danger than anything else, Barkley answered, "It may be; I am not disputing that; but what I am trying to ascertain is whether the Senator from New Hampshire thinks that Germany would wait if Germany saw it to her interest to declare war, or whether Hitler would wait, for I do not really like to associate Hitler with Germany, because I have great respect for the German people; I have none for Hitler, and I hope the time will come when they will themselves recognize the difference between the German people and Hitler."[52]

Tobey continued to press the point that convoying would only lead Americans to war, proposing a resolution that would prohibit convoying:

> The Congress and the President having assured the American people they were going to do all they could keep out of war, then it logically follows that the Congress should take every step to keep this Nation out of war and use all the powers vested in it by the Constitution to prohibit the use of our ships of peace for war purposes. To that end I am introducing a joint resolution which I will take the liberty of reading. It is as follows: "Joint resolution prohibiting the use of the armed forces of the United States and American vessels and aircraft for transporting, delivering, or convoying articles or materials to belligerent countries. Resolved, etc., That, except in time of war, hereafter no part of the land or naval forces of the United States, and no vessel documented, or aircraft registered or licensed, under the laws of the United States, shall be used, directly or indirectly, beyond the limits of the territorial waters of the United States and its territories and possessions, to transport or deliver, or in connection with the transportation or delivery of, or for convoy purposes in connection with the transportation or delivery of, any articles or materials to or for the use of any foreign country with respect to which the President has issued a proclamation under section 1 of the Neutrality Act of 1939, or which is engaged in actual hostilities with one or more foreign countries, even though a state of war has not been declared or recognized in any such proclamation."[53]

The arguments became more technical, particularly the clause "except in time of war." It was a time of war. The United States just wasn't in it.

The debates continued, and on April 17, an article appeared in the *New York Daily News* stating, "Charges that battle craft of the Navy and Coast Guard are now giving armed escort to munition-laden British merchantmen leaving Atlantic ports for the European battlefront exploded in the Capitol tonight."[54] Detailed information followed. The president reported that the navy was only observing and reporting on keeping war from America's front doors.

Senator Tobey now charged that the White House was sitting on thousands of letters "from the rank and file of the American people demanding to know what the President's policy is on convoys and where the administration stands on this issue."[55] He even produced one himself that he had received from one of his constituents who had obtained firsthand information of the Atlantic convoys. This letter to Tobey stated:

> A young relative is in the Navy. He has been at sea on service. He was taken ill and put ashore in order to go to a hospital. I cannot tell you the name of the port. In fact I should not write this at all, but I think you should know.
>
> He tells me that the United States Navy has been convoying ships for about 1 month. His ship was one of the convoys. If I tell you the name of the ship or the lad's name I would perhaps get him in trouble. He has been worried and thinks someone should know.
>
> He says that they in the service know that the President's delay on the subject of convoying—the "put off"—as he expresses it, is because it is secretly going on.
>
> I trust you to use this information as you see fit, and only wish I could have given more details.[56]

In response to these charges, Senator Barkley then reported that after a conference with both the secretary of the navy and the chief of naval operations, he had been unequivocally assured that no ship carrying war materials was being convoyed by an American ship and that no future such orders were contemplated.

Still not satisfied, Senator Tobey now read a telegram that he had prepared for the president:

The White House, Washington, D.C.

The people of America are aroused on the issue of convoys. The time has come for a frank, unequivocal, and complete statement from you on this vital matter.

For several weeks word-twisting phrases of avoidance and indirection have been used to conceal rather than reveal the policy of the Chief Executive on the matter of convoys. Please review in your mind the events of the past several weeks. During the period when the administration was soliciting support of the people for the lease-lend bill the question of convoys came up, and you stated that convoys mean shooting, and shooting means war, thereby implying to the people that you were opposed to convoys.

Your Secretary of the Navy expressed his opposition to convoys in public testimony before the House and Senate Committees at their hearings on the lease-lend bill, but added that he would change his mind in favor of convoys if you gave the word.

During the first week of April reliable newspapers reported that Secretary Knox was in favor of convoys. When queried by the press as to whether he had, in fact, changed his mind, he replied, "I have no comment." Thus the American people were not enlightened. Then the Associated Press reported your statement to legislative leaders that suggestions for convoys were "too absurd to talk about at this time."

The next step was a *New York Times* report of conferences between British and American naval representatives to determine how a joint convoy system could be operated. The *Christian Science Monitor* and other leading papers reported that detailed plans for the use of convoys had already been drawn up and submitted to you.

During this time you, Members of the Senate and House, and I were receiving thousands of letters from the American people seeking definite assurance that the Navy was not going to convoy.

Then the Chairman of the House Military Affairs Committee sounded the note for convoys.

Then you in a press conference admitted that the plan for convoys was under consideration.

Then your spokesman, Representative Sol Bloom, chairman of the Foreign Relations Committee, issued a public statement denying the right of the Congress to prohibit convoys and asserting that you and you alone had the unrestricted authority in the matter. Then your White House Secretary, Mr. Stephen Early, said that you were very much amused at newspaper reports that American ships would be convoying.

During this time, the American people in increasing numbers were continuing to write to Washington for information as to your policy on convoys.

Then in your latest press conference you stated that on the convoy question more nonsense was being written and more statements made by people who did not know a hill of beans about it than you had ever seen before. You stated that you knew more about it than the writers and orators, but that you were not talking about it. Thus again the American people were left unenlightened because you did not care to discuss the subject.

Yesterday reports persisted that the Navy is already being used to escort merchant vessels carrying war materials to belligerents. This morning your Secretary of the Navy said that there was not a syllable of truth in the report. Later this morning your White House Secretary, Mr. Stephen Early, branded the report as a deliberate lie, and still, regardless of these conflicting reports, you are silent in the face of the people's justified desire for direct, complete information from you.

On different days of the past 3 weeks you have alternately advised the people that the suggestion of convoys was too absurd to talk about, that a plan for convoys was under consideration, and finally, that you know more about the subject than anyone else but do not care to discuss it.

Is not this issue of vital concern to the millions of American people? Have you not stated that convoys mean shooting and shooting means war for this country? Are not the people entitled to frank and honest dealing on this vital issue? Is this the kind of maneuvering that builds up the faith of the people in their Government?

I recall to your memory your statement made to the American people over a Nationwide radio broadcast in which you said to them, "You are, I believe, the most enlightened and the best informed people in all the world at this moment. You are subjected to no censorship of the news, and I want to add that your Government has no information which it has any thought of withholding from you."

In this hour when the men and women of the United States are asking for a statement from you, their national leader, in this hour when it is imperative in the national interest that the people be enlightened, and informed on the vital issue of convoys, which holds in the balance the question of our involvement in the war, I respectively [*sic*] urge that you give me at this time a frank, informative, and unequivocal statement of your position on the issue on convoys.

I further ask for direct replies to the following questions:

1. At any time during the past several weeks, have United States aircraft or naval vessels or Coast Guard cutters been used to convoy, escort, or otherwise used in conjunction with merchant vessels carrying goods to belligerent countries?
2. Are any such aircraft or vessels now being so employed?
3. Is there contemplation of such use of such aircraft or vessels in the near future?
4. What instructions have been given to the officers of any such aircraft or vessels with regard to action in the event that any of these merchant vessels carrying goods to belligerents are attacked?

A few weeks ago on another matter of importance to the people, you were asked for a statement of your position and you replied to me in a letter marked "personal and confidential." I emphasize at this time that this is an issue vital to the people of America on which they are entitled to information, and I therefore respectfully request that your reply be of such a nature that I may give the people the assurance which they are entitled to.

Charles W. Tobey
United States Senator[57]

Posing straightforward questions that deserved straightforward answers, Tobey now suggested that there was suspicion on the part of the whole nation concerning American convoys.

The president blatantly denied the convoy rumors, calling them absurd, but within just a few days after this, he reported that convoys were under consideration. And then a naval seaman confirmed to a relative that he had been on a convoy ship for a month. Suspicion and doubt were growing. As Tobey put it, anyone who was not suspicious of the contradictions "ought to go to a school for feeble-minded."[58] Congress and the American public were growing more concerned but unable to get a "yes" or "no" answer from Roosevelt.

On April 10, 1941, an announcement of an aggressive nature was released by the State Department. By permission of the Danish Minister in exile in Washington, an arrangement was made whereby the Americans would occupy areas of the Greenland coast for the establishment of air bases and military installations, all to be incorporated into U.S. defense and control of the western Atlantic, and specifically to allow for better management of delivering Lend-Lease.

On April 24, in a reversal of his previous inference, Navy Secretary Frank Knox announced, "We cannot allow our goods to be sunk in the Atlantic—we shall be beaten if they do [are]. We must make our promise good to give aid to Britain. We must see the job through. All of this is needed for our own safety and our future security. This is our fight."[59]

President Roosevelt continued to reject that the government had any plans for armed American ships to escort British convoys. However, he did suggest that the United States had some warships and aircraft involved in patrolling. Within just the preceding twelve months, patrolling had been as close as one hundred miles out to sea. But with the absorption of the British colonies in the Destroyers for Bases Agreement, it was now determined necessary to increase the distance to many hundreds of miles.

The president compared the current patrols with those of the Old West. Although wagon trains had guards to protect them, the reports from scouts or patrols were what determined when and in what direction to proceed. Roosevelt's policy was that when an aggressor vessel was reported in the Western Hemisphere, the details were sent directly to him and he would make any decision necessary. What would that decision be? Again, there were no answers for the American public.

As the Lend-Lease debates wore on, and more pointedly, the unresolved issues of convoying, tensions on the high seas were mounting. Americans received news of the torpedo sinking of the SS *Robin Moor* in the South Atlantic, officially announced by Roosevelt in his June 20 message to Congress. This was the first American-owned and -operated ship to be sunk by a German U-boat. The *Robin Moor* was en route from the United States to South Africa when it was stopped by the German submarine, U-69, on May 21. Allowing the crew and passengers to board the lifeboats, the U-69 torpedoed the *Robin Moor*, which took only about thirty minutes to go down.

The passengers and crew wound up spending eighteen days in rafts before being picked up. Although there were no fatalities, the incident fueled FDR's agenda, and he took advantage and delivered a very vindictive message, citing Germany's complete disregard "for the most elementary principles of international law"[60] and branding the German government as an international outlaw. Others, however, didn't see it that way. Senator Burton Wheeler, claiming the *Robin Moor* had been carrying contraband, actually defended Germany's right to sink the ship, and in turn, accused Roosevelt of taking the country one step closer to war.

By early summer, American patrols had increased in both numbers and distances into the Atlantic. There were rumors of confrontations at sea, but nothing would be officially verified. Articles would appear in leading national newspapers on incidents reported from unnamed sources, and again, no confirmation from the administration.

In a radio broadcast to the nation on May 27, President Roosevelt announced that U.S. naval patrols were, in fact, trailing Axis vessels and broadcasting their positions in efforts to protect Lend-Lease shipments. "All additional measures necessary to deliver the goods will be taken."[61] Then came a bombshell: "Therefore, with profound consciousness of my responsibilities … to my country's cause, I have tonight issued a proclamation that an unlimited national emergency exists and requires the strengthening of our defense to the extreme limit of our national power and authority."[62] Again, what did that mean?

By the middle of 1941, the *Washington Post*, the journal that had been most supportive of the president's policies, was now criticizing his actions of provoking an incident that would serve as the pretext for war in the Atlantic. The paper even suggested that such an event had already occurred when an American destroyer had attacked a German submarine. The *Post* accused the president of hoping that the Germans would shoot first in an episode that he could document in order to activate the escalator clause, "if we are attacked," of the Democratic platform, which would put the country at war. The incident involved the sinking of a British ship in the vicinity of Greenland. An American destroyer arrived on the scene, and while it was picking up survivors, the destroyer's underwater detection gear disclosed the presence of a submarine, most likely German. Fearing an attack, the American commander ordered the dropping of depth charges. The overseeing naval committee concluded that the destroyer captain was only exercising the right of self-preservation.

Now there were follow-up stories that up to 40 percent of British ships carrying American manufactured supplies were never reaching their destination, giving more fuel to the anti–Lend-Lease advocates in Congress, a figure that Roosevelt insisted to be excessively high.[63] In addition to confrontations and accusations, stories appeared that ships from the Pacific Fleet were being sent to the Atlantic, not by way of the Panama Canal where they could be monitored, but all the way around Cape Horn. Secretary Knox now served notice to a group of about 40 newspaper correspondents at a press conference. He informed them that they were to print only such news about navy operations as his office considered proper, clearly a censorship of news.

The next step to war, stoking the congressional fires, was the Americans' occupation of Iceland. In agreement with their government on July 7, 1941, the U.S. First Provisional Marine Brigade landed in Iceland along with elements of the U.S. Atlantic Fleet. Their mission was twofold: to protect the sea area shipping from German U-boats, and to free up British troops that were desperately needed elsewhere. FDR's critics had a field day. For occupying Iceland, he was compared to Hitler and the Japanese, because he was simply marching into foreign lands because it suited the American goals. The real reason for the U.S. occupation was to aid Lend-Lease deliveries. Lend-Lease could now be sent as far as Iceland, now an American satellite, with the British picking it up from there.

On July 8, Americans learned of the Marine landing that now occupied Iceland. The British invaded Iceland in May 1940 and then occupied the island, historically under Danish control, as a base for their North Atlantic operations. Now, U.S. forces would take over from the British with the logic that American shipping would be protected all the way. Iceland would also have a U.S. naval force that would include two battleships, two cruisers, and twelve destroyers.[64] The navy would now escort merchant ships of any country participating in aid to Britain.

For the Germans to occupy west in the Atlantic, or for the Americans or Canadians to occupy east, both sides recognized what the Vikings had ten centuries earlier: that Iceland was an important stepping stone either way. And now with British losses in Greece and North Africa, their troops were unquestionably needed elsewhere. Reinforcing this argument was the rumor that Germany was now planning the occupation of Spain and Portugal. The Portuguese government was signaling a move to the Azores.

With a stretch of the imagination, Iceland could certainly be encompassed into the Monroe Doctrine area necessary for U.S. defense. The Monroe Doctrine had been established in 1823 to protect North and South America from external acts of aggression. It further stipulated that the United States would refrain from interfering in European internal conflicts. This, along with the Neutrality Act of 1939, would allow the Americans to send vessels anywhere with anything. The War Council met in Washington with the president and asked General Marshall for his recommendation. He had preferred Iceland to the Azores.

Republicans in Congress instantly charged that not only was the occupation of Iceland illegal, but it was an unlawful step toward an undeclared war with Germany. Now it was the turn of Senator Robert Taft (R–OH), one of Roosevelt's most bitter opponents. He accused the president of taking militant action without the consent of Congress, contrary to his 1940 campaign pledges. In a radio address on May 28, Taft reminded Americans:

The Constitution provides that only Congress can declare war, and rightly so, because the Members of Congress are the most direct representatives of the people whose vital interest is at stake; rightly so, because no nation should go to war unless a majority of the people approve that action. The President has no right to declare war whether a national emergency exists or not. It follows inevitably that he has no right to engage deliberately in military or naval action equivalent to war except when the country is attacked.

There is another reason why this great issue today must be submitted to the people. Less than 7 months ago the President gave his pledge, "We will not send our Army, naval and air forces to fight in foreign lands outside of the Americas except in case of attack." … The American people do not want war. They have no idea whatever of joining in any conflict, whether on the Atlantic or the Pacific. They are determined to keep America at peace. In this determination I stand with them.… We now face the fundamental question whether we shall abandon the position of both political parties in the last election. Surely that cannot be done without submitting the question directly to the representatives of the people.

The President's broadcast last night was a disappointment to millions of people because it still avoided the basic issue. It still indicated an intention on his part to push further and further toward war without consulting the people. In recent months there has been a tremendous growth of public sentiment against war and against convoys. Because the President sensed that feeling, he carefully avoided any direct advocacy of convoys or of war. He talked of patrols and defense and freedom of the seas. His arguments with regard to Hitler, if they are valid at all, are arguments for war, but he did not dare to advocate war itself because the people are opposed to it. His speech contains vague threats of aggressive, warlike action to be undertaken in his sole discretion. He hints that the term "defense" will be interpreted by him to mean the occupation of islands 3,000 miles from our eastern shore, within 400 miles from Africa, belonging to a neutral nation. In short, he is suggesting that he may, in dictator style, take warlike action without submitting to the people whose vital welfare is concerned the question whether or not we shall go to war. That is not democratic procedure.[65]

And only a couple of months later, Roosevelt would engage U.S. naval operations in what could be described as closely resembling the "equivalent to war."

On July 11, several days after Americans learned of the occupation of Iceland, the president issued a directive through his chief of naval operations that the navy would now protect U.S. shipping to and from Iceland, Greenland, and Newfoundland from hostile forces which threaten such shipping. The order included the protection of "shipping of any nationality which may join such convoys between United States ports and bases and Iceland,"[66] and to wage war on any enemy forces that "threatened such shipping."[67] In essence, an order to shoot on sight was issued. This directive was announced to neither Congress nor the public. Even to the most uninformed, the occupation of Iceland was only the means of protecting ships between two U.S. ports that were involved in delivery of Lend-Lease. On August 28, this order would be broadened to include the southeastern Pacific.

While Congress had not approved, and the American public had not been officially informed, the U.S. Navy was now in the business of convoying, and the United States was at war, as the events of September and October would bear out.

Britain needed American war production and could continue to resist Nazi Germany only so long as it continued. If Hitler could eliminate Lend-Lease or reduce its effect, Britain would fall. But would sinking ships on the high seas bring on a declaration of war from America? Unknown to Washington at the time, and according to German naval-conference documentation, Hitler had ordered his naval commanders in 1941 that U-boat targets were to be absolutely identified as British before sinking to eliminate any possibility of provoking the United States. He wanted to avoid any incident that could result in war.

Any aggressiveness appeared to be on the part of FDR and his State Department with the reiterated statement assuring the American people, "We will not participate in foreign wars … except in case of attack."[68] But the Germans were under orders not to attack. FDR froze German assets in this country, and they did not attack. Then in June, he closed their embassy altogether, and they did not attack. He sent cash-and-carry war goods to Britain in direct violation of the U.S. Neutrality Act and international law, and they did not attack. Americans traded destroyers for bases in Newfoundland and the West Indies. Americans then occupied Greenland and Iceland and still, no attack. Now there were news reports of confrontations at sea, not coming from the administration but from eyewitness accounts. What was needed was a major confrontation at sea that could be documented to unite the anger of the American people, necessary to demand a state of war and send U.S. armed forces to Britain.

Perhaps that time had arrived on September 4, 1941, when the Navy Department announced that the American destroyer, the *Greer*, was attacked. The destroyer was part of the new Atlantic patrol established during July and was carrying passengers, freight, and mail for the Marines stationed in Iceland. While en route, she was attacked with two torpedoes, both of which missed, by an unidentified submarine. On the following day, the *Greer* arrived safely in Iceland, and that same day, the president issued orders to the navy to seek out and eliminate that sub, referring to the attack as deliberate.

In the interest of avoiding war, Berlin issued its own interpretation of the incident. Its submarine was operating in the German Blockade Zone when it came under attack by the *Greer* and was depth bombed until midnight. The German statement included the comment, "Roosevelt thereby is endeavoring with all the means at his disposal to provoke incidents for the purpose of baiting the American people into the war."[69] Of course, this was officially denied by Washington with the assurance that the sub had fired first.

In his address on September 4, FDR reminded the nation that with U.S. outposts in Iceland, Greenland, Newfoundland, and Labrador, the U.S. naval convoys needed to do their part if Britain's Royal Navy was to survive. The president's official announcement of the *Greer* incident came on September 11 in a radio broadcast when he assured listeners that the *Greer* "was carrying American mail to Iceland. She was flying the American flag. Her identity as an American ship was unmistakable. She was then and there attacked by a submarine. Germany admits that it was a German submarine.... I tell you the blunt fact that the German submarine fired first upon this American destroyer without warning, and with deliberate design to sink her.... We have sought no shooting war with Hitler."[70]

Referring to the actions required to defend against Hitler and further losses at sea, Roosevelt made the comparison: "But when you see a rattlesnake poised to strike, you do not wait until he has struck before you crush him. These Nazi submarines and raiders are the rattlesnakes of the Atlantic."[71] The more control Hitler gained over the high seas, the bigger the threat he became to the Western Hemisphere, and Roosevelt reminded Americans that the defense of the Americas was now imperative:

> In the waters which we deem necessary for our defense, American Naval vessels and American planes will no longer wait until Axis submarines lurking under the water, or Axis raiders on the surface of the sea, strike their deadly blow—first....
>
> The aggression is not ours. Ours is solely defense.
>
> But let this warning be clear. From now on, if German or Italian vessels of war enter the waters, the protection of which is necessary for American defense, they do so at their own peril.
>
> The orders which I have given as Commander in Chief of the United States Army and Navy are to carry out that policy—at once.... There will be no shooting unless Germany continues to seek it....
>
> I have no illusions about the gravity of this step.... It is the result of months and months of constant thought and anxiety and prayer.[72]

After a week of headlines, the gravity of the *Greer* incident led to hearings by the Senate Committee on Naval Affairs, after which Admiral Stark was directed to write a report. Released on September 20, Stark's report revealed what he referred to as "a good picture of what happened."[73]

On September 4, a British aircraft informed the *Greer* that a German U-boat identified ten miles ahead had just crash dived. The plane dropped four depth charges, and then departed. The *Greer* tracked the sub for a few hours, after which time the sub fired a torpedo well astern of the destroyer. The *Greer* then dropped a pattern of depth charges, after which the sub responded with another wide-shot torpedo. By early evening, the *Greer* fired a second salvo of depth charges, then departed the area and continued on to Iceland. FDR and his supporters for going to war, using the *Greer* incident as their ammunition, had officially fizzled out.

And yet, the *Greer* incident reinforced FDR's desire for American ships to shoot on sight, a repeat of the original order from the chief of the Atlantic Fleet, Admiral Ernest King, who had already ordered convoy escort ships to attack enemy submarines or surface raiders on sight.

In truth, Admiral Stark was well aware of the figures of the shipping that was actually arriving in Britain. Was it enough to sustain them? Stark considered it absolutely essential that the United States enter the war before Britain collapsed.

The next opportunity that would hopefully incite the American public presented itself about six weeks after the *Greer* incident. Another confrontation had taken place about three hundred fifty miles southwest of Iceland on October 17. Strangely enough, this was at a time when Congress was debating the arming of merchant vessels, which passed the House 295 to 138.[74] One of the new destroyers, the USS *Kearny* (DD-432), arrived at Reykjavik, Iceland, with not only a gaping hole in her starboard side, but also with eleven crewmen dead and twenty-two wounded.[75] The *Kearny* had been one of the five U.S. destroyers that went to the aid of Convoy SC-48, a convoy of fifty-two ships headed for Liverpool with most of its escorts scattered in a storm, when she was torpedoed by the German submarine U-568. Using the *Kearny* incident, Roosevelt made another statement for war on October 27:

> Five months ago tonight I proclaimed to the American people the existence of a state of unlimited emergency.
>
> Since then much has happened. Our Army and Navy are temporarily in Iceland in the defense of the Western Hemisphere.
>
> Hitler has attacked shipping in areas close to the Americas in the North and South Atlantic.
>
> Many American-owned merchant ships have been sunk on the high seas. One American destroyer was attacked on September 4. Another destroyer was attacked and hit on October 17. Eleven brave and loyal men of our Navy were killed by the Nazis.
>
> We have wished to avoid shooting. But the shooting has started. And history has recorded who fired the first shot. In the long run, however, all that will matter is who fired the last shot.
>
> America has been attacked. The U.S.S. *Kearny* is not just a Navy ship. She belongs to every man, woman, and child in this Nation.
>
> Illinois, Alabama, California, North Carolina, Ohio, Louisiana, Texas, Pennsylvania, Georgia, Arkansas, New York, Virginia—Those are the home states of the honored dead and wounded of the *Kearny*. Hitler's torpedo was directed at every American, whether he lives on our sea coasts or in the innermost part of the Nation, far from the seas and far from the guns and tanks of the marching hordes of would-be conquerors of the world. The purpose of Hitler's attack was to frighten the American people off the high seas—to force us to make a trembling retreat. This is not the first time he has misjudged the American spirit. That spirit is now aroused.

If our national policy were to be dominated by the fear of shooting, then all of our ships and those of our sister republics would have to be tied up in home harbors. Our Navy would have to remain respect-fully—abjectly—behind any lines which Hitler might decree on any ocean as his own dictated version of his own war zone.

Naturally, we reject that absurd and insulting suggestion. We reject it because of our own self-interest, because of our own self-respect, because, most of all, of our own good faith. Freedom of the seas is now, as it has always been, a fundamental policy of your Government and mine.[76]

Roosevelt went on to explain the dangers of Hitler and to remind Americans that the time had come to choose the lifestyle they wanted, freedom and democracy or the oppression of Hitlerism. He went on to say, "Our determination not to take it lying down has been expressed in the orders to the American Navy to shoot on sight. Those orders stand. Furthermore, the House of Representatives has already voted to amend part of the Neutrality Act of 1937, today outmoded by force of violent circumstances. The Senate Committee on Foreign Relations has also recommended elimination of other hamstringing provisions of that act. That is the course of honesty and of realism."[77]

Referring again to Germany's navy as the rattlesnakes of the ocean, Roosevelt emphasized the need to protect American merchant ships which, in turn, needed protection by the U.S. Navy. "It can never be doubted that the goods will be delivered by this Nation, whose Navy believes in the traditions of 'Damn the torpedoes; full speed ahead!'"[78] And after summarizing all the challenges the country had faced since its birth, he closed with, "Today in the face of this newest and greatest challenge of them all we Americans have cleared our decks and taken our battle stations."[79]

On the following day, October 28, national opinion supporting the president for war was eight to one (in favor of) according to Press Secretary Stephen Early.[80] FDR's argument for war finally seemed to capture the nation with the repeated phrase, "America has been attacked." But again, the facts weren't in. On October 29, Navy Secretary Frank Knox delivered his official report to the American people of the circumstances surrounding the *Kearny* attack:

On the night of October 16–17 the U.S.S. *Kearny* while escorting a convoy of merchant ships received distress signals from another convoy which was under attack from several submarines. The U.S.S. *Kearny* proceeded to the aid of the attacked convoy. On arriving at the scene of the attack the U.S.S. *Kearny* dropped depth bombs when she sighted a merchant ship under attack by a submarine. Sometime afterward three torpedo tracks were observed approaching the U.S.S. *Kearny*. One passed ahead of the ship, one astern, and the third struck the U.S.S. *Kearny* on the starboard side in the vicinity of the forward fire room…. The U.S.S. *Kearny* was forced out of action by the explosion.[81]

Did Roosevelt's recent declarations to protect war goods in transit and his comments about the attack on the *Kearny* finally mean that American ships were actually convoying? When asked this question at a Senate committee hearing on October 27, members of FDR's State Department were supplying different answers. Secretary of State Hull responded, "That is my guess,"[82] and Navy Secretary Knox responded "That statement is not true,"[83] leaving Americans again with no legitimate answer they could count on. Yet Senate hearing information was being released to the public.

On the night of October 30 at Madison Square Garden in New York City, at an America First party rally, Charles Lindbergh accused the president of using dictatorial powers to gamble with American safety. He said, "There is no danger to this nation from without. Our only danger lies from within."[84] The mere mention of the president's name was booed throughout the evening.

That same night in the Atlantic near Iceland, an incident took place involving two American ships. The USS *Salinas* (AO-19) was one of four American tankers in a convoy with thirty-eight British ships protected by five American destroyers. The destroyers had just assumed the protection of the convoy at a point where the British warships turned back. The *Salinas* was torpedoed with no loss of life. The USS *Reuben James* (DD-245), an old destroyer veteran of the type traded to Britain in the destroyer deal of 1940, came to her aid. A number of German submarines attacked the entire convoy with the five destroyers defending the best that they could. At about dawn on October 31, the *Reuben James* was hit and sunk by the German U-boat U-562. She had taken a torpedo amidship on the port side. The abandon-ship order was given, but before she went under, her depth charges exploded, adding to the loss of life of those already in the life rafts. Only forty-five were rescued with 115 officers and men killed out of a crew of 160, and only eight suffered no wounds at all.[85] The unanswered question after a three-hour battle was whether or not the U-562 captain knew, in the semidarkness and with the bulk of the convoy being British, that the *Reuben James* was American.

The president was slow to react to these losses because he had cried wolf so many times that the country was becoming skeptical. In each incident, his logic for going to war was that America had been attacked. Yet in each instance, it was the American ships that were the aggressors, pursuant to his orders to shoot on sight. By now, even an event like the first sinking of a U.S. merchant ship, the *Robin Moor*, back in May, wouldn't raise an eyebrow.

To this day, the question remains, could Britain have survived until America came into the war without Lend-Lease? During the cash-and-carry period of 1939, when Britain was short of armed escorts, seventy-nine Allied and neutral ships were destroyed by mines. An additional 114 merchant ships were sunk by U-boats. On the credit side, fifty-five hundred convoyed vessels did make British ports, but Germany lost only nine U-boats.[86]

The fall of France and Norway in 1940 gave Germany additional bases from which to operate and extended their range into the Atlantic. By this time, Britain was stretched to the limit, withdrawing ships and planes to repel the forecasted invasion, while the existing convoys had escorts only to two hundred miles west of Ireland, whose ports were closed to Britain. In just six months during 1940, from June through December, Allied shipping losses rose to nearly three million tons.[87]

By early 1941, the Germans had been manufacturing as many as twenty U-boats per month, mastering their Wolfpack tactics (submarine warfare strategies). Adding to their conquests were the disguised surface raiders that accounted for the loss of thirty-four ships from January through March alone.[88] Early Lend-Lease shipments to Britain included consolidated PBY Catalina long-range patrol bombers that she desperately needed to provide air cover for the convoys that were otherwise at the mercy of these raiders and Wolfpacks.

Shipping losses at the hands of the Germans would eventually turn around, aided by the British when they captured the German submarine U-110 on May 9, 1941, and retrieved a perfectly intact Enigma machine. These code devices were the key to passing information to their sub commands on British convoys and ship locations. Confiscating this equipment not only prompted new breakthroughs with Britain's Ultra code-breaking efforts, but it also warned British convoys when to reroute to avoid the Wolfpacks.

But even with Lend-Lease, 1941 was not a good year. A total of 875 "Allied ships [or approximately 3.3 million tons] were lost in the Atlantic."[89] Lend-Lease deliveries to Britain, however, were not the only concern. How would the Americans get their shipments through to China?

Chiang Kai-shek, the Chinese Nationalist leader whom the Americans were morally committed to support, had been reduced to two supply routes, one through the seaport of Haiphong, French Indochina, and the other by way of the Burma Road.

Material shipped into Haiphong had to be offloaded to a single-track railroad, which was often under attack, and ran two thousand miles northwest all the way to Kunming, China. In June of 1940, when France fell to Germany, the Japanese used this as the perfect time to demand from the French Vichy (German collaborationist) government of French Indochina the use of airfields and railroads from which to support their war in China itself. The French government vainly appealed to the United States for military aid that the Americans turned down for fear of getting involved. Yet, the United States was already heavily involved on both sides, by sending material to Japan that she was using to support her war in China, and by sending war materials to Chiang Kai-shek that he was using to fight the Japanese. But with Japan's occupation of Indochina, using the seaport of Haiphong was now history. The only other means of supplying Chiang was through the so-called back door of China using the Burma Road.

Going through the back door, supplies were unloaded from ships in Rangoon, Burma, and then trucked north to Lashio, where they made a right turn to Kunming, Chiang Kai-shek's headquarters. The distance from Lashio to Kunming was three hundred twenty straight miles. But the trucking route was over a mountainous, treacherous, single-lane road that was also often under attack. And due to lack of improvements, average speed was only about 10 miles per hour. To drive the Burma Road, the three hundred twenty air miles became over seven hundred twenty miles.

In a concession to the Japanese, the British had closed the Burma Road from July to October 1940, and while fighting for their own survival at home, they could not justify supporting it. A second closure was forced by the Japanese when they invaded Burma in 1942. After this closure, the Allies were forced to fly supplies into China from India. Flying over the Himalayan Mountains, the ferrying operation became known as "flying the hump," and by the end of the war, China received approximately six hundred fifty thousand tons of supplies via this route.[90]

In the meantime, Chiang Kai-Shek was making desperate appeals to Washington and London to help keep the Burma Road open. Since FDR had included China in Lend-Lease, the problem now lay in getting the supplies to Chiang. FDR's dilemma was that if the United States was committed to Lend-Lease for China, how could the Americans accept the closing of the only route into China without direct confrontation with the Japanese? Would the voting public support him?

Perhaps Arthur Hays-Sulzberger, president and publisher of the *New York Times*, in a speech in New York City on January 31, 1944, said it best:

> I happen to be among those who believe that we did not go to war because we were attacked at Pearl Harbor. I hold rather that we were attacked at Pearl Harbor because we had gone to war when we made the Lend-Lease declaration. And we took the fateful step because we knew that all we hold dear in the world was under attack and that we could not let it perish. That declaration was an affirmative act on our part and a warlike act, and we made it because we knew that freedom must be defended wherever it is attacked or we who possess it will lose it.[91]

And in another address that Sulzberger made on June 19, he again referred to the impact of passing Lend-Lease with: "I believe that we willed our participation in this war—that we went into it affirmatively when we signed the Lease-Lend Act; that we chose our course deliberately because we knew that our future could not be as we mapped it unless we halted the aggressor as quickly as we could."[92]

In the event, Lend-Lease over the course of World War II would cost the American taxpayers an estimated fifty billion dollars in 1940s values.[93]

Chapter 6

Spy Warnings

Shortly before Congress passed Lend-Lease, Bulgaria officially joined the Axis on March 1, 1941, one more cog in a very complicated scenario. Hitler's Tripartite partner, Mussolini, had been eyeing Greece for some time and had decided to launch an invasion from neighboring Albania, which he had occupied since 1939. But the outnumbered and ill-equipped Greek Army, with local British help, not only stopped the Italians, but pushed them well back into Albania. It was apparent to Hitler that whoever controls Greece controls the Eastern Mediterranean, and based on that, he decided to occupy it himself. Controlling the land passage into Greece, which was surrounded on two sides by water, were Bulgaria, Hungary, Romania, and Yugoslavia. Unlike Germany's previous invasions in Europe, Hitler offered the Balkan countries an opportunity to join the Axis with the incentive of getting a piece of the action in occupied Greece.

In early March, Prince Paul of Yugoslavia met with Hitler at Berchtesgaden, where the Fuhrer leaned on him to join the Axis Alliance. This would secure Germany's southern flank for the upcoming invasion of Russia. The prince made no commitment, but on returning home, he became convinced that neither England nor the weakened British forces presently in Greece could offer any guarantees. As Turkey had already signed a friendship treaty with Germany, and other countries had officially joined the Axis Alliance (Bulgaria, Hungary, Romania, and Slovakia) on March 25, he, too, signed.

Then suddenly on March 27, the Yugoslav people rose and threw out Prince Paul's government and his contract with Hitler. It would now be necessary for Germany to invade Yugoslavia to have clear passage into Greece. Operation Barbarossa, Hitler's scheduled invasion of Russia, would have to be delayed while troops massing near the Russian border in Poland and eastern Germany were transferred south to occupy Yugoslavia. But with only ten days of preparation, and in spite of their abhorrence for Hitler, the Royal Yugoslav Army was ill prepared for war. The invasion of Yugoslavia was launched on April 6, 1941, and in a quick victory, the defenders surrendered three hundred thousand men at a cost to Germany of only 558.[1]

In 1945, at the Nuremberg Trials, it was testified that the Yugoslav rebellion delayed by about five weeks the scheduled invasion of Russia, with German troops not reaching the outskirts of Moscow until the dead of the winter cold. A blessing for the Russians, thanks to the Yugoslavs.

The German march through Yugoslavia and Greece took but a couple of weeks. Toward the end of April, the British were committed to a second Dunkirk: they had to abandon equipment and weapons while being rescued by the British Navy. But this time the ships, in doing so, took a merciless pounding by the Luftwaffe.

The island of Crete in the Mediterranean, commanding the approach to Greece, would be of strategic importance. The island was occupied by the Greek Army and the newly arrived British evacuees from Greece. Equipment and weapons that could not be spared were rushed from British forces in Egypt for the defense of the island.

On May 20, the Germans mounted an airborne invasion with five hundred aircraft, some of which towed eighty gliders. Historically, this would be a first for an airborne invasion, dropping thirteen thousand troops on the island.[2] The defenders saw them coming but had little time to prepare. The Germans were able to send reinforcements by air, where neither the Greeks nor the British could provide support. By May 31, it was over. Although the Germans were victorious, the entire invasion had cost them four thousand killed and two thousand wounded. As a result, Hitler now decided to discontinue large airborne operations, as they were too costly in troop attrition. Again, the Royal Navy slipped in and rescued about sixteen thousand of the same troops they had rescued one month earlier, but about twelve thousand were left behind.[3]

It was on April 13, 1941, that the world learned that Russia and Japan had just signed the Russo-Japanese Non-Aggression Pact. It was the result of a courtesy call by Japanese Foreign Minister Yosuke Matsuoka and was supposedly concluded in the record time of ten minutes. A key clause stated that "if either nation should 'become the object of hostilities' by a third party, the other would 'observe neutrality throughout the duration of the conflict.'"[4] Hypothetically, this freed up Japan to concentrate on the British, Dutch, and Americans without having to worry about her back door.

On June 22, Germany started its invasion of Russia, Operation Barbarossa, on a front stretching from the Baltic to the Black Sea. Included were 117 infantry and seventeen panzer divisions, plus many supporting organizations.[5] Then, four days later on June 26, Finland joined with the Germans with an attack on Leningrad.

The German invasion of Russia raised many educated controversies. It opened some optimism in the Free World that perhaps Adolf Hitler had bitten off more than he could chew. Within hours, Winston Churchill changed his rhetoric on the vagaries of Communism and offered unconditional support to Russia.

In the United States, the extremes of every possibility were all voiced, and FDR found himself in the middle. He had recently associated Communism, Fascism, and Nazism as all "enemies of Democracy."[6] Undersecretary of State Sumner Welles was quoted as saying that the "principles and doctrines of communistic dictatorship are as intolerable and as alien to their own [Americans'] beliefs as are the principles and doctrines of Nazi dictatorship."[7] After Hitler's invasion, Welles changed his tune: "Any rallying of the forces opposing Hitlerism, from whatever source these forces may spring, will hasten the eventual downfall of the present German leaders, and will therefore redound to the benefit of our own defense and security. Hitler's armies are today the chief dangers of the Americas."[8]

Not everyone saw it that way. Senator Taft told an audience that the "victory of Communism in the world would be far more dangerous than a victory of Fascism."[9] Progressive Party Senator Robert LaFollette, Jr., of Wisconsin, another isolationist who had supported Roosevelt until it came time to pass the naval expansion bills, warned that soon Americans "would be told to forget the purges by the OGPU [Russia's state security organization], the persecution of religion, and the confiscation of property."[10] Another member of the Wheeler-Nye-Taft camp was America Firster Senator Bennett Champ Clark (D–MO). Clark asked his constituents, "What profit is it … in helping one system of heathenism against another?"[11] Former President Hoover suggested that now American worries were over because the two totalitarians would destroy each other without American help, which might have been the case without American Lend-Lease.

In reference to two nations at war that were not God-fearing, the Rev. Dr. John O'Brien, best-selling author and educator at Notre Dame University, evangelized, "The American people cannot be driven by propaganda, trickery, or deceit into fighting to maintain the Christ-hating despot, Stalin, in his tyranny over one hundred million enslaved people. The propaganda that we must eventually enter the war in order to save Democracy and Christianity has now received its death blow."[12] Although the political influence of the Catholic Church had always been recognized, the opinions of most Americans fell somewhere within these statements.

The professional military opinions of the U.S. Joint Chiefs of Staff held somewhat less water. Their official estimate gave the Russians six weeks at the most, in which case any aid wouldn't get there in time anyway. The Joint Chiefs had good reason to be concerned. Lend-Lease had been at the expense of the army and the air corps. Of the four hundred combat aircraft manufactured in a one-month period, all were sent abroad.[13] Not one stayed in the United States. If FDR extended Lend-Lease to Russia, it would only increase the hardship on the U.S. armed forces.

To that end, Admiral Stark was of the opinion that if the Americans agreed they could not let Great Britain fall, full-scale escorting of Lend-Lease supply ships to Britain would have to be started, which sooner or later would get the United States involved in a shooting war. Every day America hesitated was a day lost. This gave clout to the argument of arming American merchantmen who were delivering Lend-Lease to Britain, although not officially admitted to, and to the final decision to escort these ships with the U.S. Navy. It was during this controversy, Communism versus Fascism, that FDR announced that he would send his advisor, Harry Hopkins, to Russia before confirming his tentative decision to support the Russians.

The German invasion of Russia hit Tokyo like a bombshell. Japan had just concluded in April a nonaggression pact with Moscow, and "The ink was scarcely dry on Foreign Minister Yosuke Matsuoka's neutrality treaty."[14] So Germany's attack on Russia could totally reverse any hope of leaving the back door to the Asian continent unguarded. Matsuoka had not gone to Moscow to make a deal at Tokyo's behest. He had done this on his own. Japan may suddenly be left with one of three options, of which there may not be time to deliberate, all a Catch-22.

Matsuoka's term as foreign minister would be short-lived. In spite of the neutrality pact he had signed with Russia, he believed strongly that Japan should attack Siberia. At the same time, his hostility toward the United States grew, since he believed that the Americans were provoking Japan into war, a war that the Konoye cabinet wanted to avoid. Becoming unpopular with the military as well as with the cabinet, Konoye and his cabinet (including Matsuoka) resigned in July 1941, and when Konoye was promptly reinstated, he filled Yosuke Matsuoka's foreign minister post with Admiral Teijiro Toyoda. Toyoda, too, wanted to avoid war with the United States, and shortly after his new appointment, he dispatched Ambassador Nomura to the United States to strengthen negotiations with the Americans.

Fumimaro Konoye was first appointed prime minister of Japan in June of 1937, just before the Marco Polo Bridge incident. Becoming disillusioned with the Chinese conflict, and tired of being manipulated by the military, he resigned in January 1939. However, it was the Japanese Army that called for his reappointment in July of 1940. The army had drafted a policy to continue its conquest of China and to move into Indochina, but the policy also called for a peace negotiation with Russia. Any additional moves would be determined on responses from the Americans and the British. Preferring peace with the United States rather than war, Konoye's proposal included, among other things, the withdrawal of Japanese troops from China, and he strongly encouraged a meeting with President Roosevelt. Similar to Matsuoka's fate, his views were unpopular with the emperor and the military, and in October 1941, he resigned for the second time. And the entire cabinet went with him.

Foreign Minister Toyoda's fate, of course, would be sealed with the rest of Konoye's cabinet. After the second cabinet resignation in October, Toyoda would accept a position with Japan Iron and Steel Works. Having studied steel production earlier in his career, he was able to improve industrial work methods and conditions in Japan's efforts to meet her wartime needs.

With Hitler's invasion of Russia in June, Berlin may suddenly advise Tokyo of its obligation to the Tripartite Pact and expect Japan to attack Russia from the east, forcing Russia to fight on two fronts. This could be the golden opportunity for Japan to complete the once-intended invasion north into Russian territory toward Vladivostok, with Siberian divisions headed west to meet the German threat. But none of this would be possible without first getting control of the British and Dutch colonies, assuring the supplies of oil, rubber, and tin, which would probably bring the United States into the war.

If Japan honored the Tripartite obligation, she would automatically break the nonaggression treaty with Russia, in which case, she would have to guard against a Russian advance against Japanese-occupied territory in China and Manchuria. Consequently, forces available for the conquest of the colonies would be reduced. And she would possibly be entering a two-front war herself. There had been no diplomatic exchange warning Tokyo of Berlin's intentions, but now the diplomacy came, after the fact, but still months before Germany would be desperate for any outside help.

On July 1, the anticipated, dreaded announcement arrived in Tokyo in the form of a telegram from German Foreign Minister Joachim Von Ribbentrop. Although very unpopular among other Nazi party leaders, Von Ribbentrop was one of Hitler's most avid "yes men" and had devoted his earlier efforts to getting Adolf Hitler appointed chancellor of Germany in 1933. Appointed ambassador to Great Britain in 1936, Ribbentrop was the leading influence behind the Anti-Comintern Pact of 1936, but then later, as Hitler's Reich minister of foreign affairs, he also signed the German-Soviet Non-Aggression Pact of 1939.

The wording of Von Ribbentrop's message to the Japanese on July 1 wasn't exactly what had been anticipated. Instead, it was an invitation to a "unique opportunity"[15] that read:

> It seems to me, therefore, the requirement of the hour that the Japanese Army should, as quickly as possible, get into possession of Vladivostok and push as far as possible toward the west. The aim of such an operation should be that, before the coming of cold weather, the Japanese Army advancing westward should be able to shake hands at the half-way mark with the German troops advancing towards the east ... and that finally the whole Russian question should be solved by Germany and Japan in common in a way which would eliminate the Russian threat to Germany and Japan for all time.[16]

As tempting as it was, Japan's petroleum supply had to be first priority. Foreign Minister Matsuoka, perhaps in an effort to save his reputation, had tried to convince the Japanese cabinet to scrap his own nonaggression pact in favor of entering the Russo-German conflict on the side of Germany. But he was alone. The Konoye cabinet was convinced that by removing themselves from Hitler, they might be able to secure oil concessions from the Dutch or Americans. In the July 1941 cabinet reorganization, however, when Matsuoka was replaced by Admiral Toyoda, Tokyo assured Berlin that Japan would remain faithful to the Tripartite Pact.

The risk for Japan just seemed too great to move militarily into Russia with her back to the precious oil resources behind her. The Konoye cabinet came to two decisions: self-sufficiency and a compromise with the army. In exchange for an army move into Russia, it would occupy all of French Indochina, which could serve as a bargaining chip in future negotiations in Washington.

Since 1939, the Dutch East Indies and Japan had maintained an informal trade agreement. However, in 1940, the German occupation of Holland and Japan's membership in the Tripartite Pact had the potential of leaving Japan on the short end. The Dutch refused to be tied down with export quotas so they could remain flexible in a changing world situation. Since the East Indies were key to Japan's requirements of petroleum, rubber, tin, and other raw materials, Tokyo had to protect her interests. To that end, many diplomatic missions were sent to Batavia to seek commitments in negotiations which ran from the end of 1940 through May of 1941. The Japanese had infiltrated most aspects of Dutch domestic affairs and business and had a labor force ready, all in the vain hope of control or disruption if and when necessary. Then there was the highly publicized Matzuoka trip to Berlin that only served to reinforce Dutch suspicions of how much export was actually going to Germany.

In the interest of a guaranteed flow of oil to Japan, Kenkichi Yoshizawa, hand-picked by Prime Minister Konoye, was dispatched to Batavia, Dutch East Indies. Yoshizawa, a career diplomat, had served as minister to China and ambassador to France, and was also Japan's representative to the League of Nations. In his role as special envoy to the Netherlands East Indies, he faced a "no holds barred" confrontation. The Dutch negotiator was Dr. Herbertus Van Mook, more than ably qualified for his task. Van Mook, a Dutch administrator, had been born and raised on the island of Java and considered it home. With the Japanese, he would not back down. Japan's demands were intentionally unacceptable, and included, among many things, increased shipments of oil, tin, rubber, and foodstuffs such as coconut oil and sugar. With the Dutch government at home in exile, Van Mook couldn't count on outside help, but he held his ground. The Japanese argument included the threat that to not give in to Japanese demands meant the Dutch would have to deal with the Germans, who were also eyeing the East Indies' oil reserves. But again, Dr. Van Mook was concerned that exports from the Dutch to Japan were finding their way to Germany anyway.

After it was obvious that negotiations were going nowhere, Tokyo called Yoshizawa home in June. Van Mook well understood that this was only round one. Would round two be conducted at the bargaining table or with flying lead?

With the German invasion of Russia, Japan now became convinced that Batavia would reduce trade with Japan in favor of Russia, since they were fighting Germany. Japanese diplomatic efforts to convince the Dutch that in spite of the Tripartite Pact they would remain neutral, had little effect. Because of Japanese espionage activity, the Dutch on July 29, 1941, prohibited the use of the Japanese language in the Dutch East Indies. The Dutch considered the Japanese invasion of southern French Indochina a threat to their security and placed an embargo on all shipments to Japan. The result was a seesawing of asset- and goods-freezing. After President Roosevelt and Great Britain froze trade with Japan on July 26, Batavia immediately sided with the Allies and warned Japan that continued aggression would result in a military alliance with the United States and Britain.

The Japanese occupation of southern French Indochina was ostensibly a move to place them in a better position to strike at Singapore and the Dutch East Indies. But in Washington, Ambassador Nomura was reminded that this occupation could hardly be justified for Japan's defense. For food, raw materials, and economic security, the Dutch, British, and American harbors would open if Japan would only follow a peaceful policy in the Far East.

Kichisaburo Nomura had achieved the rank of full admiral before retiring from the Japanese Imperial Navy in 1937. Earlier in his career, he had also served as naval attaché to Austria, Germany, and the United States, diplomatic roles that would later qualify him for his 1939 appointment to foreign minister of Japan. Then in November 1940, Nomura was appointed ambassador to the United States, and throughout his negotiations with Secretary of State Cordell Hull, he made numerous pleas for concessions to his own government that were ignored.

It was also in July of 1941 that FDR sent Harry Hopkins, who was now in charge of the entire Lend-Lease program, to London again and then on to Russia to meet with Stalin. "Of course,"[17] the president said, Americans would give their support to the Russians. He did. They received $1 billion worth.[18] Much of FDR's later belief in Stalin was the result of what some thought was the spell Stalin had on Hopkins.

There was no one more loyal to Franklin Roosevelt than Harry Hopkins, who would become FDR's closest advisor throughout most of the war. During World War I, Hopkins had been rejected by the draft due to poor eyesight, and with his experience in social and public-health roles prior to the war, he served as a director for American Red Cross. Hopkins continued his health-project work after the war, and by 1924, he became the executive director of the New York Tuberculosis Association, building on his reputation by significantly growing that organization.

While Roosevelt was governor of New York in 1931, Hopkins had been appointed executive director of the Temporary Emergency Relief Administration (TERA) by its president, Jesse Straus. Roosevelt was so impressed with Hopkins's efficient management practices that in 1932, he appointed Hopkins president of TERA.

After Roosevelt was elected to his first presidential term, he brought Hopkins to Washington to supervise the Federal Emergency Relief Administration (FERA), the Civil Works Administration (CWA), and the Works Progress Administration (WPA), all programs sponsored by FDR's New Deal. By 1938, Roosevelt would appoint Hopkins secretary of commerce, but due to his fragile health, he would step down from the role in 1940.

There were those in Congress who opposed Roosevelt's appointment of Hopkins to head up Lend-Lease, and one in particular was Senator Taft. One of Roosevelt's harshest critics in the Senate, condemning the New Deal as socialism, and staunchly defending isolationism, he made his concerns about Harry Hopkins perfectly clear: "Harry Hopkins' administration of the W.P.A. could hardly be called a success except perhaps from a political viewpoint, and the same is true of his efforts as Secretary of Commerce. I say that any administration which takes away the administration of the seven-billion-dollar lend-lease program from Knudsen and gives it to Harry Hopkins brands itself as completely incompetent and inefficient."[19]

But it was Hopkins's meeting with Stalin in July of 1941 that was the deciding factor in extending Lend-Lease to Russia, and eventually, Hopkins would become the primary negotiator with the Russians. With all the different hats he was wearing, many believed he held more power and influence than all of the State Department put together. Some referred to him as Roosevelt's "alter ego," while others referred to him as "deputy president."

On Thursday, July 24, Ambassador Nomura was called to the White House, where, in the presence of the Assistant Secretary of State Dean Acheson and Admiral Stark, the president tried to convince Nomura of the error of Japanese policy. He pointed out that it was difficult to convince American citizens that they should continue exporting gasoline to Japan to supply their aggression while American public supply was being reduced. FDR bluntly stated that for the last two years, the only reason that he had continued to allow the export of oil to Japan was that had the supplies stopped, the Japanese would have had an excuse to forcefully take the East Indies. The British would have come to the aid of the East Indies, and of course, the Americans were now aiding the British. A war in the Pacific would result. U.S. policy was the maintenance of peace, but Japan's move into Indochina "created a serious problem for the United States."[20] Nomura stated that he personally objected to the move, but he was caught embarrassingly in the middle. His hands were tied.

The president took one last shot. If Nomura could convince Tokyo to reverse the advance into Indochina, pull out altogether, and return it to Vichy control, he would try, from China, Britain, and the Netherlands Indies, to recognize Indochina as neutral, and this would open up her raw materials and food products to Japan. Although Nomura would pass it on, both knew that nothing would come of it. That same day, the Vichy government officially welcomed the "protection" of Japan.

On July 25, General Marshall and Admiral Stark issued a joint message to the Hawaiian commanders, informing them that the final embargo order was about to be issued: "Chief of Naval Operations and Army Chief of Staff do not anticipate immediate hostile reaction by the Japanese through the use of military means, but you are furnished this information in order that you may take appropriate precautionary measures against any possible eventualities."[21]

And on July 26, the White House issued an executive order to freeze all Japanese assets in the United States, requiring the U.S. government to assume control of all Japanese import and export activities. All U.S. ports would be closed to Japanese vessels, including the Panama Canal, which was closed at the time for technical reasons. By the weekend, Britain, its dominions, and the Dutch East Indies had virtually duplicated the White House order.

For Japan, the freezing of all assets and the suspension of all trade was almost a death blow. This act alone ended 75 percent of foreign trade and cut off 90 percent of her oil supply.[22] Prime Minister Konoye's bargaining chip had worked in reverse. Japan's economy was suddenly dead in the water. Oil alone was a necessity for survival. All previous temporary sanctions were child's play by comparison. The freeze had accomplished exactly what FDR had expected. There were now only two alternatives: to fight, or to lose face by submitting to the Allied strategy. On July 28, Japan responded by freezing American, British, and Dutch assets.

Members of the U.S. Joint Chiefs of Staff were not among FDR's retaliation enthusiasts. They had recommended against the embargo with the conclusion that it would only force Japan into war. Their estimate of the situation gave Japan eighteen months of oil under war conditions.[23] How long could they or would they wait to build a reserve? In addition, the

Panama Canal was now closed to Japan. The likely scenario that Japan might soon act in her oil interest meant that the time had come to better organize U.S. defenses in the Pacific.

Meanwhile, Marshall was concerned that the first draftees, enlisted under the Selective Service Act of 1940, would be completing their one-year obligations, making them due for discharge starting in October. The original act applied to all males from ages twenty-one to thirty-five to serve a minimum of twelve months.[24] He had spent the month of July trying to convince Congress of the necessity to revise or mainly extend the law. Now, since the embargo, at a time when the United States needed a larger army, it wasn't there. Compulsory military service had always been unpopular with the politicians, especially at re-election time, but the Democratic minorities had to support the president. In the House, the vote to extend service by eighteen months passed by one vote, provided by Majority Leader McCormack. In the Senate, the vote was 45 to 30, but the age was reduced from thirty-five to twenty-seven.[25] Starting at age twenty-eight, draftees would be separated from service. The draft would now be for two and a half years, and to counter the draft extension, the isolationists across the nation created the Ohio Movement. It had nothing to do with the state of Ohio, but was an acrostic for the slogan, "Over the hill in October," and was intended to encourage desertion on the one-year anniversary date of the Selective Service Act.[26] With the attack on Pearl Harbor in December, this became a nonissue.

Apparently, the recent depression had taken its toll on the health and education of the draftees. In 1941, many of them were rejected for military service due to bad teeth, bad eyes, and illiteracy. Many of them had to make a mark because they could not sign their own names. The balance of draftees consisted of those with children, those going out of their way to avoid service, and finally those who just couldn't pass the physical. Because the army was the only service drafting, it had already set its standards lower than the others.

At the other end of the spectrum, many American flyers apparently felt quite differently about the war in Europe and Asia. From September 1940 through August 1941, over two hundred forty American pilots turned up in England to fill the ranks of over three flying squadrons. These men became known as the Royal Air Force Eagle Squadrons and carved for themselves a record against the Luftwaffe.

Likewise, a retired Army Air Corps captain by the name of Claire Chennault accepted an appointment by Chiang Kai-shek, a promotion to general, and was allowed to recruit among air corps, navy, and Marine flying units. Chennault eventually recruited ninety pilots and one hundred fifty ground personnel. By the fall of 1941, the recruits all casually arrived in Rangoon, Burma, to form the Flying Tigers.[27] Their three squadrons would establish an unprecedented record by destroying three hundred enemy aircraft in the first seven months of the war. But due to their limited resources, the Flying Tigers would officially be disbanded by July 1942.[28]

Slowly, the scales were turning and various polls were indicating that the Americans should support Britain, almost to the point of going to war. While the isolationists were becoming more hardened, their membership numbers were falling.

On August 3, 1941, the president disappeared from Washington, where educated speculation was an overdue fishing trip. The unpublished destination was actually Placentia Bay, Newfoundland, where the president with his military staff secretary met with Winston Churchill and his military advisers. The meeting took place aboard the newest and fastest battleship in the British Navy, HMS *Prince of Wales*, which had carried Churchill across the

North Atlantic to this meeting. Its purpose was to draft an outline of the common principles of the two countries in looking toward the future.

With the aid of Undersecretary of State Sumner Welles and British Undersecretary of State for Foreign Affairs Sir Alexander Cadogan, an eight-principle document was created. There were many issues involving the Axis to be resolved, but first there had to be a common ground from which to work. This portion became known as the Atlantic Charter. It contained eight principles that included commitments to the rights of peoples, no territorial interests, self-government, and cooperation among nations, among others.

When news of the conference was given to the press, the details released included the charter, as well as discussion of aid to Russia, which would involve some type of return commitment. Not given to the press were any details on how to deal with Japan in various likely scenarios. Churchill wanted a pledge from FDR as to U.S. intentions should the Japanese advance beyond a certain point or attack either Malaya or the East Indies. Would the president ask Congress for war, or at least for the authority to aid them? The president would not commit to either. Nor was there any discussion of organizing the various Pacific commands.

The Atlantic Conference conclusions included FDR's reassurance to the American people that no commitments had been made that would draw the United States into war. During the 1945–46 congressional investigation of the Pearl Harbor attack, the only man who had sat in on the Roosevelt-Churchill conversations, Undersecretary Welles, was called to testify to report on what was actually discussed. Welles reported that it was Churchill who actually suggested a mutual-aid document to be signed by the United States, Great Britain, the Netherlands, and possibly Russia in the efforts to restrain Japan, and that in the absence of such a document, the Allies might fall one by one.

As America was the powerhouse of the Pacific, such sponsorship would fall on the president, who did nothing. In hindsight, as a result of Harry Hopkins's return from Moscow and the decision to extend Lend-Lease to Russia, this could have been contingent on Stalin's signature on such a document that would certainly have offered some fear of exposure of Russia's eastern border to Japan. And it also would have recognized the far greater advantage of her only source of outside help. The extent of FDR's plan simply warned that any action against Britain might draw the United States into the war.

Also on the agenda in Newfoundland was the occupation of the Azores. There was apprehension that Germany might invade both Spain and Portugal. This would naturally include the Azores, from which Germany would be in a position to hamper U.S. sea traffic and communications. FDR and Churchill both agreed on a thirty-day notice for its occupation. However, the reality of the situation recognized that Germany's main attention was now on the eastern front.

Though many details of the Conference have never been released, there was a great deal of speculation. Some insist it was at Placentia Bay that FDR convinced Churchill that, in order to defend British interests in the Far East, Americans would have to reclaim some Lend-Lease. At the time, one out of every three B-17 Flying Fortress long-range bombers rolling off the assembly line at Seattle was going to Lend-Lease.[29] The United States would reclaim one of three of the one of three and fly them to the Philippines, where American airpower would be introduced to the Far East, to deal with any Japanese aggressive moves. All through the Atlantic Conference, British officers were briefing their American counterparts. Present at the conference, of course, was Harry Hopkins, who, on his return from Moscow, sailed with Churchill to meet with Roosevelt.

Another interesting event that occurred in August of 1941 was the arrival of Dusko Popov. There would be a number of individual warnings provided Washington of the Japanese plans to attack Pearl Harbor that were not acted on for various reasons, mostly because of the mindset of lower officials who were only reacting to the mindset of those above them who, in turn, had no sense of urgency.

One such example of intelligence not acted on in Washington exemplified the frustration of the most dashing and flamboyant double agent operating in the United States. Dusko Popov, an aristocratic Yugoslavian, was educated in Germany, where he received a law degree, and then in short order was arrested by the Gestapo on suspicion of being a Communist sympathizer. Family connections arranged for his release, and after returning to German-occupied Yugoslavia, he was approached by the German Abwehr Dienst (counterintelligence) to become an agent and operate in Britain. His upper-class status and attraction to women and fast cars would make him an ideal, unsuspected hopeful. Being first a patriot with the full understanding that the best way to destroy something was to become part of it, he agreed. But it wasn't long before he also offered his services to the British Security Service and soon was passing information to the Germans, all of which was orchestrated by the British intelligence organization, MI6.

After the successful British attack on the Italian fleet in November 1940, the Japanese became so dedicated to getting the minute details that it could mean only one thing: virtual duplication. But where could they get this information? Conferring with their Axis partner in Berlin, it was determined that what was needed was a top agent to go to Hawaii, a Caucasian who could move and mingle more easily than could an Asian. Popov was the man, now code-named Tricycle because of his preference to bed down with two women at the same time. He would be armed with Germany's new technology of the microdot system, with which an entire page could be reduced to the size of a period.

Popov's instructions from the German Abwehr Dienst were to provide as many details as possible about the military operations at Pearl Harbor. Their inquiry included details on not only airfields and ammunition dumps, but also on "pier installations, number of anchorages and depth of water."[30]

En route to Hawaii, his first stop was in New York City, where he was to establish a new German spy ring. The FBI had whittled down the existing one to the point where it was time to build one with new blood. As planned, he was met by an FBI agent. And after setting himself up with a penthouse, a new car, and his movie star contacts, he got down to the business of explaining his mission of the spy ring, the microdots being utilized, and his anticipated mission to Hawaii. Surprisingly, the FBI didn't believe him. Everything was too detailed, too complete, and was thought to be an attempt to throw them off.

At a meeting with the FBI director, J. Edgar Hoover took an immediate dislike to Popov. His lifestyle of enjoying two women at once was particularly repulsive to Hoover's homosexual tendencies; plus, Hoover had no stomach for double agents, and thus chose not to believe a word Popov said. Popov failed to impress on Hoover that the Japanese were going to attack Pearl Harbor before the end of the year and that he should be allowed to leave at once. All the director showed interest in was the microdot system, and Hoover postponed Popov's permission to leave for Hawaii.

The British observed J. Edgar Hoover's handling of Popov's mission and intelligence with disbelief. Hoover, who was so used to closing down foreign intelligence rings, had the complete inability to establish one. And While the FBI did not take his information seriously, Popov enlisted the help of William Stephenson, British envoy to the United States, as well as Sir John Masterman, who recruited German agents to work for the Allies. They, too, were unsuccessful in getting the administration's attention.

Although Tricycle was not permitted to go to Hawaii, he was allowed to make a trip to Rio de Janeiro several months later to receive particulars from the Abwehr Dienst on setting up a two-way radio in New York City that the FBI would control. It was on his return trip that he heard of the Pearl Harbor attack. Popov was personally elated that, thanks to information he had passed on to the FBI, the U.S. Navy had been waiting. Upon his arrival, he discovered that it was the other way around. But Popov had the satisfaction of knowing that J. Edgar Hoover had been warned, and thanks to Hoover's ego, had failed to pass it on. In fact, Hoover had failed to share the microdot system with army and navy intelligence operations even though such sharing of information had been mutually agreed upon. (It was Tricycle and his lifestyle that would later be the inspiration for British author Ian Fleming to create James Bond in the image of Dusko Popov.)

At least two more, similar warnings would be presented later in October. Another glaring case in point was that of Kilsoo Haan, whose attempts to pass on Japanese intelligence proved futile. Since the Japanese occupation of Korea in 1910, there were a number of patriots and organizations dedicated to throwing off the bonds of oppression. One such organization was the Sino-Korean Peoples' League, and one of their agents, Kilsoo Haan, while born in Korea, was raised in Honolulu, where he became active with the league. And in 1938, he moved to Washington, D.C.

Passed on to Haan was intelligence from their agents in Japan and Hawaii that Japan would attack Pearl Harbor in December. One had even seen detailed blueprints of the harbor laid out on a desk in the Japanese consulate. But Haan was frustrated by his inability to create any interest in officials at the State Department, all of whom promised to pass it on, and yet, no one ever got back to him. Finally, in October, he found someone who would listen, Senator Guy Gillette (D–IA). As one of the conservative Democrats, Gillette had opposed Roosevelt's third and fourth terms, and it was his opposition to Lend-Lease that would cost him his own re-election in 1944. His attempts to pass on the Haan intelligence fell on deaf ears. In addition to Pearl Harbor, the Japanese would make coordinated attacks on the Pacific islands of Guam, Midway, Wake, and the Philippines. Gillette informed the State Department, as well as army and navy intelligence operations, and personally met with the president. The response from Roosevelt was, "Thank you, the matter will be looked into."[31]

Now Haan's updated information indicated that it would be the weekend of December 7, and he passed this on to Maxwell Hamilton, the State Department's chief, Division of Far Eastern Affairs, and to Senator Gillette, who again passed it to the president. Through an aide, Roosevelt responded to Gillette that "the matter had been taken care of."[32] Gillette's apprehension turned to a sigh of relief in that it had been officially acted on and passed to Pearl Harbor. The Haan dilemma ended the day after Pearl Harbor was attacked when he received a call from Hamilton at the State Department threatening him not to breathe a word of his warnings: "If you do, I can put you away."[33] Kilsoo Haan reluctantly agreed not to say a word until after the war.

But Senator Gillette's story continues. The FBI and naval intelligence had been well aware of Japanese espionage activities in Honolulu. Just by renting a plane and flying as close as possible to military installations would reveal everything. The agencies could not stop photos from going to Japan, nor could they monitor the mail. So while espionage activity was being observed, nothing was being done. Diplomatic immunity was home free, and those observing the espionage were helpless. It was thought by some that the Japanese spy system in this country would put the Germans to shame.

Representative Martin Dies (D–TX), head of the Special Committee to Investigate Un-American Activities from 1938 to 1944, had been encouraged by Roosevelt to confine the committee's investigations to Nazis and Fascists, but Dies expanded his efforts to include any subversive activities, right-wing and left-wing, inside and outside the government. Now he found an even greater threat, the Japanese. He found a staunch ally in Senator Guy Gillette, and between them they planned to hold hearings in the fall of 1941 to make America aware of the Japanese threat. Witnesses had even been subpoenaed to testify as to the magnitude of the threat. But in early October, the whole investigation ground to a halt when the State Department advised against its continuance as it might offend the Japanese during the negotiations between Hull, Nomura, and Kurusu. FDR's sensitivity to Tokyo's concerns brought the last word on the subject. Both Dies and Gillette were later convinced that had they been permitted to continue their investigation, the flow of intelligence to Tokyo would have stopped. And it would have been unlikely that Admiral Nagumo would have chanced the Pearl Harbor attack with only old information on the ship locations. Later, Democratic majorities in both Houses would absolve the president of anything that could have been construed as aggressive or warmongering.

And yet another warning that went unheeded was from perhaps the most brilliant Russian agent in all of World War II, Richard Sorge. Educated in Germany, he was operating out of the German Embassy in Tokyo, from where he was forwarding to Moscow intelligence weeded from both Berlin and Tokyo. Sorge is credited as being the one who warned Joseph Stalin weeks in advance of Germany's June invasion, which provided ample time to reposition Siberian divisions to the west. And it was Sorge who advised Stalin that Japan had no plans for an attack on Russia, thereby freeing up those divisions guarding Russia's eastern frontiers for the German front. But Sorge did not have the confidence of Stalin, who either did not believe or perhaps did not trust him, with the result that nothing was done in either case.

In October 1941, Sorge was arrested by the Japanese Secret Police, and before his execution in 1944, he made a lengthy confession containing the sum of his activities as an espionage agent. Included in his disclosure was the fact that Japan was going to attack Pearl Harbor in sixty days. Russia, by then a recipient of American Lend-Lease, would have been very anxious to forward such information to Washington to get the United States into the war to take the pressure off Russia's western front. This would have passed through diplomatic channels; however, again there is no such record in the Capitol.

That Moscow knew in advance of the Japanese plan to attack Hawaii was authenticated in files discovered by U.S. Army intelligence in postwar occupied Japan. But the Washington copy is somewhat abbreviated in that there is no reference to an attack at Pearl Harbor in sixty days. Had someone done some editing, and if so, who had ordered it? (After Richard Sorge's arrest, there was an opportunity to exchange him for an agent held in Russia. Stalin refused.)

Even Major Warren Clear, who during 1941 worked for army intelligence operations in the Far East, was ignored. He had tried to warn Washington that Japanese intentions in the Pacific included attacks on Guam and Hawaii, but like all the others, he got no response. He would later write that Washington had "solid evidence, prior to P.H. that Japan would take the whole chain of islands, including attacks on Guam and Hawaii."[34] Similar to Ralph Briggs, Major Clear would be another individual who would not be asked to testify before the joint congressional committee convened in 1945–46.

Meanwhile, the embargo imposed on Japan in July had hit every level of Japanese commerce. This could not continue. It was time to reopen dialogue with the Americans. But concessions would be demanded. To what could, or would, the Japanese concede? In Washington, Ambassador Nomura was expecting instructions. Japan was not about to bend, based on economic pressure, but on what could they bend? The message to Nomura read in part, "With this instrument we hope to resume the Japanese–U.S. negotiations which were suspended because of the delay of the delivery of our revised proposals of July 14 and because of our occupation of French Indo-China which took place in the meantime."[35]

Ideally, a settlement should be reached before Japan would have to tighten the belt to the strangling notch. In desperation, the Japanese military finally conceded to Prince Konoye not to venture south of Indochina, with Indochina itself to be evacuated after settlement of the China issue.

In exchange, the United States would have to resume normal trade and aid to Japan, and at the same time, convince China to accept Japanese terms and undertake suspension of U.S. measures in the southwest Pacific. And finally, the United States would offer a priority status for Japan in Indochina, even after the removal of their troops, based on settlement of the China issue. Armed with this proposal, Ambassador Nomura was at the State Department the next day, August 6. The secretary of state read the document, listened, and concluded that Japan obviously wanted everything in exchange for giving nothing. Two days of discussion made crystal clear both positions.

Then, out of the clear blue, Nomura inquired as to whether the two heads of government might actually meet. Suggesting Honolulu as the location, Nomura proposed that Prince Konoye and President Roosevelt sit down and try to work out their differences, the first hint of a leaders' conference. But it was a conference that would never take place.

Chapter 7

Negotiations

The last days of August 1941 would produce many history-shaping events. In support of the Monroe Doctrine, the U.S. Navy would now guard against the German intrusion of the Atlantic waters of South America by establishing the sporadic, irregular appearance of American cruisers.

On the last Thursday of August, a squadron of B-17 Flying Fortresses departed Hamilton Field, San Francisco, for Clark Field, Luzon, to introduce American air power to the Far East. The route would take them to Pearl Harbor, Midway, Wake, and on to Rabaul and Port Moresby in Papua New Guinea. This was not the most direct route. A natural last stop would have been Guam. But the Americans had refrained from building an airfield on Guam in order to appease the Japanese hardliners, an airfield that could have accommodated the heavy bombers. It was believed that the presence of the bombers in the Philippines, however, would discourage any Japanese moves toward British Malaya or the Dutch East Indies in their efforts to recoup their losses from the July 26 American embargo. While all discussions at Placentia Bay between FDR and Churchill (Atlantic Charter) were not released to the public, some believe that the decision to fly the bombers to Luzon was reached at that time.

Per Brereton's inventory of early November, this brought the total of B-17s at Clark up to thirty-five. Supplying the Philippines with bombers from San Francisco represented the first land-based bomber crossings of the central Pacific. They proved that the Philippines could be reinforced by air. And had the Japanese ever entertained bypassing the Philippines, the arrival of the B-17s ended that plan, because it now threatened any Japanese moves in the southwestern Pacific.

In the waning days of August, Ambassador Nomura, who had been negotiating with Secretary Hull throughout the year, arrived at the State Department armed with a startling proposal: a face-to-face meeting between the Japanese prime minister, Prince Konoye, and the president. It had been almost a month since Konoye had approached the Japanese navy and war ministers with the thought that perhaps a new method of appeal to Washington would bear better results. He requested their support for a direct, person-to-person discussion with the president. Because there had been no success so far, there was certainly nothing to lose. In fact, procrastination could make such a meeting more difficult if the German advance into Russia slowed or stopped altogether, in which case, the American position would become very hard-line.

And by late summer of 1941, the German offensive in Russia was slowing down. The

Red Army would eventually mobilize another three hundred divisions by the end of the year.[1] So it would not be the quick defeat of Russia that Germany initially predicted.

The Japanese needed to act before Americans took the hard line. General Tojo, who would later succeed Konoye as prime minister, reminded Konoye that this, a meeting of the prime minister and the president, could be a breach of the Tripartite Pact and demanded assurances that he was not softening on Japan's demands or position. The evidence suggests that Prince Konoye was a sincere man who hoped to strengthen his position with his ministers by meeting with the president to discuss their differences, and hopefully return with the start of something that would be acceptable to them. A new beginning. Anything positive would certainly strengthen his position at home.

Armed with the support of Emperor Hirohito, who had chosen to reign and not rule, the proposal suggested Hawaii as the possible site for the leaders' conference. Konoye communicated his proposal to Ambassador Grew, who immediately cabled Washington and pointed to this as the best occasion to set a new course, by laying both sides on the table.

Nomura even succeeded in getting FDR's interest in the "'frank exchange of views' on 'all important problems between Japan and America covering the entire Pacific area.'"[2] Roosevelt encouraged Nomura's optimism by responding that it was at least a step in the right direction. FDR's counter to a leaders' conference in Hawaii was possibly aboard a battleship off Alaska. He was even prepared to deny the existence of such a proposal to throw off German fears that the Japanese were undermining the Tripartite Pact. Had the isolationists gotten a hint of the Konoye offer, they would have had a field day with demands for such a meeting. For a start, Secretary Hull drew up four basic principles that the president forwarded to Konoye via Nomura:

1. Respect for the territorial integrity and sovereignty of each and all nations.
2. Support the principles on non-interference in internal affairs of other countries.
3. Support the principles of equality, including equality of commercial opportunity.
4. Non-disturbance of the status quo in the Pacific except … by peaceful means.[3]

In an attempt to pacify his war ministers and the emperor, Konoye drew up his "Plans for the Prosecution of the Policy of the Imperial Government."[4] Although in contrast to FDR's four principles, they were meant to smooth over or soften tensions until he could get concrete concessions at the conference.

But it was FDR's own State Department that pulled the plug on any hope of top-level discussions, using the argument that an agenda of particular or specific demands should first be established before going blind into such a meeting. This was the same department that had refused to accept warnings from Grew that Pearl Harbor had been singled out for attack earlier in the year, the same department that refused to acknowledge that Japan was preparing for war and would take on the United States. Secretary of State Hull was insisting on handling Japanese concessions in China as good faith for a meeting, which eventually sabotaged the whole idea. With the disastrous British appeasement at Munich still fresh in American memories, Hull was reluctant to court a potential repeat performance. With this concern, Hull indicated to Secretary of War Stimson that nothing could be discussed unless a preliminary agreement with Japan was reached first. And Stimson agreed with Hull.

Since becoming prime minister in 1937, Konoye had worked diligently to bring all of Japan's adversaries together. Meeting with Roosevelt would have been his shining opportunity, even though the military considered him too moderate for a Japan with a military future. This moderation forced his resignation October 17. He was replaced by General Hideki Tojo, who now held the dual position of prime minister and war minister.

Known as a Fascist, as a nationalist, and as a militarist, Tojo was certainly less relenting than Konoye. Favoring expansion in China, and supporting the Tripartite Pact with Germany and Italy, he had no qualms about taking on the United States. With Hirohito's blessing, it was only a matter of weeks after his appointment as prime minister that the plans to attack Pearl Harbor would be finalized.

Unfortunately for the United States, it was known that Konoye's influence was on the decline, and the leadership conference would have returned his popularity. But if toppled, his replacement would be the hard-line militant, Tojo. Not considered in Washington was that the failure of such a leaders' conference would prove to the Japanese people that war was unavoidable, further supporting the Japanese war ministers' positions. This in itself would strengthen their resolve for final victory. With this diplomatic failure in Japan's gravest hour, it was obvious that no smooth future diplomacy by the Japanese ambassador would persuade the Americans to stop aid to China or to give up the Burma Road. War preparations must press ahead.

As late as early September 1941, Emperor Hirohito, who had reigned since 1926, appeared to favor diplomatic negotiations over war preparations. At the Imperial Conference on September 6, he put his army and navy leadership to the test. Breaking with tradition, he directly questioned the military leadership and found that most were in favor of war.

None of this sat well with Hirohito, who believed that the ministers, too, were giving precedence to war over diplomacy. It was in this atmosphere that he recited a line from an old, historic Japanese poem: "Since all are brothers in this world, why is there such constant turmoil?"[5] To this, the ministers promised diplomatic attempts first. Both ambassadors, Nomura and Grew, expressed disappointment with the prospect of no leaders' conference with Konoye and Roosevelt, and both agreed that this would seal the fate of the Konoye government and its replacement with a "less moderate leader."[6]

On October 2, the no-meeting decision was handed to Nomura. But on October 18, the day after the fall of the Konoye government, the Magic machines in Washington decoded a message to Nomura stating that regardless of who runs the new cabinet, negotiations with the Americans had to continue. By this time, however, after more meetings with General Tojo, Hirohito had started leaning toward war, and on November 5, he approved the plans to attack the United States.

The following message from Admiral Stark to Admiral Hart in Manila and Admiral Kimmel in Hawaii illustrates how the State Department well understood that unwillingness to deal with Prince Konoye would end any peaceful attempts to negotiate with his hard-line, militaristic replacement. It read in part: "The resignation of the Japanese cabinet has created a grave situation. If a new cabinet is formed it will probably be strongly nationalistic and anti–American."[7] But just a few days later, Stark toned down that message in a personal letter to Kimmel with the comment, "Personally I do not believe the Japs are going to sail into us and the message I sent you merely stated the 'possibility.'"[8]

The argument for diplomacy was fast reaching an end. Every waiting week of anticipated diplomacy may have meant concessions for the Japanese and additional strength in the Philippines for the United States. Japan's naval minister, Admiral Koshiro Oikawa, who was opposed to Japan's taking on either Russia or the United States, favored going "all the way with the policy of bringing the negotiations to fruition."[9] But General Tojo would not budge, and by October, he asked for the resignation of Konoye and his cabinet.

The failure of the proposal did signal the end for Prince Konoye, who spent the balance of the war as an outsider. By 1945, he was active in attempts to bring about the end of the war. But later on, hearing that he could be charged with war crimes because of his office at the start, he committed suicide with poison.

Surprisingly, the Japanese would make one last-ditch effort to get something on the table. Foreign Minister Toyoda inquired through Ambassadors Grew and Nomura as to exactly what it would require to get FDR to a leaders' meeting. Again, nothing developed, but now there was a new concern on the part of Tokyo. In a conversation with Grew in the second attempt for a session, Toyoda commented that he would have to rely mostly on Grew because response from Nomura was uncharacteristically vague. Perhaps the workload had finally caught up with him. Toyoda confessed to Grew that he was wrestling with the thought of sending another top diplomat to Washington to help Nomura. This was still exactly one week before Prince Konoye stepped down, which refutes the claim that the Kurusu Mission to Washington, thought by some to be a delay tactic, was an invention of the Tojo government.

Historically, it was on September 24 that the so-called *bomb plot message* was sent from the Tokyo foreign office to the Japanese consulate in Honolulu and decoded by Magic in Washington. These were the instructions: to inform Tokyo of all ship movements in and around Pearl Harbor. By the time it was decoded in early October, it was already over ten days old, and at the time, the message sounded no alarms. It read:

> Henceforth, we would like to have you make reports concerning vessels along the following lines in so far as possible:
> 1. The waters of Pearl Harbor are to be divided roughly into five sub-areas. We have no objection to your abbreviating as much as you like.
>   Area A. Waters between Ford Island and the arsenal.
>   Area B. Waters adjacent to the island south and west of Ford Island. This area is on the opposite side of the island from Area A.
>   Area C. East loch.
>   Area D. Middle loch.
>   Area E. West loch and the communicating water routes.
> 2. With regard to warships and aircraft carriers we would like to have you report on those at anchor (these are not so important), tied up at wharves, buoys, and in dock. Designate types and classes briefly. If possible, we would like to have you make mention of the fact when there are two or more vessels alongside the same wharf.[10]

A follow-up message dated November 15 read, "As relations between Japan and the United States are most critical, make your 'ship in harbor report' irregular, but at a rate of twice a week. Although you already are no doubt aware, please take extra care to maintain secrecy."[11] And finally a third message: "We have been receiving reports from you on ship movements, but in the future, will you also report even when there are no movements."[12] This last message was sent on November 29 and decoded on December 5.

Pearl Harbor might be compared to a modern-day corporate parking lot where everyone has an assigned place to park. Every ship at Pearl Harbor had a designated berth. If the berth was empty, the ship was either out to sea or in dry dock. Of the one hundred forty-five ships at Pearl Harbor, ninety-six of them were combat vessels.[13]

The Washington intelligence reception of these messages ranged from "interesting" to "nicety of detail," to "nonsense," because in the event of war, the ships wouldn't be in port anyway. These responses came from officers of both services authorized to read Magic, who either thought the information should be forwarded to Hawaii, to decision makers who refused to pass it on for any one of many reasons. Interestingly, no officer who ever guessed Pearl Harbor as the target was ever advanced in grade or promoted in his job.

There were two such officers who insisted on warning Kimmel of the bomb plot message: Captain Alan Kirk, the director of naval intelligence, and Captain Howard Bode, head of the foreign intelligence section of ONI. Both officers had extensive backgrounds in intelligence, and clashed with Admiral Richmond Turner, Director of War Plans, concerning the Magic decrypts and how they should be distributed. When Turner heard of their urging to notify Kimmel, both men were relieved of their duties and reassigned elsewhere, a warning for others. Kirk would later serve as an amphibious commander in the invasions of Sicily and Italy in 1943, as well as senior naval commander at Normandy on June 6, 1944. Bode would eventually be assigned to the *Oklahoma*, which was torpedoed at Pearl Harbor. After Pearl Harbor, he went on to command the USS *Chicago* (CA-29), which would later be sunk in the Battle of Rennell Island in early 1943.

Admiral Turner had been appointed Director of War Plans in 1940, and technically, he reported to Chief of Naval Operations Admiral Stark, but he involved himself with both naval intelligence and naval operations. Some in the intelligence operations in Washington believed that Turner intimidated Stark, and therefore Stark acquiesced to his demands. And it was Turner who decided not to share the most recent Japanese diplomatic communications with Kimmel.

Admirals Stark and Turner later denied ever seeing such messages. Perhaps to cover themselves, they easily convinced their director of naval intelligence, Rear Admiral Theodore Wilkinson, to do nothing because Wilkinson was new to the job. Wilkinson had just joined the Office of Naval Intelligence in October 1941, and while it was the responsibility of his staff to collect and evaluate intelligence, Turner had already started calling the shots. Because Stark thought Turner was much too valuable to alienate, he allowed Turner to operate in whatever way suited him, and Turner was making the decisions on which decrypts were shared with the fleet commanders. Strangely, he was one of the few in Washington who would admit that there was a fifty-fifty chance that the Japanese would start with Pearl Harbor in their conquest of the Pacific, and yet he didn't feel it necessary to share with Kimmel what could have helped him the most.

Another player involved in the bomb plot controversy was Rear Admiral Leigh Noyes. As the director of naval communications, he had been caught in the crossfire between Admiral Turner and Admiral Wilkinson. But thinking that the Japanese were bluffing, he failed to see the importance of the message. Oddly enough, Noyes was known for his indecision, and yet, he would later be put in tactical command of the USS *Wasp* (CV-7), which was sunk by the Japanese on September 15, 1942, just after the invasion of Guadalcanal. The *Wasp* would be Noyes's last sea command.

Being the most feared and disliked officer on the naval staff, Turner had been nicknamed "Terrible Turner." He had a personality conflict with Admiral Kimmel and felt that Kimmel was getting too much information already. Yet Kimmel had been assured by Admiral Stark that he would receive anything and everything necessary for him to make command decisions.

As the director, Admiral Wilkinson did, however, send the December 2 message to the fleet commanders, advising them that the Japanese consulates had been ordered to destroy their codes. As this was a standard operating procedure, Wilkinson would have been in the clear of Terrible Turner. After his brief time with ONI, Wilkinson was assigned commander of Battleship Division 2, Pacific Fleet, and later deputy commander in the south Pacific under Admiral Bull Halsey.

Army intelligence suffered from the same leadership issues that navy intelligence did. Brigadier General Sherman Miles, Assistant Chief of Staff G-2 and head of Military Intelligence Division (MID), refused to warn General Short of the bomb plot message with the logic that the Japanese were seeking this information from ports all over the Pacific. When Miles was later challenged to name just one port of all those under surveillance by the Japanese, he could not.

In 1939, General Miles had been appointed military attaché to Britain, and after serving about six months in that capacity, he returned to the States to join General Marshall's staff. By 1941, he was promoted to assistant chief of staff, taking on his new responsibilities as head of the MID. Whether he, too, was scapegoated, or simply did not fulfill his duties, this would be the last general staff role that he would hold.

Incompetence, negligence, and the lack of experienced codebreakers have all been suggested in the failure of MID to properly alert those in Washington, and in turn, those in the field commands. Some believed that the Magic intercepts coming into MID before the attack on Pearl Harbor were not being properly and thoroughly analyzed. For whatever reason, MID did not see the significance of the pre-attack messages, and as a result, they failed to interpret the true meaning of the intercepts.

Colonel Rufus Bratton, the chief of Far Eastern Section of MID, and Lieutenant Commander Alvin Kramer, a section chief in naval intelligence, both considered the bomb plot message, at the least, an aide to sabotage.

After the war, the joint congressional committee's findings of 1945–46 would reveal how the bomb plot message was actually distributed in Washington. The "Minority Report" prepared by those who dissented from the congressional committee's majority opinion points out that Kramer had "promptly distributed the Pearl Harbor 'bomb plot' message to the president, the Secretary of the Navy, the Chief of Naval Operations, the Director of Naval Communications, the Director of War Plans, and the Director of Naval Intelligence."[14] In distributing the message, Kramer had added a summary: "Tokyo directs special reports on ships in Pearl Harbor which is divided into five areas for the purpose of showing exact locations."[15]

Additional conclusions of the "Minority Report" also indicate that Colonel Bratton "delivered the 'bomb plot' message to the Secretary of War, the Chief of Staff, and the Chief of War Plans Division."[16] Bratton would also testify to the subsequent conversations with the War Department's general staff, debating its significance, and concluding with the implication that it was a Japanese "plan for an air attack on ships in Pearl Harbor."[17] The 1945–46 congressional committee, however, never determined why the bomb plot messages were not forwarded to Pearl Harbor.

After the attack on Pearl Harbor, General Miles would be assigned to perform installation inspections in South America, and later, to a support service role until his retirement in 1946. Regardless of the perceived notion that Miles was not on top of things, it seems that the bomb plot message did reach all the right places.

Today, what seems so obvious to ask is: why were the intelligence officers in Washington not exercising intelligence and doing what seemed so logical, warning the Pearl Harbor commanders? But one can only speculate as to what difference it would have made.

What also seems so incredible today is that, thanks to the presence of a Magic machine at Station CAST on Corregidor in the Philippines, even General MacArthur was aware of the attention to detail of the ships berthed at Pearl Harbor, information that was of absolutely no value to him, and yet the Pearl Harbor commanders themselves were kept in the dark.

In early October, just after the bomb plot message was sent, Japanese aviators were introduced to the Japanese war plans in progress. In a statement made after the war by a former Japanese naval aviator, he confirmed that in a briefing to about one hundred aviators held aboard the carrier *Akagi* in home waters, they were told that the war with America would start on December 8 (Tokyo time) with an attack at Pearl Harbor.

On November 4, both Ambassadors Grew and Nomura were informed by Tokyo that a special envoy would be sent to Washington to assist Nomura with his negotiation efforts. Saburo Kurusu, another career diplomat, had previously served as ambassador to Belgium in 1937, and then was reassigned as ambassador to Germany in 1939. In this role, he represented Japan when the Tripartite Pact was signed in September 1940. As Ambassador Nomura was making little progress with the U.S. State Department, Special Envoy Kurusu was being dispatched to the States to reinforce his efforts.

On his way to Washington, Kurusu had stopped off in the Philippines, where he confided to friends that he was not hopeful about having any success in Washington. By the time he reached San Francisco, however, he tried to convince reporters otherwise. Kurusu told a throng of reporters there, "I hope to break through the line and make a touchdown…. If I didn't have a hope, why do you think I came such a long way?"[18]

Anticipating Kurusu's arrival, whispers around Washington began to spread. Would he bear something solid or merely bring more of their status quo? Would he be able to change the tide of the negotiations?

On November 5, 1941, the day after Kurusu left Japan, the Japanese navy issued to its top commanders the Combined Fleet Top Secret Operation Order #1, Admiral Yamamoto's plan for the attack on Pearl Harbor, which also included cutting Americans' supply lines to the Orient, cutting British supply lines on the Burma Road, and the occupation of British Malaya.

Also on November 5, a new twist appeared in the routine of reading Purple (Magic) intercepts. Instructions came to Nomura to move ahead with Proposal A, one of Japan's final efforts to negotiate a settlement with the Americans in the interest of turning exports back on to Japan. (Proposal A, which provided only a partial withdrawal of Japanese troops from China, was presented by Nomura to the State Department on November 6 and was later rejected by the Americans.) Per Tokyo's message to Nomura, there would also be an amended Proposal B if the State Department refused Proposal A: "If the United States expresses too many points of disapproval to Proposal A … we intend to submit our absolutely final proposal, Proposal B…. Be sure to advise this office before Proposal B is submitted to the United States…. We wish to avoid giving them the impression that there is a time limit or that this proposal is to be taken as an ultimatum. In a friendly manner, show them that we are very anxious to have them accept our proposal."[19]

But in a later message that same day, a time limit for acceptance of either proposal was given: "Because of various circumstances, it is absolutely necessary that all arrangements for the signing of this agreement be completed by the 25th of this month."[20]

Whenever dealing with a contract or negotiation that stipulates a time limit, it is accepted that upon the arrival of the deadline, something will change. The Japanese had just signaled that on or after November 25, something would happen. There were twelve authorized readers of Magic with four of those authorized to alert overseas commands: General Marshall, Admiral Stark, and the two officers heading up their respective war plans divisions, General Leonard Gerow and Admiral Richmond Turner.

Considering all the senior officers who were reading Magic, and with a suspense date in their hands, why no warning was sent to Admiral Kimmel or General MacArthur defies the most elementary logic. Bearing in mind that Corregidor had a Magic machine, MacArthur could have deduced this himself, if he saw it. Kimmel was out in the cold.

In Tokyo, Foreign Minister Shigenori Togo (not to be confused with Tojo) was encouraging Ambassador Grew to recommend to Washington a quick but favorable settlement of either Proposal A or Proposal B. Togo had joined the cabinet in October 1941. Ultimately opposed to war with the United States, he would be among those pushing at the last minute for a conference between Konoye and Roosevelt. (By September of 1942, Togo would resign from the cabinet over political differences concerning Japan's newly occupied territories.)

At the same time, Togo also wired Nomura to emphasize the urgency in getting the American State Department to respond:

> The United States is still not fully aware of the exceedingly criticalness [*sic*] of the situation here. The fact that the date [November 25] set forth in my message #736 is absolutely immovable under present conditions. It is a definite dead-line and therefore it is essential that a settlement be reached…. You can see, therefore, that the situation is nearing a climax…. When talking to the Secretary of State and others, drive the points home to them…. At the same time, do everything in your power to have them give their speedy approval to our final proposal.[21]

But by November 12, intelligence reached Tokyo that all was not well in the United States.

In an attempt to defeat Nazi Germany, FDR had initiated military, industrial, and economic measures, which many considered as dictatorial as Hitler's. The America First Committee was feverously involved in attempting to impeach the president for his foreign policy agenda. At the end of October, twenty thousand AFC members had gathered at Madison Square Garden make this demand.[22] Even the *New York Times Herald* advised that FDR may find himself in impeachment proceedings.

On Saturday, November 15, Kurusu arrived in Washington, where again the news media were waiting for a statement. "I greet you with all my heart,"[23] he said, commenting that he anticipated a "fighting chance for peace."[24] There was no response to the question of any proposal in his possession to end the standoff, although he already had an appointment for Monday morning at the White House.

Meanwhile, Nomura had been personally wrestling with what he considered a lost cause in trying to sway the State Department into the slightest sign of conciliation. Tokyo was making its own demands, and he was caught in the middle. He sent a long, cautious personal appeal to Togo. In it, he warned that any move toward the south would bring war with Britain and America. He cautioned the foreign minister not to be misled by American entanglement in the Atlantic. It could still launch its "main strength"[25] in the Pacific. Interestingly, he forecast that Germany had already reached its zenith in Russia and that Tokyo should exercise "patience for one or two months in order to get a clear view of the world situation."[26] His answer came in record time and was in his possession on Sunday, November 16, and by the following day, Magic recipients were reading it: "In your opinion we ought to wait and see what turn the war takes and remain patient. However, I am awfully sorry to say that the situation renders this out of the question. I set the deadline for the solution of these negotiations in my #736 and there will be no change…. Press them for a solution on the basis of our proposals."[27]

And at this point, Grew sent a wire through to Secretary Hull, warning of "sudden Japanese naval or military actions in the Pacific,"[28] as Japan was amassing troop concentrations in Formosa and Manchuria. Although his information was not firsthand, it might suggest a Japanese move north or south in the near future. But Grew pressed that opportunities for him, from the standpoint of being a diplomat, were "negligible."[29] After the hour-long meeting between Kurusu, Nomura, Hull, and Roosevelt, it became obvious that Kurusu had brought nothing new to the table but a reminder that the Pacific was a "powder keg"[30] and that Tokyo had attained the "explosive stage."[31]

On Tuesday, November 18, the Japanese ambassadors met with Hull again. The full three hours consumed only three subjects: the trade embargo, China, and the Tripartite Pact, with no agreement reached on any. While Hull should be applauded for safeguarding America's long-range interests, using the advantage of reading Magic as fast as the Japanese ambassadors could, and pleading to the U.S. Joint Chiefs of Staff to buy time in order to sufficiently reinforce the Philippines and Hawaii, there should have been caution against bullheaded diplomacy. The door was open to explore stopgap measures in the interest of obtaining that time, and yet he feigned ignorance of their deadline, suggesting nothing with any promise to extend it. Nomura even suggested that to ease the tense atmosphere they should start with the situation that existed prior to the freeze order. But Hull showed little interest and even suggested that there was no guarantee that the troops withdrawn from southern Indochina wouldn't be sent someplace "equally objectionable."[32] Was a commitment to withdraw troops from Indochina not worth exploring in the bid for time?

While the Japanese ambassadors were putting forth their solid proposal of vacating all of Indochina, Hull was getting bogged down in what seemed like unrelated issues: the Tripartite Pact and China. In forwarding the progress or lack of progress to Tokyo, Tokyo responded that the tradeoff of southern Indochina for an end to the freeze would still leave the United States in a position to introduce "rather complicated terms."[33] The message continued, "The Ambassador [Kurusu] did not arrange this with us beforehand, but made the proposal … for the purpose of meeting the tense situation existing within the nation, but this can only result in delay and failure in the negotiations. The ambassador, therefore … will please present our B Proposal of the Imperial Government, and no further concessions can be made. If the United States' consent to this cannot be secured, the negotiations will have to be broken off; therefore, with the above well in mind, put forth your very best efforts."[34]

Foreign Minister Togo was not convinced that the Americans appreciated how critical the situation in the Far East was. Even Berlin was pressuring Tokyo, requiring Nomura to demand that the United States cease in its actions against the Axis powers. Nomura then attempted a clarification of what the details concerning the Tripartite Pact involved. Hull had been insistent that as long as Japan continued with alliances such as the Anti-Comintern Pact and the Tripartite Pact, it would be difficult to convince the United Sates of their sincerity.

Almost unbelievably, the ambassadors requested and received another appointment with Secretary Hull on Thanksgiving Day, at which time they presented him with Proposal B:

1. The Governments of Japan and the United States agree that neither will militarily invade any area in Southeast Asia and the South Seas with the exception of French Indo-China.
2. The Governments of Japan and the United States will cooperate mutually in guaranteeing the obtention of the materials they need in the Netherlands Indies.
3. The Governments of Japan and the United States will mutually return to the situation prior to the freezing of their respective assets and the government of the United States will agree to furnish Japan with the petroleum she needs.
4. The Government of the United States will engage in no activity which might put an obstacle in the way of Japan in her efforts to make peace with China.[35]

The addendum to Proposal B assured everyone that if the main points could be agreed upon, and if peace in the Pacific became a reality, Japan would withdraw her troops from China, as well as revisit the terms of the Tripartite Pact.

While Hull found Proposal B to be completely unacceptable, he had no doubt that the Japanese ambassadors were laboring under a deadline. Reiterating the deadline of November 25, Magic intercepts had revealed that no further concessions could be made and that negotiations would have to be broken off. At the congressional investigation of 1945–46, Hull would describe the Americans' position:

The plan thus offered called for the supplying by the United States of as much oil as Japan might require, for suspension of freezing measures, for discontinuance by the United States of aid to China, and for withdrawal of moral and material support from the recognized Chinese Government. It contained a provision that Japan would shift her forces from southern Indo-China to northern Indo-China but placed no limit on the number of armed forces which Japan might send into Indo-China.... There were no provisions which would have prevented continued or fresh Japanese aggressive activities in ... for example, China and the Soviet Union.[36]

The only certainty was that Japan would not take on the Soviet Union with her oil prospects unresolved. Suddenly there was a desperate need for time—time to create a temporary alternative solution that would be satisfactory to Tokyo and to give the Americans a little more time. Such a possibility came from Secretary of the Treasury Henry Morgenthau, Jr.

Morgenthau had been serving in Roosevelt's cabinet since 1934, and while he didn't agree with all aspects of Roosevelt's New Deal, he did help with designing and financing it. With war approaching, he felt strongly that financing for the war should come on a voluntary basis, as opposed to increasing taxes again. So with the help of others, he was instrumental in developing the War Bond Program, similar to the Liberty Bond Program of World War I. And by the end of World War II, Americans would make loans to their government to the tune of roughly $185 billion.

Dabbling in foreign policy, it was Morgenthau, in December of 1940, who had prepared a draft, outlining the move to freeze Japanese funds. But now, with negotiations with Japan going nowhere, he outlined another proposal for Roosevelt, in the interest of avoiding the inevitable. Members of the State and War Departments studied it. There was some skepticism, but overall, it had merit. In essence, as FDR sketched out:

1. U.S. to resume economic relations—some oil and rice now—more later.
2. Japan to send no more troops to Indo-China or Manchurian border....
3. Japan to agree not to invoke tripartite pact....
4. U.S. to introduce Japs to Chinese to talk things over but U.S. to take no part in their conversation.[37]

And as roughed out by General Gerow, Chief of War Plans: "The adoption [of the Morgenthau proposals] would attain one of our present major objectives—the avoidance of war with Japan. Even a temporary peace in the Pacific would permit us to complete defensive preparations in the Philippines and at the same time ensure continuance of material assistance to the British—both of which are highly important.... War Plans Division wishes to emphasize it is of grave importance to the success of our war effort in Europe that we reach a modus vivendi with Japan."[38]

The alternative in submitting to Proposal B was, in Secretary Hull's view, "clearly unthinkable. It would have made the United States an ally of Japan in Japan's program of conquest and aggression and of collaboration with Hitler. It would have meant yielding to the Japanese demand that the United States abandon its principles and policies. It would have meant abject surrender of our position under intimidation. The situation was critical and virtually hopeless."[39]

And simply not to reply was equally not a valid alternative in that it would offer the same result as a complete rejection. Then suddenly, in the midst of near panic, Magic disseminated a new dispatch from Togo to the ambassadors in Washington:

> To both you Ambassadors:
>   It is awfully hard for us to consider changing the date we set in my #736. You should know this, however, I know you are working hard. Stick to our fixed policy and do your very best. Spare no efforts and try to bring about the solution we desire. There are reasons beyond your ability to guess why we wanted to settle Japanese-American relations by the 25th, but if within the next three or four days you can finish your conversations with the Americans; if the signing can be completed by the 29th (let me write it out for you—twenty-ninth), if the pertinent notes can be exchanged, if we can get an understanding with Great Britain and the Netherlands; and in short if everything can be finished, we have decided to wait until that date. This time we mean it, that the deadline absolutely cannot be changed. After that things are automatically going to happen. Please take this into your careful consideration and work harder than you ever have before. This, for the present, is for the information of you two Ambassadors alone.[40]

"Things are automatically going to happen." Those authorized to read Magic read this on Saturday, November 22. What alternative could it have meant but war? Could Washington have been so consumed by a stopgap modus vivendi that they neglected to warn the Pacific commanders for two days that war could come in just a matter of days? The idea of the modus vivendi, a temporary agreement to buy time, certainly appealed to both Admiral Stark and General Marshall, but now it appeared to be too late.

That same day, Hull managed to muster the representatives of Britain, China, and the Netherlands (the ABCD powers), along with Australian representatives, and presented them with the modus vivendi, the Americans' alternative to Proposal B, as well as the Japanese deadline. The plan called for an amnesty or temporary reprieve for three months, during which time Japan would make no military moves in any direction, they would evacuate southern Indochina, and they would reduce their occupation forces in the north. In return, the United States would suspend the freeze and export to Japan food, medical supplies, cotton, and enough oil to meet civilian consumption.

The Chinese ambassador to the United States was Hu Shih, an academic who had studied at both Cornell University and Columbia University in the States, and served as ambassador from 1938 to 1942. Although the issue of China was not approached in the modus vivendi, Ambassador Shih was at least consoled by the fact that the terms laid down in the modus vivendi would keep the Burma Road open for another ninety days. Secretary Hull admitted that the Japanese more than likely would not accept the offer of "a little chicken feed."[41] The other representatives at this meeting seemed satisfied.

Marshall and others pleaded with Secretary of War Stimson, who opposed the three-month stall, to add his recommendation to the president, but Stimson was convinced that it offered nothing more than appeasement.

Early that evening, the Japanese ambassadors were back in Hull's office, at which time they were presented with the counteroffer and were informed that it already had the approval of the other foreign representatives. The ambassadors hurriedly returned to their embassy to forward the American counterproposal.

Hull spent the weekend making two more revisions to the modus vivendi, attempting to make it more digestible to the Japanese. But the ABCD and Australian representatives would disagree on technicalities affecting their respective geographical areas. Hull later wrote:

> I remarked that each of their governments was more interested in the defense of that area of the world than this country, and at the same time they expected this country, in case of a Japanese outbreak, to be ready to move in a military way and take the lead in defending the entire area. And yet I said their Governments ... do not seem to know anything about these phases of the questions under discussion. I made it clear that I was definitely disappointed at these unexpected developments, at the lack of interest and lack of a disposition to co-operate.[42]

Tokyo wasted no time in answering the modus vivendi submitted by the ambassadors:

> Our expectations ... go beyond the restoration of Japanese-American trade and a return to the situation prior to the exercise of the freezing legislation and require the realization of all points of Proposal B.... Therefore, our demand for a cessation of aid to Chiang (the acquisition of Netherlands Indies goods and at the same time the supply of American petroleum to Japan as well) is a most essential condition. In view of the fact that this is a just demand, the fact that the Government of the United States finds it hard to accept makes us here in Japan suffer inordinately.[43]

Magic's revelation of this communication now seemed like a blow to Stark and Marshall's near demands for more time.

The chiefs of staff met and decided to send the first recorded alert by Stark to Admiral Hart in Manila and Admiral Kimmel in Pearl Harbor:

> Top Secret.
> Chances of favorable outcome of negotiations with Japan very doubtful. This situation coupled with statements of Japanese Government and movements of their naval and military forces indicate in our opinion that a surprise aggressive movement in any direction including attack on Philippines or Guam is a possibility. Chief of Staff [Marshall] has seen this dispatch concurs and requests action addressees to inform senior Army officers their areas. Utmost secrecy necessary in order not to complicate an already tense situation or precipitate Japanese action. Guam will be informed separately.[44]

And on Tuesday, November 25 (Wednesday, November 26, in Japan), the Kido Butai strike force departed the Kurile Islands for the Pearl Harbor mission. Its six carriers carried over four hundred aircraft of Japan's First Air Fleet, of which approximately three hundred fifty would be used in the actual attack.

In addition to the five submarines carrying the two-man midget subs, three of the other submarines were each equipped with a float plane, tethered in a waterproof hangar on deck, which would be used for scouting ahead. Aboard his flagship, the *Akagi*, Admiral Nagumo was under strict orders: the task force could be recalled at any time during the ten-day trip in the event of a diplomatic breakthrough in Washington.

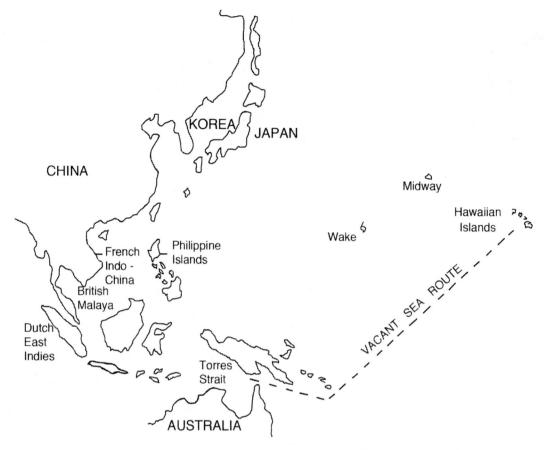

Vacant Sea (Vacant Sea Order route)

Also on November 25, there occurred what would become one of the most unbelievable events surrounding Pearl Harbor. An order, known as the Vacant Sea Order, was passed to the Fourteenth Naval District Hawaii to reroute all ship traffic from the regular, most direct shipping routes to and from the Orient to a most indirect route dramatically south through the Torres Straits, between New Guinea and Australia. The order was signed by Rear Admiral Royal Ingersoll, Stark's assistant chief of naval operations. In essence, it would clear the route of the Kido Butai in that if they were sighted by any commercial or military ship, it could blow the surprise, and Nagumo would be tempted to cancel the attack. In short, this order cleared the way for them. Such an order would certainly have been in accordance with FDR's demand that Japan must strike the first blow. "Top Secret: Route all transpacific shipping through Torres Straits. CINPAC and CINAF provide necessary escort. Refer your dispatch 230258."[45]

The order applied to shipping originating as far east as the west coast. This order then ensured the attack FDR needed to justify a war with Germany to the American voters. This one event alone should refute any possible argument by those who insist that Pearl Harbor was a surprise, because this order actually vacated the route of the approaching Japanese.

Given that ships sailing west to east were also affected by the order, in anticipation of war, the USS *Hugh L. Scott* (AP-43) and the SS *President Coolidge*, loaded with American service dependents, were escorted by the heavy cruiser USS *Louisville* (CA-28) from Manila to Honolulu by way of the Torres Straits. Even Kimmel was caught in the web of the Vacant Sea Order.

Based on Kimmel's own intelligence, he had ordered a search of the "vacant sea" area without White House approval. His attack force was in the exact area from which Admiral Nagumo would launch his aircraft within the week. When Washington got word of this, Kimmel was ordered to return to Pearl Harbor immediately. This event refutes the arguments that Kimmel did not conduct adequate searches. The war warning to Hawaii that followed on November 27, the warning that could have alerted the Hawaiian commanders to everything that FDR knew, had said nothing because they were based only on what the intelligence officers knew, which was next to nothing.

Then came the sudden order from Washington to Kimmel on the November 26 to get both carriers loaded and out of

The Vacant Sea Order issued from Washington to Admiral Kimmel, November 25, 1941.

port immediately and to take with them only the fastest escorting ships. Kimmel was being ordered to "get the valuables out of the safe."

In the interest of buying time to reinforce the Philippines, Tuesday, November 25, also brought a third modification to the modus vivendi for Japanese consideration which, like the first two, offered next to nothing. But before it could be presented to the Japanese ambassadors, it would first have to be approved by the war council and the president. At noon, Hull, Stimson, Knox, Marshall, and Stark met with Roosevelt at the White House. During the congressional investigation of 1945–46, Stimson's testimony revealed that:

> The President at once brought up the relations with the Japanese. Mr. Hull said that the Japanese were poised for the attack—that they might attack at any time. The President said that the Japanese were notorious for making an attack without warning and stated that we might be attacked, say next Monday, for example.

> One problem troubled us very much. If you know your enemy is going to strike you, it is not usually
> wise to wait until he gets the jump on you by taking the initiative. In spite of the risk involved, however,
> in letting the Japanese fire the first shot, we realized that in order to have the full support of the American
> people, it was desirable to make sure that the Japanese be the ones to do this so there should remain no
> doubt in anyone's mind as to who were the aggressors.[46]

Off the record, Stimson wrote in his diary, "The difficult proposition was how we should maneuver them [the Japanese] into the position of firing the first shot without allowing too much danger to ourselves."[47]

At the war council conference, the question arose as to how Americans would respond if the Japanese made an attack that was not specifically directed at the United States. Roosevelt responded by indicating that that would still be a violation of American safety.

Within a day or two, American allies started to unknowingly play into the hand of the Japanese in sabotaging the modus vivendi plan for time. British Foreign Secretary Anthony Eden, who criticized Churchill at times for the confidence he placed on the Americans for help, advised that the modus vivendi was not strong enough, asserting that total withdrawal of all Japanese forces from all of Indochina should be demanded. He did not have the spirit of buying valuable time, nor did the advisor to Chiang Kai-shek, Owen Lattimore. Lattimore, an expert on Chinese affairs, contributed significantly to the public debate on the Americans' involvement with China, and he told one of FDR's assistants that Chiang was livid. Any agreement between the United States and Japan could dissolve the Chinese trust in the Americans. China could go down as a result of American diplomatic treachery. Hull's response was that China could be no worse off than she is now.

Stimson confided to Hull that not only would the Japanese not accept the new revision, but that the British and Chinese were determined that it shouldn't even be presented. His only support had been from the Dutch.

Around midnight on November 25, a cable arrived from Churchill for FDR expressing his concern for the Chinese reaction to the latest proposal, as well as Churchill's fear of Chiang Kai-shek's potential collapse. In closing, however, he stated, "We are sure that the regard of the United States for the Chinese cause will govern your action."[48] Even Churchill was against it.

Now Stimson received a G-2 intelligence report of a Japanese expedition sailing from Shanghai south toward Indochina, and immediately he passed the report up to the White House, inquiring if the president had seen it. He had, and according to Stimson's diary, FDR exploded, criticizing the Japanese for their bad faith "that while they were negotiating for an entire truce—an entire withdrawal (from China)—they should be sending this expedition down there to Indo-China."[49] As far as Roosevelt was concerned, everything had changed. And this negated the entire principle of the modus vivendi, which would have been the relaxation of trade restrictions on Japan in exchange for no further Japanese aggressive moves in Asia.

Winston Churchill's cable of November 25 would be followed up with a call to Roosevelt on November 26. Although the Americans had the ability to decode and read Japanese diplomatic intelligence and to conceivably piece together the overall picture, it would be the British who would actually shape the Americans' response.

In 1937, the American Telephone and Telegraph Company (AT&T) had invented a scrambler system for telephone conversations. If monitored, each end would be unintelligible or jumbled, but crystal clear at the receiving end. The system was first purchased by Germany, and in September 1939, the scrambler system was installed in the White House. There were conceivably an infinite number of scrambling mechanisms, so to possess one did not give access to another. A seemingly innocent article appeared in the *New York Times* dated October 8, 1939, titled, "Roosevelt Protected in Talks to Envoys by Radio Scrambling to Foil Spies Abroad."[50] The Germans immediately saw this as a challenge to break that particular scrambler, and by late 1940, they were monitoring White House conversations between FDR and Churchill.

Interestingly or suspiciously, of all secret U.S. intelligence files and the massive recorded conversations between the two, all scrambler phone and telegraphic exchanges for November 26, 1941, were locked up and withheld from the Public Records Office in London for the next seventy years. The accompanying statement from the British foreign secretary simply said that to release it would harm national security. What is known is that the Germans had a descrambler monitoring station in the occupied Dutch coastal town of Noorwijk aan Zee.

As revealed in Gregory Douglas's book, *The 1948 Interrogation of Heinrich Muller*, the Dutch station monitored a scrambler call to FDR by Churchill in the early morning hours of November 26 advising that British Far East Intelligence, and decoded Japanese secret messages, revealed that a large Japanese task force of six carriers and two battleships had departed northern Japan and were headed east toward Pearl Harbor. The confusing part was that the date given for the attack was Monday, December 8. FDR knew that the ships were mainly in port only on the weekends. Neither realized that December 8 referred to the date in Japan.

With less than two weeks left, the president expressed the concern that if one of his intelligence people got this same information, all intelligence people would know it and want to meet the Japanese head-on. And there would go the excuse to go to war with Germany, the number one enemy. FDR decided that he simply would have to be unavailable to make the decision to attack the Japanese task force if sighted. He then commented that he should distance himself from Washington while the scenario unfolded.

Gregory Douglas's accounting of the Muller interrogation remains highly suspect by many to this day. Since Muller's disappearance on May 1, 1945, there has been no documented proof of his whereabouts after the war or whether or not he even survived the war. And without that proof, many consider *The 1948 Interrogation of Heinrich Muller* to be fictitious.

And yet, the November 26 phone call between Churchill and Roosevelt has been corroborated by William Casey, who served as director of the Central Intelligence Agency from 1981 to 1987. Casey mentions the call in his book, *The Secret War Against Hitler*, in which he discusses the war years while he worked for William Donovan. Donovan had been the head of the OSS (Office of Strategic Services), which was the predecessor of the CIA, and at the time, Casey served as head of the Secret Intelligence Branch for Europe. To refute a statement from such a personage would require an overabundance of conviction.

And finally, Rear Admiral Edwin Layton, still a captain in December 1941, would later describe an event on Wednesday, November 26, that changed everything by one hundred eighty degrees. An expert linguist and cryptanalyst, Layton had been assigned to Kimmel's staff exactly one year prior to the attack on Pearl Harbor. A strong supporter of Admiral Kimmel, he would spend a considerable amount of time trying to determine how much intelligence Washington was withholding, blaming Admiral Turner specifically for controlling the flow of information to Hawaii. Layton would later be instrumental to the team of cryptanalysts who helped the Americans win the Battle of Midway in June 1942.

According to Layton, the modus vivendi suddenly turned into the Ten Point Note, and diplomatic accommodation took an about-face. Without specifically identifying the phone call from Churchill, Layton states that clearly something had happened: "An event occurred that caused the President to override his diplomatic and military advisors to stop negotiations."[51]

Totally unaware of Tokyo's plans for war, Ambassador Nomura and Special Envoy Kurusu, while waiting to hear from Secretary Hull for two days, impatiently sent a message to Tokyo indicating that "there is hardly any possibility of having them consider our 'B' Proposal in toto. On the other hand, if we let the situation remain tense as it is now, sorry as we are to say so, the negotiations will inevitably be ruptured, if indeed they may not already be called so. Our failure and humiliation are complete."[52]

To illustrate the ambassadors' innocence and sincerity in trying to turn things around, they continued: "We might suggest one thing for saving the situation. Although we have grave misgivings, we might propose, first, that President ROOSEVELT wire you that for the sake of posterity he hopes that Japan and the United States will cooperate for the maintenance of peace in the Pacific ... and that you in return reply with a cordial message, thereby not only clearing the atmosphere, but also gaining a little time."[53] Understanding that the Americans and the British would protect the Dutch East Indies, they closed by saying, "We should propose the establishment of neutral nations, including French Indochina, Netherlands Indies and Thai[land, as Roosevelt had proposed the previous September]."[54]

It would be Hull's decision, and in the early afternoon hours on November 26, he presented himself to the President Roosevelt for official approval of his recommendation, which read:

> In view of the opposition of the Chinese Government and either the half-hearted support or the actual opposition of the British, the Netherlands, and the Australian Governments, and in view of the wide publicity of the opposition and of the additional opposition that will naturally follow through utter lack of an understanding of the vast importance and value otherwise of the modus vivendi, without in any way departing from my views ... I desire very earnestly to recommend that at this time I call in the Japanese ambassadors and hand them a copy of the comprehensive basic proposal for a general peaceful settlement, and at the same time withhold the modus vivendi proposal.[55]

History does not indicate army or navy approval of this recommendation, considering the three months needed in the Philippines, but the president approved it, and Hull returned to his office.

It is interesting to note that while the modus vivendi would have given the temporary, three-month time advantage to the United States, each one of the objecting nations would expect the United States to save their situation in the event that they were attacked. They were only concerned with their particular interest, not considering that strengthening the Philippines could be the fundamental blueprint to save the entire theater.

Meanwhile, General Marshall departed Washington for a two-day trip to the Carolinas to observe army maneuvers.

It was also on November 26 that President Roosevelt ordered the Census Bureau to document, by state, all Japanese residing in the United States for future internment. And by December 3, they would complete the task, providing names of nearly one hundred twenty-seven thousand Japanese living in the United States.[56] Concerning Hawaii alone, there were thirty-seven thousand five hundred foreign-born Japanese residing on the islands who were not American citizens,[57] and who would dare to guess as to whom their allegiance would be?

After meeting with Roosevelt, Hull returned to his office and sent for the Japanese ambassadors who arrived about 5:00 p.m. By this time, Admiral Nagumo's task force was one day at sea. Each ambassador was given the proposal of an agreement between the United States and Japan. They were dumbfounded. Was this the Americans' answer to a modus vivendi? This was the Ten Point Note that was in reality an arrogant demand, as they saw it, to the settlement of unresolved issues. It included the following proposals:

Section 1.
   Draft mutual declaration of policy.
   The Government of the United States and the Government of Japan both being solicitous for the peace of the Pacific affirm that their national policies are directed toward lasting and extensive peace throughout the Pacific area, that they have no territorial designs in that area, that they have no intention of threatening other countries or of using military force aggressively against any neighboring nation, and that, accordingly, in their national policies they will actively support and give practical application to the following fundamental principles upon which their relations with each other and with all other governments are based:
   1. The principle of inviolability of territorial integrity and sovereignty of each and all nations.
   2. The principle of non-interference in the internal affairs of other countries.
   3. The principle of equality, including equality of commercial opportunity and treatment.
   4. The principle of reliance upon international cooperation and conciliation for the prevention and pacific settlement of controversies and for improvement of international conditions by peaceful methods and processes.
   The Government of Japan and the Government of the United States have agreed that toward eliminating chronic political instability, preventing recurrent economic collapse, and providing a basis for peace, they will actively support and practically apply the following principles in their economic relations with each other and with other nations and peoples:
   1. The principle of non-discrimination in international commercial relations.
   2. The principle of internal economic cooperation and abolition of extreme nationalism as expressed in excessive trade restrictions.
   3. The principle of non-discriminatory access by all nations to raw material supplies.
   4. The principle of full protection of the interests of consuming countries and populations as regards the operation of international commodity agreements.
   5. The principle of establishment of such institutions and arrangements of international finance as may lend aid to the essential enterprises and the continuous development of all countries and may permit payments through processes of trade consonant with the welfare of all countries.
Section 2.
   Steps to be taken by the Government of the United States and by the Government of Japan:
   The Government of the United States and the Government of Japan propose to take steps as follows:
   1. The Government of the United States and the Government of Japan will endeavor to conclude a multilateral non-aggression pact among the British Empire, China, Japan, the Netherlands, the Soviet Union, Thailand and the United States.
   2. Both Governments will endeavor to conclude among the American, British, Chinese, Japanese, the Netherland and Thai Governments an agreement whereunder each of the Governments would pledge itself to respect the territorial integrity of French Indo-China and, in the event that there should develop a threat to the territorial integrity of Indo-China, to enter into immediate consultation with a view to taking such measures as may be deemed necessary and advisable to meet the threat in question.
      Such agreement would provide also that each of the Governments party to the agreement would not seek or accept preferential treatment in its trade or economic relations with Indo-China and would use its influence to obtain for each of the signatories equality of treatment in trade and commerce with French Indo-China.
   3. The Government of Japan will withdraw all military, naval, air, and police forces from China and Indo-China.

4. The Government of the United States and the Government of Japan will not support—military, politically, economically—any Government or regime in China other than the national government of the republic of China with capital temporarily at Chungking.

5. Both Governments will give up all extraterritorial rights in China, including rights and interests in and with regard to international settlements and concessions, and rights under the Boxer Protocol of 1901.

   Both Governments will endeavor to obtain the agreement of the British and other Governments to give up extraterritorial rights in China, including rights in international settlements and in concessions and under the Boxer Protocol of 1901.

6. The Government of the United States and the Government of Japan will enter into negotiations for the conclusion between the United States and Japan of a trade agreement, based upon reciprocal most-favored-nation treatment and reduction of trade barriers by both countries, including an undertaking by the United States to bind raw silk on the free list.

7. The Government of the United States and the Government of Japan will, respectively, remove the freezing restrictions on Japanese funds in the United States and on American funds in Japan.

8. Both Governments will agree upon applying the stabilization of the dollar-yen rate, with the allocation of funds adequate for this purpose, half to be supplied by Japan and half by the United States.

9. Both Governments will agree that no agreement which either has concluded with any third powers shall be interpreted by it in such a way as to conflict with the fundamental purpose of this agreement, the establishment and preservation of peace throughout the Pacific area.

10. Both Governments will use their influence to cause other Governments to adhere to and to give practical application to the basic political and economic principles set forth in this agreement.[58]

Kurusu's only response was "that when they reported our answer [in essence, Hull and FDR's approval not to negotiate] to their Government it would be likely to throw up its hands."[59] All the ambassadors could do was to ask for an appointment the next day to report Tokyo's response, which was granted. The ambassadors retired to their embassy to cable Tokyo. After summarizing, they added:

> In view of our negotiations all along, we were both dumbfounded and said that we could not even cooperate to the extent of reporting this to Tokyo. We argued back furiously, but HULL remained solid as a rock. Why did the United States have to propose such hard terms as these? Well, England, the Netherlands and China doubtless put her up to it. Then, too, we have been urging them to quit helping CHIANG, and lately a number of important Japanese in speeches have been urging that we strike at England and the United States. Moreover, there have been rumors that we are demanding of Thai[land] that she give us complete control over her national defense. All this is reflected in these two hard proposals, or we think so.[60]

These Purple communications (Magic decryptions) to Tokyo definitely refute the claims of some historians that the ambassadors were trying to deceitfully promise things that were fantasy, and that they themselves were buying time to allow Nagumo's task force to cross the Pacific. In actuality, they were stunned, with no comprehension that the negotiations were virtually meaningless.

Stimson's diary records the question as to whether Secretary Hull had even presented the modus vivendi on Wednesday. Hull's response to Stimson was that "he had broken the whole matter off,"[61] and that "I have washed my hands of it and it is now in the hands of you and Knox—the Army and the Navy."[62] Did Hull have FDR's permission to "wash his hands" of negotiations, or was he ordered to replace the modus vivendi with the harsh Ten Point Note?

Top priority consideration for FDR and the war council was that the modus vivendi termination was two full days prior to the Japanese deadline of November 29. Was this an invitation to war? With FDR's isolationist opposition in Congress, could he be accused of maneuvering a war? On the other hand, if he reached an interim settlement with Tokyo, and then they attacked, Roosevelt could be compared to Britain's Neville Chamberlain as an unsuccessful appeaser, which would make it impossible for him to get his congressional support for promises made to Britain. And finally, if he did nothing, he could be accused of dereliction of duty. All secret evidence that had been gathered from Magic about Japanese movements and the deadlines would have to be kept under a high state of security.

There was still time that day, November 26, to get a message from Roosevelt off to the High Commissioner of the Philippines, Francis B. Sayre. As high commissioner of the Philippines, Sayre had little authority, serving mainly as the personal representative of the president of the United States. Roosevelt's message to Sayre read, "Preparations are becoming apparent ... for an early aggressive movement of some character although as yet there are no clear indications as to its strength or whether it will be directed against the Burma Road, Thailand, Malay Peninsula, Netherlands East Indies, or the Philippines. Advance against Thailand seems the most probable. I consider it possible that this next Japanese aggression might cause an outbreak of hostilities between the U.S. and Japan."[63]

This warning leaves little doubt that Washington expected a hostile response from Japan. Yet the subsequent warnings to the field commanders would be watered down, leaving them with the assumption that they would be kept informed of any updates.

That night, the Washington newspapers made a brief press release from the State Department to the effect that the United States had deserted the modus vivendi and had presented so-called final terms to the Japanese. Although there were no details, Washington was awaiting for an official Japanese response. Washington would have to wait until Saturday evening, December 6. Diplomatically, the key had been to somehow buy three months' time without showing any sign of weakness. But in the event of war, the president had insisted that the Japanese must strike the first blow directly at the United States.

Not knowing what the Japanese response or action would be to Hull's surprising proposal, Americans had to be prepared for any and all eventualities. There were war warnings to be sent to overseas commands. The nation should be alerted, but not to a point of ringing the alarm.

General Hap Arnold was busy making final preparations to dispatch two of the army's long-range B-24s requested by the navy for photo reconnaissance missions to the Marshall and Caroline Islands. Army Chief of War Plans General Gerow was meeting with Navy Secretary Knox and CNO Admiral Stark to compose a war warning for MacArthur that would require General Marshall's signature as soon as he returned to Washington.

Hull called a news conference for selected correspondents in order to tell the nation as much as he dared, mainly of what the Japanese were doing. He passed on reports of the Japanese landing twenty thousand fresh troops in Saigon. There was a reported movement of ten thousand troops from the north to the south of Indochina.[64] It appeared that the next logical move would be to the west to occupy Siam (Thailand). This would put them in an ideal position to launch an invasion of Burma. Indochina seemed to be the key to moving west or south toward Malaya or the Indies.

What Hull did not disclose to the correspondents was the justification to the American public of going to war if an attack was not directed at the United States. Although the Japanese ambassadors were granted their request to speak directly to the president, they had nothing new to report. FDR had already received a briefing from Stimson, Knox, Stark, and Gerow, stating, "If the current negotiations end without agreement … Japan may attack: the Burma Road; Thailand; Malaya; the Netherlands East Indies; the Philippines; the Russian Maritime Provinces."[65] There was no mention of the likelihood of a combined attack on several at once or of a strike from Japan thirty-five hundred miles east to Pearl Harbor, considered to be in the backwaters of the Pacific.

Between Stimson and Gerow, a war warning was drafted for General MacArthur and Admiral Hart (and sent to MacArthur), which read:

> Negotiations with Japan appear to be terminated to all practical purposes with only barest possibilities that Japanese Government might come back and offer to continue. Japanese future action unpredictable but hostile action possible at any moment. If hostilities cannot, repeat cannot, be avoided the United States desires that Japan commit the first overt act. This policy should not, repeat not, be construed as restricting you to a course of action that might jeopardize the successful defense of the Philippines. Prior to hostile Japanese action you are directed to undertake such reconnaissance and other measures as you deem necessary. Report measures taken. Should hostilities occur you will carry out the tasks assigned in revised Rainbow 5 which was delivered to you by General Brereton. Chief of Naval Operations concurs and request you to notify Hart.[66]

Hawaii also had to be alerted, but obviously the same warning would not apply. In addition, there were the concerns for sabotage and alarming the civil population. However, as much concern as there was for the sabotage issue, it could not overshadow the military threat. So, with the first three sentences the same as for the Philippines, the warning for Hawaii and Panama was issued. Message No. 472 read:

> This policy should not, repeat not, be construed as restricting you to a course of action that might jeopardize your defense. Prior to hostile Japanese action you are directed to undertake such reconnaissance and other measures as you deem necessary but these measures should be carried out so as not, repeat not, to alarm civil population or disclose intent. Report measures taken. Should hostilities occur you will carry out the tasks assigned in Rainbow 5 so far as they pertain to Japan. Limit dissemination of the highly secret information to minimum essential officers.[67]

In Washington, General Miles of G-2 didn't think that the sabotage alert was strong enough and sent a follow-up message to General Short's G-2, Lieutenant Colonel Kendall Fielder, emphasizing, "Hostilities may ensue. Subversive activities may be expected."[68]

This message put on record at least two warnings from commanders concerning the threat or fear of sabotage on Oahu, including the G-2 himself, Miles. In response to the order to report to Washington as to what steps were being taken, Short responded the following day that he had initiated Alert No. 1, the alert against sabotage. In essence, this should have gotten Short off the hook because his response was on file for the next nine days with no negative reply from the War Department.

The wording of the war warning itself would account for Short's actions. His orders were specifically not to alarm the civil population. How could he possibly activate Alert No. 3 and not alarm the populace or disclose intent? His orders included carrying out tasks assigned in Rainbow 5 only after hostilities commence. He was also under orders to limit dissemination of this information to a minimum of essential officers. How could he alert all commands to prepare for a major attack and limit this knowledge to only essential officers?

A more likely answer would appear that the war warning was covering Washington's knowledge of events rather than notifying Hawaii to prepare for war.

The more logical interpretation of "not to alarm the civil population" in Short's mind was Washington's fear that Tokyo would charge him with undue harassment of the local Japanese civilian population rather than the thought of an external military attack. Thus, the anti-aircraft artillerymen remained in their barracks, and the ammunition remained in the magazines.

And finally, it is difficult to accept the War Department's claim, where everything goes up in the chain of command, that Marshall did not see Short's response and the activation of Alert No. 1 for nine days. It is difficult to accept, especially considering the urgency of the war warning that was issued just hours after the Hull Note was delivered to the Japanese.

Armed with the Alert No. 1 order, General Frederick Martin, chief of the air corps in Hawaii, ordered all aircraft at the army airfields of Hickam, Wheeler, and Bellows to be parked in the center of the fields and close together in compliance with the sabotage alert, so they would be inaccessible to saboteurs. And the guard was doubled.

When General Short received no response from Washington, he assumed that the action he had taken was approved. It is difficult to believe that, with his nearly forty years of military experience, he would have lined up the planes as he did if he had had any inclination or related orders concerning a possible air strike. That simply makes no sense.

And where some historians have credited part of the success of the Japanese attack to Short's misinterpretation of the November 27 war warning, those same historians totally disregard the fact that the same war warning was ignored by MacArthur in the Philippines. "Prior to hostile Japanese action, you are directed to undertake such reconnaissance and other measures as you deem necessary." Hart had previously advised MacArthur that the navy PBYs could not maintain reconnaissance north toward Formosa and west of Luzon with any degree of adequacy. A change put the air force in charge of reconnaissance north to the International Treaty boundary between the Philippines and Formosa. The order was to make such flights to Formosa, five hundred miles to the north, even at the risk of a shooting match. But when General Brereton asked permission to make such flights, to check out the obvious place from which Japan would launch such an attack on the Philippines, his request was denied.

MacArthur informed Brereton that his limit would be the International Treaty Line, south of Formosa. Brereton argued that that was not close enough to observe Japanese activity. What about oblique photos from high altitude? Again, the answer was "No."[69] When one B-17 returned from an unofficial mission and reported airfields stacked with bombers, it was reported that MacArthur was convinced that they were intended for an attack on Malaya or Thailand. While MacArthur had his staff of officers, he never sought their advice. His selection of his staff included "yes men," those readily accepting his point of view. Only his point of view was ever released for publication. It has even been stated that he did not want an official history of the Philippine campaign published because it might be critical of him. (While Admiral Hart outranked him with four stars, MacArthur occupied the entire top-floor penthouse at the Manila Hotel while Hart lived in a small third-floor apartment.)

General MacArthur's reply to the November 27 war warning was in sharp contrast to reality. He replied, "Everything is in readiness for the conduct of a successful defense. Air reconnaissance in conjunction with Navy and ground security measures taken. The inability of an enemy to launch an attack on these islands is our greatest security which leaves me with a complete sense of security."[70] Unlike General Short, MacArthur was never called to account, and his disaster in the Philippines paled in comparison to that of Pearl Harbor.

Although MacArthur's message instructed that it be shown to Hart, this communication would not suffice for Pearl Harbor. To make the point a little stronger, Admiral Stark sent his own warning to both Hart and Kimmel:

> Top Secret.
> This dispatch is to be considered a war warning. Negotiations with Japan looking toward stabilization of conditions in the Pacific have ceased and an aggressive move by Japan is expected in the next few days. The number and equipment of Japanese troops and the organization of naval task forces indicates an amphibious expedition against either the Philippines, Thai, or Kra Peninsula or possibly Borneo. Execute an appropriate defensive deployment preparatory to carrying out the tasks assigned in WPL 46 (Rainbow 5). Inform district and Army authorities. A similar warning is being sent by War Department. SPENAVO (the naval mission in London) inform British. Continental district Guam, Samoa directed take appropriate measure against sabotage.[71]

In the not too distant future, Americans would be told that the sabotage threat was Short's invention. Sabotage, here, specifically references Guam and Samoa, where nothing had been done for fear of provoking the Japanese. But as of February 1941, Congress had approved expansion of bases on both islands.

Had Washington been paying more attention to military planning in Hawaii, a far more powerful and effective alert would have included an order to the commanding general of the Hawaiian Department and the commandant of the Fourteenth Naval District to execute the Joint Coastal Frontier Defense Plan. This advance warning would have provided ample time for the two services to trade their aircraft to beef up the long-range patrols as well as the army's island air defense, rather than having the planes parked in neat rows awaiting destruction on the ground.

Even Admiral Stark had voiced his concern for sabotage. Concerning the November 27 war warning itself, no one had addressed it better than Rear Admiral Robert Theobald. Theobald had previously served as chief of staff to Admiral Bloch while Bloch was commander in chief of the U.S. Fleet. And at the time of the attack, he was serving as the commander of Pacific Fleet, Destroyers. It would be Theobald who would assist Admiral Kimmel during the Roberts Commission's investigation of the Pearl Harbor attack, and as he later wrote, "Critics of Admiral Kimmel and defendants of the Washington Administration magnify the significance of the Navy Department dispatch of November 27 because it contained the sentence, 'This dispatch is to be considered a war warning.' They would have us believe that this one message counter-balanced the withholding of the mass of information which made the Japanese attack possible."[72] Theobald went on to say that had the two messages to Hawaii included the fact that Secretary Hull had, for all practical purposes, ended the negotiations, the warnings would have been greatly strengthened.

Fridays were the regular press conference day, but on Friday, November 28, there was nothing to report. The only news was that after a two-day delay, FDR would travel to Warm Springs, Georgia, to the Little White House for a belated Thanksgiving with the patients of the Infantile Paralysis Foundation he had established.

In the interest of eliminating the possibility of making premature decisions, FDR had decided that he should not be too available in Washington as the situation unfolded. For days, the trip to Warm Springs had been postponed, but now on November 28 he announced that he would leave that afternoon and would not return until Tuesday, December 2, world conditions permitting.

Japanese deception was working perfectly. Their expeditionary forces of some thirty thousand men heading south into Indochina were making no attempt to hide their positions. So all attention would be on them to cover Japan's vital operations elsewhere. But their destinations could determine peace or war. If they were headed for Indochina, there would be little relevance, but if their destinations were either the Kra Isthmus (the southern narrow neck of Thailand) or the Dutch East Indies, the British would probably fight, and the Americans would have been locked in. The simple answer would have been to strike it at sea. But how could that be explained to the voters? By the time the Japanese naval attack force passed through the South China Sea, FDR would be back in Washington.

Hull, himself, had held a press conference where he expressed fear of a Japanese attack on Thailand, and commented that Americans were most likely on the brink of war, closer to it at that point than at any other point in history.

That same Friday, November 28, Foreign Minister Togo sent a message to the ambassadors with instructions relating to the Hull Note, decoded by Magic as follows:

> Well, you two Ambassadors have exerted superhuman efforts but, in spite of this, the United States has gone ahead and presented this humiliating proposal. This was quite unexpected and extremely regrettable. The Imperial Government can by no means use it as a basis for negotiations. Therefore, with a report of the view of the Imperial Government on this American proposal which I will send you in two or three days, the negotiations will be de facto ruptured. This is inevitable. However, I do not wish you to give the impression that the negotiations are broken off. Merely say to them that you are awaiting instructions and that, although the opinions of your Government are not yet clear to you, to your own way thinking the Imperial Government has always made just claims and has borne great sacrifices for the sake of peace in the Pacific. Say that we have always demonstrated a long-suffering and conciliatory attitude, but that, on the other hand, the United States has been unbending, making it impossible for Japan to establish negotiations.... From now on, do the best you can.[73]

In Washington, this message should have served as a final wake-up call, understanding that after tomorrow, November 29, things were automatically going to happen. This latest message revealed that negotiations were officially broken off. But Japan did not want this known to the Americans. The ambassadors were under orders to drag things out, and they were to make things appear to be better than they really were, so that the American government's guard would be down.

And on November 29, things did happen. Magic translated a message from Tokyo to the Japanese ambassadors that would become a key issue in later investigations. Certain affected embassies with endangered relations were notified that upon receipt of a certain code, they were to destroy all secret codes and documents. Nomura's message read:

> In case of emergency (danger of cutting off our diplomatic relations), and the cutting off of international communications, the following warning will be added in the middle of the daily Japanese language short wave news broadcast.
>
> 1. In case of a Japan-U.S. relations in danger—HIGASHI NO KAZEAME (East Wind rain).
> 2. Japan-U.S.S.R. relations—KITANOKAZE KUMORI—(North Wind cloudy).
> 3. Japan-British relations: NISHI NO KAZE HARE—(West Wind clear).
>
> This signal will be given in the middle and at the end as a weather forecast and last sentence will be repeated twice. When this is heard please destroy all code papers, etc. This is as yet to be a completely secret arrangement.[74]

Tokyo followed this up with:

> When our diplomatic relations are becoming dangerous, we will add the following at the beginning and end of our general intelligence broadcasts:
>   1. If it is Japan-U.S. relations, "HIGASHI."
>   2. Japan-Russia relations, "KITA."
>   3. Japan-British relations (including Thai, Malaya and N.E.I.),–"NISHI."
>   The above will be repeated five times and included at beginning and end. Relay to Rio de Janeiro, Buenos Aires, Mexico City, San Francisco.[75]

This became known as the *winds* message, and once the November 29 transmissions were read, Washington established a listening watch on the most likely radio frequencies. But the Japanese now created a number of deceptive devices to confuse and lull American intelligence into following Japanese movement. While they were making no attempt to hide or deceive the movement of their task force headed south toward Malaya, they were creating a volume of false radio traffic to position Japanese ships where they were not.

To make sure that there would be no suspicion of any action to commence in early December, Tokyo announced that it would dispatch the ocean liner *Tatsuta Maru*, also known as the *Tatuta Maru*, to sail to America on December 2 to pick up Japanese nationals who wanted to return home. Her initial passengers would be many Americans anxious to leave Japan. Obviously, nothing could happen until the ship returned home. The reality was that the *Tatsuta Maru* would sail only as far as the International Date Line and then return to Japan. Her American and British passengers were imprisoned for the balance of the war, America's most forgotten.

On Sunday, November 30, Magic decoded a message from Tokyo to Berlin. Between the lines, it announced that Japan was about to go to war with the United States:

> The conversations begun between Tokyo and Washington last April ... now stand ruptured—broken....
> In the face of this, our Empire faces a grave situation and must act with determination. Will Your Honor, therefore, immediately interview Chancellor HITLER and Foreign Minister RIBBENTROP and confidentially communicate to them a summary of the developments? ... Say very secretly to them that there is extreme danger that war may suddenly break out between the Anglo-Saxon nations and Japan through some clash of arms and add that the time of the breaking out of this war may come quicker than anyone dreams.[76]

This was followed up with a December 1 message to Nomura and Kurusu in Washington that "the situation continues to be increasingly critical. However, to prevent the United States from becoming unduly suspicious we have been advising the press and others that though there are some wide differences between Japan and the United States, the negotiations are continuing."[77]

And on December 1 another message came to explain the process of destroying code machines and documentation: "When you are faced with the necessity of destroying codes, get in touch with the Naval Attache's office there and make use of chemicals they have on hand for this purpose.... The four offices in London, Hong Kong, Singapore, and Manila have been instructed to abandon the use of the code machines and to dispose of them ... the U.S. [office] retains the machines and machine codes."[78]

The destruction of codes was last-minute business before war. Those authorized to read Magic were now well aware that war was a possibility somewhere at any time. The war warnings were weak because they did not have specific information. And it must have been difficult for the president not to share what he knew, that the Kido Butai had been en route to Pearl Harbor since November 25. But sharing this information would bring the demand to meet the Japanese head-on, and that would eliminate his legitimacy for war with Germany per the Tripartite Pact. Besides, how strong could Japan be, anyway? In four years, they had not been able to defeat the poorly armed Chinese, and it was difficult to rate their air power because the only aircraft that went up to meet it were obsolete relics.

Magic received on November 30 was obviously passed on to the president because late that night, he reappeared in Washington, two days ahead of plan. When queried by the press why he returned early, he simply responded that a speech by Prime Minister Tojo in Tokyo was full of aggressive overtones, and that he wanted to be atop of developments. The Japanese were reacting to the Ten Point Note.

It has been over seventy years since Churchill made the November 26 call to Roosevelt, advising him that the Japanese were on their way and would arrive at Pearl Harbor on December 8. And while those missing intelligence files of the November 26 communications make it difficult to verify that phone call, an appeal to a sense of logic makes everything fit.

A review of the events is chronological. Regardless of who actually wrote the Ten Point Note, it had to carry FDR's final approval, which, in essence, brought all negotiations to a standstill.

Admiral Kimmel had been alerted as early as November 10 of a planned mission for the carriers to deliver planes to Wake and Midway. But suddenly on November 26, he was ordered to get the carriers out of port immediately and to take the fastest ships with them. The ships left behind consisted of eight old and slow World War I battleships.

Whether one agrees or not with Gregory Douglas's published account of the Roosevelt-Churchill call of November 26, the Vacant Sea Order issued on November 25 adds further evidence that Roosevelt was fully aware that the Japanese were on their way.

Perhaps Harry Hopkins had made the best analysis, concluding that Cordell Hull was really a man of peace and not aggressive enough with the Japanese ambassadors to meet FDR's force-them-into-a-corner policy. The Ten Point Note was forced on Hull to present a full two days before the Japanese deadline, and up to the last minute, Hull had hoped that something could be worked out. As a result, he took FDR's blame for the stubbornness or unyielding nature of the American government's foreign policy. Upon FDR's re-election in November 1944, Hull would resign.

Chapter 8

Final Warnings

For over sixty-five years the first question asked by skeptics has been: if the attack on Pearl Harbor was such a surprise, how was it that the main targets, the carriers, were gone? This one subject has been the source of heated arguments on both sides of the conspiracy theory. These are the facts.

As far back as November 10, a heads-up signal had been issued by Washington with the plan of reinforcing Wake and Midway Islands with fighters, twelve for Wake and eighteen for Midway. The islands were being prepared to accommodate the planes, and Kimmel would make his carriers available for the delivery. At the time, Kimmel's fleet still included the three aircraft carriers, the *Enterprise*, the *Lexington*, and the *Saratoga*, but the *Saratoga* had just returned to San Diego for refitting.

And with the possibility that Japan could strike somewhere in the Pacific at any moment, there was now concern in Washington that the additional forty-eight B-17s[1] that had accumulated on the West Coast for delivery to the Philippines could be attacked en route. Because of the distance involved, they would be defenseless. They could carry only minimum crews and no defensive guns or ammunition. The weight saved would provide just enough fuel to reach Hawaii, the longest leg of their trip.

On November 26, Admiral Stark forwarded the order to Kimmel to immediately prepare the two remaining carriers, the *Enterprise* and the *Lexington*, with the fastest escorting ships in his command, for the delivery of some of the army's P-40 fighters to both Wake and Midway Islands. The fighters would provide some degree of security for the bombers' refueling stops. The army had offered them to the navy, but the catch was that General Short would have to provide them. All Short had for fighter protection for all of Hawaii were the fourteen Boeing P-26s, which were of 1934–35 vintage; the thirty-nine P-36s, which were of 1939 vintage; and a total of (now) ninety-nine Curtiss P40B and C fighters with top speeds of about 350 miles per hour.

Because only the P-40s were relatively state of the art, Short was reluctant to give up 30 percent of that strength. The Joint Chiefs had promised to replace them as soon as possible, but admitted that until such time, there would be a risk involved. But to even have considered such a transfer of fighters leaves no doubt that Pearl Harbor was not considered at risk. At this time, two hundred P-40s were on their way from the United States to Russia.

The problem now arose of loading army aircraft onto an aircraft carrier. Unlike naval aircraft, army planes had no fittings to lift them onto the decks by crane. Nor were there off-

Kapiolani Park, near Waikiki Beach, before the December 7, 1941, attack (Diamond Head is in the background). In just two weeks the park would be scattered with junk to prevent enemy landings.

loading docks at the destinations, although they could fly off the carriers that they could not land on. This meant that, once there, they would have to stay.

With the urgency of the order, Kimmel decided to substitute the P-40s with Marine Grumman F4Fs that could be lifted or flown aboard. For the defense of Pearl Harbor, this left Kimmel with virtually no navy or Marine fighters. And it would eliminate the navy's ability to loan its fighter strength to the army for island defense in compliance with the Joint Coastal Frontier Defense Plan. The balance of Kimmel's protection was at the Marine air station at Ewa that was home to the SBD and SB2U dive bombers and some F4F fighters. Ford Island and Kaneohe were home to the PBY patrol bombers.

For the B-17s destined for the Philippines that required fighter protection, FDR's priority had been to send them to Britain. But Stimson had argued they be sent to the Philippines to keep Japan away from Singapore. And Marshall had preferred they go to Hawaii. Of course, no one thought to ask General Brereton, who, as commander of the Far East Air Force, considered it bad judgment to send B-17s to the Philippines, where, as events would bear out, they would have no fighter protection, nor any place to land them. Clark Field had no more room for additional bombers. There remains only the speculation on future events. If the B-17s, which were later destroyed on the ground at Clark Field, had been sent to Pearl Harbor for long-range patrol instead, would events at Pearl Harbor have vastly changed?

The author's wife observing a modern carrier departing Pearl Harbor.

At 0800, Friday, November 28, the *Enterprise*, under the command of Admiral "Bull" Halsey, carrying twelve Grumman F4Fs[2] and supporting crews, led Task Force 8 through the narrow channel leading out of Pearl Harbor, followed by three fast cruisers and a squadron of destroyers. When clear of the harbor entrance, they turned toward Wake Island, twenty-five hundred miles west. The *Enterprise* and the *Lexington*, the latter of which was preparing to take reinforcements to Midway, had identical air groups for offensive or defensive action. So with both carriers away from port, Kimmel would lose thirty-six SBD dive bombers, eighteen TBD torpedo bombers, and eighteen fighters—per carrier, a total of 144 aircraft.

At the time of the initial order, General Martin in Hawaii suggested that, regardless of which branch furnished the fighters, they send the obsolete planes "because those were the ones we could afford best to lose."[3] But General Short insisted, "If we are going up against the Japanese, we wanted the best we had instead of the worst."[4]

Not understanding the underlying purpose of Washington's order, Kimmel had asked Halsey, who would take the *Enterprise* to Wake, "Do you want to take the battleships with you?"[5] "Hell no," Halsey replied. "If I have to run I don't want anything to interfere with my running."[6] The two Annapolis classmates finally agreed that in order to cover themselves with Washington, escorting vessels should go along and make the trip look more routine to watchful eyes. But they would return to Pearl Harbor as soon as possible. In the event of trouble with the Japanese, Halsey inquired, "How far do you want me to go?"[7] Kimmel replied, "Goddamitt, use your common sense!"[8] Halsey understood , thinking that those were "the finest orders ever given to a man."[9] Halsey's interpretation of common sense would be "all ships in readiness for instant combat."[10] This meant warheads on the torpedoes, aircraft loaded with machine gun ammunition, bombs brought up to readiness position, radio silence, and daily air patrols two hundred miles ahead, with orders to sink any Japanese ship they encountered.

On December 2, twelve navy PBY patrol bombers took off from Midway for the twelve-hundred-mile trip to Wake Island to check the route and search five hundred miles around and then cover the arrival of the *Enterprise* task force. At the same time, Kimmel ordered a squadron of PBYs from Pearl Harbor to replace those at Midway.

On December 4, the *Enterprise* squadron was two hundred miles northeast of Wake when one of the Wake PBYs appeared overhead. The twelve F4Fs took off and followed it to the airfield on the island. After making a precision pass over, they landed and were cheered by all sixteen hundred-plus military and civilian personnel. On December 6, all the PBYs departed Wake for the return trip to Pearl Harbor.

And on December 5, after some delays, Task Force 12, under the brief command of Rear Admiral John Newton, departed Pearl Harbor. Led by the *Lexington*, which carried eighteen Vought SB2U-3 dive bombers[11] and supporting crews, and accompanied by three heavy cruisers and five destroyers, they embarked on their mission to Midway. These fighters would beef up the Marine Fighter Squadron 221, which was currently flying the obsolete Brewster F2A Buffalos. Their departure left eight old World War I–vintage battleships remaining in port, all tethered to Ford Island. For some, this was a little too ironic.

Adding to the irony is that after weeks of gathering the B-17s on the West Coast for delivery to the Philippines, there was suddenly the urgency of reinforcing their route (Wake and Midway Islands) on, of all days, November 26, the day of FDR's call from Churchill. And it was on this same day that Secretary of State Cordell Hull washed his hands of further negotiations, and one day after the Vacant Sea Order had been issued. Many scholars have argued that the real intention was to get the carriers, the main Japanese targets, out of port as quickly as possible, leaving behind the ships that could best afford to be lost.

In all the Philippines, there were just the two airfields large enough to handle the B-17s, Clark and Del Monte. By December 7, Clark already had thirty-five of them and could not handle the additional forty-eight waiting on the West Coast. And Del Monte was still under construction. Thus the immediate urgency to get reinforcements to Wake and Midway, requiring the carrier missions, remains highly questionable. The absence of any place to land or refuel them does not support a legitimate argument.

While the *Lexington* was en route to Midway, the daily routine scout planes were dispatched, flying out two hundred miles to secure the route ahead. One of "Lady Lex's" TBD torpedo bomber pilots, Norman Sterrie, M.D., told this author that one of these scouts reported the sighting of a Japanese single-engine, fixed-landing-gear scout plane. The mere fact that it was a single-engine plane would indicate the not-too-distant presence of the mother ship or task force in the moderate vicinity. This highly decorated American aviator, who would become the last surviving TBD pilot, has pondered all these years as to what ever happened to that report and how more attention to it may have changed history. (In five months, Sterrie would have to swim away from the sinking *Lexington* to save his life.)

Task Force 12 was at a position four hundred twenty miles southeast of Midway that Sunday morning, with the plan to launch the planes at noon, when the report of the attack at Pearl Harbor was received. Rather than launch these dive bombers so badly needed at Midway, Admiral Newton ordered the return of the fleet to Pearl Harbor with its aircraft still aboard. Whether or not he was ordered to turn around is in question, but Newton was criticized for that action with the argument that the planes would have been of more value at Midway in scouting for the Japanese. Command of the *Lexington* would next go to Vice Admiral Wilson Brown who, at the time, was one of the oldest naval officers to serve in combat operations during World War II. After Wilson took command of the *Lexington*, Newton would serve in deputy-commander roles through the early part of 1944.

In 1941, the word "radar" was a term of mystery, and the small percentage of the public or military who had heard the word considered it as futuristic, the state of the art in protection from air attack. At the time, barrage balloons were used, as well as sound locators that had a maximum range of five miles. Smoke protection was also used to obscure targets. Hawaii had none of these. The War Department recognized that unless an enemy could be detected hundreds of miles out, there was no protection.

In response to an earlier request from Marshall, Short responded that air defense for Hawaii was totally inadequate. What was needed was an aircraft warning system that could detect an enemy far enough out to sea to give the island sufficient time to respond, not just the five-mile range of the sound detectors, but hundreds of miles out. Nor did the airfields themselves have any protection, no means of aircraft dispersion, nor any bunkers. While some of the ships had state-of-the-art shipborne radar, they were useless while the ships were in port because of the high surrounding hills.

Eventually, three fixed and six mobile radar sets were promised, and by late summer, the mobile sets had arrived. The first one was set up at Schofield Barracks for installation and operator training. By mid–November, five of the six mobile sets were in place around the island.

An information center was created at Fort Shafter to disseminate the collected information, which required the training of additional enlisted personnel, as well as the training of officers to determine what to do with the gathered information. In the middle of 1939, then Lieutenant Kenneth Bergquist was posted to Wheeler Field, and by the middle of 1940, he was promoted to operations and intelligence officer of the Eighteenth Pursuit Wing, later transferring over to the Fourteenth Pursuit Wing. It was Lieutenant Bergquist who organized the entire intelligence operation at Fort Shafter.

General Short had instructed that the mobile sets should all operate between 0400 and 0700, the most critical or dangerous hours. At the field radar sites, enlisted operators were learning their trade, while at the information center, more enlisted operators were learning how to receive and plot these radar intercepts. Each morning, an unlucky pilot had the additional duty to report at 0400 and learn as much about the operation as he could and to determine what to do with the information collected. And this was just ten days prior to December 7.

While sabotage warnings to Hawaii from Secretary Stimson and Generals Gerow and Miles seemed to be the order of the day, Hap Arnold, chief of the army air force, forwarded yet another message to General Short: "Critical situation demands that all precautions be taken immediately against subversive activities.... Also desired that you initiate forthwith all additional measures necessary to provide for protection of your establishments, property, and equipment against sabotage, protection of your personnel against subversive propaganda, and protection of all activities against espionage."[12]

With so much emphasis being placed on sabotage, General Arnold would later testify, "We had been having a lot of trouble with our airplanes all over the United States.... We had had many accidents that we could not explain.... In certain cases the finger pointed right directly at sabotage; in certain other cases, looking back on it now, I know it was inexperienced workmen.... But at that time we were so convinced that it was sabotage that we had sent sabotage messages all over the United States."[13]

For Admiral Kimmel, about the only defense without alarming the civil population was defense against submarine attack. During the preceding year, there had been many incidents of unidentified underwater propeller sounds in the vicinity of Hawaii, but Admiral Stark had given strict orders not to attack such contacts. But after receipt of the November 27 war warning, Kimmel had apparently changed his mind and issued an "order that any submarine contacts in the operating areas around the island of Oahu should be depth bombed."[14] After passing a copy of his order to Washington, he received no negative response, and consequently, it was on file in Washington. This order would constitute the justification of the *Ward*'s attack and sinking of the Japanese sub in one week.

By the end of November, all Japanese radio could talk about was the Ten Point Note with extreme severity. The United States had broken the peace and established an ultimatum, and would be solely responsible for whatever happened next. These sharp radio commentaries brought a plea from Kurusu in Washington. In a call to Tokyo on November 30, he stressed, "Unless greater caution is exercised in speeches by the Premier and others, it puts us in a very difficult position. All of you over there must watch out about these ill-advised statements. Please tell Mr. Tani."[15]

Kurusu was confused on what appeared to be the main issue. First, Tokyo was in a hurry to settle negotiations, but now it appeared that they wanted them stretched out. Trying to clarify the direction he was to take, Kurusu said, "We will need your help. Both the Premier and the Foreign Minister will need to change the tone of their speeches!!! Do you understand? Please use all discretion."[16] This was sent on the last Sunday of peace.

Formal approval of hostilities against the Americans, British, and Dutch was approved by the Japanese cabinet on Monday, December 1, and the orders were issued accordingly from Chief of the Naval General Staff, Admiral Osami Nagano, to Admiral Yamamoto and to Vice Admiral Mineichi Koga, who was the commander in chief of China Area Fleet:

1. It has been decided to enter into a state of war between the Imperial Government on one side and the United States, Great Britain, and the Netherlands on the other during the first part of December.
2. The C-in-C Combined Fleet will destroy the enemy forces and air strength in the eastern seas [and] at the same time will meet any attack by the enemy fleet and destroy it.
3. The C-in-C Combined Fleet will, in co-operation with the Commander of the Southern Army, speedily capture and hold important American and British bases in eastern Asia and then Dutch bases. Important strategic points will then be occupied and held.[17]

An additional order was sent specifically for Yamamoto: "Japan under the necessity of self-preservation has reached a decision to declare war on the United States of America, British Empire, and the Netherlands. The C-in-C Combined Fleet shall at the start of the war direct an attack on the enemy fleet in the Hawaiian area and reduce it to impotency using the First Air Fleet as the nucleus of the attack force."[18]

At the end of November, there was also a sudden, complete change of direction by British Foreign Secretary Lord Halifax and Australian Minister to the United States Richard Casey. On November 29, they appeared at the State Department, bent on extending negotiations to allow more time for military preparations. But by this time it was too late. They had finally come to the realization that time was of the essence. Upon departing, Lord Halifax left this message in Hull's office:

> There are important indications that Japan is about to attack Thailand and that this attack will include a sea-borne expedition to seize strategic points in the Kra Isthmus…. R.A.F. are reconnoitering on an arc of 180 miles from Tedta Bharu for three days commencing November 29 and our Commander-in-Chief, Far East has requested Commander-in-Chief, Asiatic Fleet at Manila to undertake air reconnaissance on line Manila-Camranh Bay on the same days. Commander-in-Chief, Far East has asked for permission to move into Kra Isthmus, if air reconnaissance establishes the fact that escorted Japanese ships are approaching the coast of Thailand, and he asks for an immediate decision on this point.[19]

The bottom line to all of this was that the British now considered it necessary to invade the Kra Isthmus themselves in order to beat Japan to the draw, as the Japanese would consider it important to get all the troops ashore before the shooting started in the move into Malaya. Lord Halifax wondered what the reaction in Washington would be. Hull's only answer was that he would show it to the president.

Almost as if timed to the moment, the Japanese consulate in Bangkok reported to Tokyo that the majority of the Siamese wanted to remain neutral. Therefore, whoever occupied Siam would be considered the aggressor. The message even suggested that Japan should land troops in the area of Kota Bharu, just across the Malay border, which would almost force British occupation of Thailand to keep from being boxed in.

That same day, November 29, Tokyo also received a communiqué from Berlin. It contained a low-key hint that while Russian forces were engaged on the western front, this would be the pristine time for Japan to start the occupation of Siberia through Russia's back door. It would provide the expansion from Manchuria that Japan had always hungered for. But of course, the underlying motive was that such a move would take some of the pressure off Germany's eastern front, where the advance into Russia had slowed to a halt.

On Monday, December 1, the America First Committee advertised that it would enter the primary and general election the following year pledging support of an isolationist candidate. It argued that Americans had been too content to do nothing while the real threat of going to war "lay in the irresponsible and dictatorial leadership of the 'one man,' Franklin D. Roosevelt."[20] In addition to Charles Lindbergh, their ranks had swelled with powerful names like Alfred Landon, the 1936 Republican presidential candidate; Senator Robert Taft; and Republican Minority Leader Joseph Martin, Jr. It was also announced that the nationwide rail strike set for Sunday, December 7, had been settled.

Ambassadors Nomuru and Kurusu arrived at the State Department on Monday and were set upon by an army of correspondents asking if they were armed with Tokyo's answer to the Ten Point Plan of November 26. They replied that it would be another two or three days.

The big question that still looms after seventy years is what the president and top military leaders actually knew by reading Magic. With the Allies all counting on the United States to save them in the military emergency when it could happen at any moment, why was there no attempt to organize the Australians, British, Dutch, Chinese, and Americans? It cannot be accepted that it would have been considered as warlike to the American voter opposition. The Allies knew that their fate hung in the balance of negotiations being conducted in Washington. Was the American government looking after their best interests? With their resources of oil, rubber, and tin, as valuable to the Americans as to the Japanese, why there was no attempt to keep them from falling into Japanese hands so quickly defies any form of rationale. If the president was negotiating for the Allies, he was not keeping them informed, and not even FDR's staff knew what possible deals were being negotiated in the almost daily conversations with Churchill on the scrambler phone. Maybe the isolationists were right: he was dealing the country into certain oblivion.

To create a solution by adding the knowns with the unknowns and achieving the correct answer was in reality going to be total guesswork. The two knowns were the attack force headed for Pearl Harbor and the one headed south that had departed northern Indochina on November 26, which the Japanese had made no attempt to hide so all attention would be on it. But what was its destination: Malaya, the Kra Isthmus, or the Dutch East Indies? If the strike force aimed at Pearl Harbor attacked first, the United States was legitimately in the war, but what if the southerly force hit first and not directly at America? How would FDR rationalize any retaliation to the voters? Obviously, it would be strategically desirable to hit an invasion force at sea before it landed, using the thirty-five B-17s at Clark Field, Luzon.[21]

Under the provision of the current war plan, Rainbow Five, in which the United States was allied with Britain and France, Europe would represent the primary target, and until mastery was achieved, any Pacific action would be mainly defensive. If Japan, a member of the Tripartite Pact, shot first at the United States, that would trigger the action FDR had hoped for, justifying an offensive war in Europe. There were two lines on the map that could activate this action. If a Japanese invasion force sailed south of ten degrees north latitude or west of one hundred degrees east longitude, their motive would obviously be aggressive. With the advantage of hitting them while at sea, the burden of this response would fall on the president, who had failed to organize the Allies. If he responded with the B-17s, he would be branded a warmonger by U.S. voters. If he did nothing, he would encourage the resentment of the Allies, the ABCD powers, and Australia for breaking a moral commitment. The obvious answer was to make sure that Japan shot first directly at the United States. Because his information from Churchill indicated that the attack at Pearl Harbor would not commence until December 8, a move against the southerly force couldn't wait.

On December 3, FDR sent a secret message to Admiral Hart in Manila to immediately prepare and dispatch three seagoing yachts. The yachts would have three requirements: they must fly the American flag; they must be commanded by American naval officers (the crews could be Filipinos who would volunteer for the money); and the yachts must have mounted on them what could easily be recognized at a distance as a deck gun. It was also required that at least one flexible machine gun be mounted. The yachts were to sail out into the South China Sea with the mission to sacrifice themselves by encouraging Japan to shoot first. It was even hoped that the loss of the crewmen would rally the Philippines behind the war effort. If the yachts were attacked in short order, orchestrating an international incident or act of war, it would hopefully leave time to meet Admiral Nagumo's force head-on.

By December 7, only Admiral Hart's personal yacht, the USS *Isabel* (PY-10), had been dispatched in time. FDR had personally ordered their destinations in harm's way. To her captain, John Walker, it was puzzling as to why he should be ordered to sail the coast of Indochina, virtually daring to be shot at. His understanding was that he was going to be monitoring and reporting Japanese shipping. He was sighted several times by Japanese aircraft, but none took the bait, so the *Isabel* was recalled from her failed mission.

The second yacht, the *Lanikai*, was one day out at sea when she was recalled, and the third, the *Molly Moore*, was still in port. The *Lanikai*'s captain, Kemp Tolley, recalled that with a questionable receiver and no operative transmitter, he would have had to sail all the way back to Manila to report a sighting.

In Washington, the military intelligence estimates focused on the Kra Isthmus as the Japanese destination. The question was asked if the overseas commanders had been adequately warned. Admiral Stark and his war plans director, Admiral Turner, advised to the affirmative.

In Tokyo, all that remained was submitting the plan of the Pearl Harbor attack to Emperor Hirohito himself. In doing so, Admirals Nagano and Yamamoto emphasized with Hirohito that it was essential to neutralize Pearl Harbor, explaining many of the details. The date that hostilities would commence would be December 8, to which the emperor seemed comfortable. Thus the order was issued:

> From: The Chief of the Naval General Staff
> To: C-in-C Combined Fleet
>   The hostile action against the United States of America, the British Empire, and the Netherlands shall be commenced on 8 December. Bear in mind that, should it appear certain that Japanese-American negotiations will reach an amicable settlement prior to the commencement of hostile action, all forces of the Combined Fleet are to be ordered to reassemble and return to their bases.[22]

This order leaves no question that virtually up to the last minute the recall order could go out in the event of a breakthrough in talks in Washington. But in relatively short order, it seemed so obvious that any favorable outcome in negotiations seemed so remote that on the night of December 2, Admiral Nagumo received his final order, "Climb Mount Niitaka, 1208 Repeat 1208," which confirmed that diplomacy had failed, and the attack was set for December 8 (Tokyo time).

By this time, the Japanese fleet was located nine hundred forty miles north of Midway Island. Mount Niitaka was the highest mountain, not only in Japanese-held Formosa, but in all of the Japanese Empire. To climb its thirteen thousand feet was considered the most formidable challenge. Back in Japan, it would be recognized that to win at Pearl Harbor would be considered an act of genius. To lose the attack would be labeled ludicrous.

On Tuesday, December 2, General Brereton's B-17s were patrolling north toward Formosa, but not actually over it. The crews were reluctantly following the orders of General MacArthur, who only allowed reconnaissance as far as the international boundary so as not to create an overt act in defiance of his actual orders. Hart's PBYs operating out of the Philippines were patrolling the South China Sea, where they identified nine Japanese submarines heading south, and in Camranh Bay, twenty-one Japanese transports were spotted at anchor.

This was also the day that those in Singapore gave a sigh of relief with the arrival of the HMS *Prince of Wales*, Britain's capital battleship of thirty-five thousand tons, along with the cruiser HMS *Repulse*. The promise of a battle fleet had become a reality.

There was more intrigue in Washington. The Japanese ambassadors were given a message from the president to pass on to Tokyo: "The stationing of these increased Japanese forces in Indo-China would seem to imply the utilization of these forces by Japan for purposes of further aggression.... Please be good enough to request the Japanese ambassador and Ambassador Kurusu to inquire at once of the Japanese Government what the actual reasons may be for the steps already taken and what I am to consider is the policy of the Japanese Government."[23]

Undersecretary Sumner Welles, filling in for Cordell Hull, who was down with a cold, reminded the Japanese ambassadors that the American government still had not received any answer from the Ten Point Note of November 26. For a couple of days, FDR had been considering sending a message directly to the emperor. In casually mentioning it, he had received no support. As a matter of fact, everyone on his war council was against it.

To keep the Americans guessing and to throw off American intelligence, the Japanese had changed all of their call signs on November 1, and on December 1, they did it again. But on the contrary, this helped alert U.S. combat intelligence that something was up. Kimmel asked his fleet intelligence officer, then Captain Edwin Layton, for a chart on the approximate location of the principal Japanese ships, and on December 2, Layton reported back that he was drawing an absolute blank on the location of the carriers. They could be in home waters, but he didn't know. Kimmel fired back, "You mean they could be coming around Diamond Head, and you wouldn't know it?"[24] Almost apologetically, Layton replied, "Yes, sir, but I hope they'd have been sighted before now."[25]

Early on December 3, Nagumo's task force refueled at sea. Once this operation was completed, having no further need of the tankers, the Kido Butai could pick up the pace for the balance of the mission.

Over the next three days, conversations took place between Kimmel and Short that would refute the Roberts Commission claim that the two never conferred in coordinating commands. On Monday, December 1, both officers received word from Washington to start making arrangements for the replacement of the Marines in the farther western islands with army personnel. With those Marines presently under navy command, once they were replaced, the issue arose as to who would control the islands under army occupation. Kimmel wanted his Marines back, but not at the expense of surrendering control of his harbors to the army. Nor was Short interested in placing army troops under navy command. "The Army should exercise no command over Navy bases,"[26] Kimmel retorted. Hawaii was an excellent case in point. Both individually communicated with Washington and shared their messages with each other. This was an excellent example of the army relying on the navy to warn of an attack. Their meetings continued for three days, but there was so little time remaining that it would become a dead issue.

FDR's previous demand for an answer to Japanese troop movements prompted this message from Nomura to Foreign Minister Togo in Tokyo: "I presume of course, that this reply was a result of consultations and profound consideration. The United States Government is attaching a great deal of importance on this reply.... If it is really the intention of our government to arrive at a settlement, the explanation you give, I am afraid, would neither satisfy them nor prevent them from taking a bold step.... I would like to get a reply which gives a clearer impression of our peaceful intentions. Will you, therefore, reconsider ... and wire me at once."[27]

Whereas on Monday, Magic had revealed the two messages about destroying the code machine, Tuesday, December 2, brought a third order from Tokyo to Nomura and Kurusu:

1. Among the telegraphic codes with which your office is equipped burn all but those now used with the machine and one copy each of "O" code and abbreviating code (L). (Burn also the various other codes which you have in your custody.)
2. Stop at once using one code machine unit and destroy it completely.
3. When you have finished this, wire me back the one word "HARUNA…."[28]

The problem in the intelligence business is that if the enemy senses that his intelligence is being read, its value comes to an end. It had taken almost two years to break the Purple code and to develop the Magic machine to quickly decode and translate the communications. And the greater the distribution of that intelligence, the higher the risk of security compromise became. These critical days were not the time to risk losing a primary source of intelligence. Therefore, the Americans had to be careful not to react to information that would reveal that intelligence personnel were reading the messages as fast as the Japanese ambassadors were. But now distribution suddenly seemed worth the risk.

On Wednesday, December 3, Admiral Stark sent a duplicated message to both Hart and Kimmel: "Highly reliable information has been received that categoric and urgent instructions were sent yesterday to Japanese diplomatic and consular posts at Hong Kong, Singapore, Batavia, Manila, Washington, and London to destroy most of their codes and ciphers at once and to burn all other important confidential and secret documents."[29]

It is difficult to lay any blame on the Pearl Harbor commanders for what was to come when messages that they had never even seen were only decoded after lying in Washington for two weeks, messages that rang no bells or even lifted any eyebrows. There were a sufficient number of these accumulating in piles on the desks of both the army and the navy. And concerning the bomb plot messages, there were no such requests from Tokyo for ship information for any other location. Some of the messages were not even translated or distributed until after December 7, at which time they took on a frightening aspect. Additionally, when it was later revealed that these had been withheld from the Hawaiian commanders, more than one commander confirmed that the plotting information being requested by Tokyo was a clear sign that an attack plan was in the works.

On Luzon, Hart's returning PBY patrols toward Camranh Bay reported that the Japanese transport that had been under U.S. observation for three days had virtually disappeared. But Iba radar on Luzon's west coast, sixty miles due west of Clark Field, had been experiencing nightly visitors snooping in the direction of Clark. Being inaccessible to searchlights and fighter planes, they had to be Japanese. The order to let Japan fire the first shot would not apply here. If they returned, U.S. antiaircraft would respond.

At Clark Field rested the thirty-five B-17s of the Nineteenth Bombardment Group, so all the American offensive eggs were in one basket there.[30] And with no spare parts, the flyable total had already been reduced to thirty-three. And about ninety fighters on Luzon, used to protect the bombers, were experiencing the same problems, not to mention the other issues with the Swedish P-35s. The fighters were all scattered across the six airfields on the southern half of the island, not the ideal arrangement for proper dispersal. Anything resembling desired defense was a major problem. Antiaircraft protection for the airfields was inadequate or missing altogether, as were the communications.

Telephone lines through the jungle were insecure and ground-to-ground radio was no better through the mountains. The enemy that faced them was all speculation, and since the Philippine forces were not allowed to reconnoiter Formosa, the odds against them were all guesswork. By December 8, only two of the seven radar sets in the Philippines would be operational.

With a total lack of training in the utilization of airpower, both MacArthur and Richard Sutherland, MacArthur's chief of staff, were at odds with Brereton, who was subordinate to MacArthur. Major Sutherland had arrived in the Philippines in March of 1938 and was initially posted to the office of the military advisor. It wasn't long, only a few months later, when he, too, was promoted to lieutenant colonel, easing out Lieutenant Colonel Dwight Eisenhower, and taking over the role as MacArthur's chief of staff. Completely loyal to MacArthur, Sutherland served as an effective bootlicker, which antagonized American and Australian officers alike. Working his way up the ranks, Sutherland would eventually be promoted to major general by the end of 1941.

MacArthur maintained the typical infantry attitude that the B-17 was an extension of coastal artillery and not an offensive weapon. But it was obvious that the B-17s at Clark, which was overexposed and overcrowded, were a targeted disaster waiting to happen. The only alternative was to send the planes six hundred miles south to Del Monte Airfield on Mindanao. But with construction there still underway, there were as yet no refueling facilities. Thus any offensive action would require the B-17s to return to Clark to refuel, which brought them back to square one.

Although the Japanese were still unaware of the existence of Del Monte, to put Clark out of business would ground the B-17s no matter where they were. Sutherland recommended against the move, but with no alternative plan, he reluctantly approved the transfer provided, that they return as soon as conditions would allow. Thursday night, they waited for the irregular night intruder to return. It did not. The following evening, sixteen B-17s, eight from the Fourteenth Squadron and eight from the Ninety-Third Squadron, were prepared for a 2200 departure for the three and one-half hour trip to Del Monte.[31] Ground personnel would go by ship.

Brereton had also been informed that two squadrons from the Seventh Bomb Group were to leave the States the first week of December for the Philippines, and these, too, would have to be based at Del Monte. But because they arrived at Hawaii in the midst of the Pearl Harbor attack, they would never make it to the Philippines.

Across the road from Clark was the army's Camp Stotsenburg, General Jonathan Wainwright's headquarters, where he was busy selecting a staff that would attempt to train inexperienced Filipino recruits into an army that would be capable of defeating an enemy landing force on the beaches, the task which MacArthur had years before reported to Washington was well under way.

Friday, December 5, Admiral Sir Tom Phillips arrived in Manila by plane. Having the complete confidence of Winston Churchill, Phillips had previously served as naval advisor to King George VI, and in 1940, Churchill appointed Phillips to acting vice-admiral. In late 1941, Phillips was then appointed commander in chief of the China Station, departing Britain aboard his flagship, the *Prince of Wales*, and accompanied by the *Repulse* and four destroyers. What Phillips did not have with him was any air cover, which would, in the not-too-distant future, seal his fate.

He was desperate to confer with Admiral Hart because the aircraft carrier he had been promised had not materialized. The carrier HMS *Ark Royal* had been sunk in the Mediterranean, and its replacement, the HMS *Indomitable*, had run aground in the West Indies; in addition, two of Phillips's four battleships were overdue. Hart was sympathetic but had nothing to offer other than the careful loan of four destroyers currently in the Dutch East Indies. They could be in Singapore in forty-eight hours and would increase the number of Phillips's destroyers to eight. Hart made the loan carefully because he had no authority to turn American warships over to the command of a nation at war with Germany and Italy. On the other hand, FDR had been doing this for some time in the Atlantic in the name of Lend-Lease.

During the two-day discussion, Hart invited MacArthur and his chief of staff Sutherland to join in. Phillips had been concerned that there were too few airfields in the Philippines and commented that the defense of Luzon depended on the ability of fighters to operate from any location. In response, MacArthur made the statement, one he would have to live with, that "the inability of an enemy to launch his air attack on these islands is our greatest security,"[32] and that it left him "with a sense of complete security,"[33] similar to his response to Washington when he received the November 27 war warning.

The American sighting of some Japanese ships that could be headed for Malaya hastened Phillips's departure on Saturday. In just a couple of days, Hart had done more for the ABCD powers than anyone in Washington had thought to do.

As commander in chief of the British Far East, Sir Robert Brooke-Popham was responsible for the defense of Singapore, Hong Kong, Burma, and Malaya. He had served with the Royal Air Force since its inception in 1918 in numerous roles, including commander in chief of the RAF Middle East. Retiring from the RAF in 1937, he was posted to the governorship of Kenya, but by 1939, he was recalled to the RAF, and in November 1940, he took over the British Far East command.

Brooke-Popham faced the same challenges that Kimmel and Short dealt with on Hawaii. With Britain's focus on the European theater, he lacked sufficient forces and aircraft to defend the colonies, and had little success in getting the needed reinforcements. From a command standpoint, both the naval units and the civil servants all reported to London. Considering the disparity between the responsibility he was given and the actual authority he had, as well as the limited resources, he had been placed in an untenable situation. And in spite of other career successes, he would always be associated with the fall of Singapore in February 1942.

That night, Admiral Hart received the shock of his life when he received a message from Captain John M. Creighton, the official navy observer in Singapore. Creighton told Hart that Air Marshal Brooke-Popham had just received word from the British War Office in London that under certain eventualities, Britain could expect help from the United States to defend British interests in the Far East. Specifically, the message read: "We have now received assurance of American armed support in cases as follows: (A) We are obliged to execute our plans to forestall Japs landing on Isthmus of Kra or counteract invasion elsewhere in Siam. (B) Defend against attack of Dutch Indies. (C) If Japs attack U.S. put plan into action without reference to London if you have good info. If Dutch are attacked put into action plans agreed on by Dutch and British."[34] That Hart, in the absence of a formal plan, would be expected to start the shooting war was news to him.

This message has long been considered proof that FDR and Churchill had agreed on conditions to get the United States into the war without being directly fired upon. Neither the British documents nor the president's personal papers, however, are available to public scrutiny. Hart immediately sent off a request for confirmation to Washington that, on his deathbed, he still had not received. It is difficult to consider the transmission of a message from London to Singapore, with such repercussions, that could not be confirmed by the initiating authority.

The Japanese ships at anchor in Camranh Bay four days prior suddenly reappeared on Saturday and were spotted by one of Hart's PBYs, which prompted Phillips to return to Singapore. Still in Camranh Bay, the count was thirty transports and one cruiser. Hart forwarded the information to Washington and Pearl Harbor which, again, would leave the impression in Hawaii that the only known action would be in the western Pacific.

Still later the same day, a British patrol aircraft identified another Japanese convoy of about thirty-five transports escorted by cruisers and destroyers. The only question was the destination.

Late Wednesday night, December 3, Ralph Briggs, a Japanese language expert and senior radio operator, reported for duty at Station M, the navy's east coast Japanese radio monitoring station at Cheltenham, Maryland. Briggs, who had worked with naval intelligence for four years, reported to Chief Petty Officer Daryl Wigle. Upon reporting for duty, he was briefed to listen closely to the Japanese weather reports. It was early Thursday morning when suddenly was broadcast "higashi no kazeame," known as the *winds execute*. The message would be timed to the eve of war. On receipt, the embassies were to destroy codes and secret documents and expect a termination of international communications.

The message was repeated a second time, then a third. Briggs logged it in, along with the date, time, and frequency. Then he teletyped the winds execute to the Washington office of Captain Laurence Safford, head of OP-20-G, the cryptanalysis section of Office of Naval Communications.

Safford was a firm believer in collaborating with the army whenever possible. So when he received the winds execute from Briggs, he passed it on to his opposite in the army, Colonel Otis Sadtler, head of U.S. Army Signal Intelligence, who was responsible for the distribution of Magic decrypts for the Army. Safford also passed the message on to the director of naval communications, Admiral Leigh Noyes, where it was again passed up to Admiral Theodore Wilkinson, the chief of naval intelligence, who passed it to the White House, where, for all practical purposes, it disappeared off the face of the earth.

Briggs had had the weekend of December 7 off, and when, along with the rest of America, he heard of the attack, he assumed, based on the winds execute he had passed on, that the Japanese had taken a beating. Upon returning to work, he was told that it was the other way around. He immediately checked the file for the duplicate copy. It was missing. Upon inquiring with his supervisor, Chief Petty Officer Wigle, Wigle told him that he did not know what was going on, just that nobody was talking. Captain Safford had also made copies, seven of them, and they, too, eventually vanished. That same day, two more messages arrived in Washington from Batavia and Bandoeng that the Dutch had intercepted the winds execute. Again, they disappeared. Safford would later testify at the joint congressional investigation that he had last seen the winds execute when he was gathering documentation for the Roberts Commission in December of 1941.

The Dutch, too, had been working to break Japanese codes. When U.S. Brigadier General Elliot Thorpe, serving as a military attaché on Java, was informed by a Dutch general in early December that Hawaii, the Philippines, and Thailand would soon be attacked by the Japanese, he cabled Washington right away. The "east wind rain" message had been intercepted by the

Dutch on Japanese radio. Thorpe just assumed he wasn't getting a confirmation of receipt because of atmospheric conditions. But after sending four messages, with the final message going to General Miles of G-2, he received an order from the War Department: "Send no more on this subject."[35]

The last reference to the winds execute was when it was passed on to the Roberts Commission, after which time its existence would be denied forever, at least by many of those who had seen it. And during the congressional hearings on Pearl Harbor in 1945–46, Briggs was not asked to sign anything. Nor was he asked to testify. He had been ordered by his commanding officer, Captain John Harper, not to appear in the interest of saving his navy career.

With the Japanese order to destroy codes, ciphers, and papers, it was now imperative that the Americans do the same. Instructions were sent to the army and navy military attaches in Tokyo, including the alert that "early rupture of diplomatic relations with Japan has been indicated."[36] Attaches in the threatened areas of Shanghai, Peiping, and Bangkok would all receive the additional instruction to send the word "jabberwock" when completed.

The naval message sent to Guam was more imperative: "Be prepared to destroy instantly all classified matter you retain in event of emergency."[37] Admirals Kimmel and Bloch received the same message, but being in the backwaters of the Pacific, they assumed that it was for informational purposes only. It should be recalled that the Hawaiian commanders had no knowledge of events in their own backyard. The so-called bomb plot messages requesting U.S. ship berthing positions and sailing activity had not even made an impression in Washington, nor were they passed on to Hawaii.

On Friday morning, the Japanese ambassadors presented themselves at the State Department with Togo's answer to FDR's question about the southerly movement of Japanese troops:

> As Chinese troops have recently shown signs of movements along the northern frontier of French Indo-China bordering on China, Japanese troops, with the object of mainly taking precautionary measures, have been reinforced to a certain extent in the northern part of French Indo-China. As a natural sequence of this step, certain movements have been made among the troops stationed in the southern part of the said territory. It seems that an exaggerated report has been made of these movements. It should be added that no measure has been taken on the part of the Japanese Government that may transgress the stipulations of the Protocol of Joint Defense between Japan and France.[38]

Thanks to Magic, U.S. intelligence had already read it. Secretary Hull's reaction was that it was news to him that the Japanese were on the defensive in Indochina. Hadn't it been the other way around? If they themselves were in danger of attack, the easiest move would be to get out of Indochina altogether. The ambassadors had little to say in defense. Meanwhile, at the Japanese foreign office, the deception continued that Japan's viewpoint was being misinterpreted by the Americans, and that despite the cessation of negotiations, Japan hoped they could continue negotiations with the impression of sincerity.

The change in Japanese call signs for the second time in a month, the inability to track much of their fleet, and the order to their embassies to destroy codes and secret papers finally prompted a meeting of Admiral Turner and Admiral Ingersoll. They considered what more they needed to do. Perhaps send more warnings. Turner, who put his personality conflict with Kimmel ahead of common sense, was adamant. No more warnings. Kimmel had received sufficient alert.

They also consulted with Admiral Stark, who was swayed that sufficient warning had been sent. They would later admit that all were under the assumption that Kimmel had more information and intelligence than he actually had received.

There had been friction in the Navy Department since early 1941, when Admiral Turner convinced Admiral Stark that all intelligence from Office of Naval Intelligence should not be deciphered or forecast by it, but should instead be forwarded to War Plans. There, Turner would interpret it using his own analysis, but he made some incorrect estimates of the direction that the Japanese would move. All along, he was not entirely convinced that Japan would attack the United States, but would only use scare tactics. Up until November 26, Turner's War Plans directives indicated that Japan would most likely attack Siberia.

An earlier explanation of the Vacant Sea Order, or an order to activate the Joint Coastal Frontier Defense Plan from those in Washington, would have meant more to the Pearl Harbor commanders than all of the precautionary advice they actually received.

On Friday, December 5, Magic decoded two more messages sent earlier by Tokyo to Honolulu. One was three weeks old and gathering dust before it was finally decoded. It was specific on requesting reports on "Area N., Pearl Harbor" ship anchorages. By comparison, the second one was fresh, dated just November 29: "We have been receiving reports from you on ship movements, but in the future will you also report even when there are no movements?"[39] Top U.S. military intelligence in Washington apparently weren't even curious enough to wonder why Japan would want specific information on ships that did not move. They were busy accumulating the request by the president to make an estimate of Japanese strength in Indochina, which seemed more pressing. The high estimate was one hundred twenty-five thousand troops and four hundred fifty aircraft, as well as forty thousand troops and four hundred planes on Formosa. The strength for Hainan Island, located off the southern coast of China, was estimated at fifty thousand troops and two hundred planes.[40]

And that same night, the order went out to U.S. embassies and consulates in Tokyo, Hong Kong, Chungking, Bangkok, Saigon, and Hanoi to destroy secret papers and to deal with the emergency when it arose.

Meanwhile, as reported by one of the Lexington's TBD pilots, the two American task forces were actually within reconnaissance distance of each other with the twelve PBYs at Midway watching for their approach. The other twelve PBYs from Wake were returning to Pearl Harbor to increase Admiral Bellinger's patrol aircraft number to sixty-nine, which would be shared between Ford Island and the Kaneohe Naval Air Base just north of Bellows. A dozen were down for maintenance with no spare parts, but he would also have the other twelve PBYs due in from Midway. For Kimmel, his dilemma was how best to utilize the PBYs. With his fighters gone, they were all he had. During the week, they would patrol out as far as four hundred miles and be down for maintenance on the weekends. He preferred not to squander their long-range capability on defense. Admiral Kimmel would later be charged with failure to conduct sufficient air reconnaissance, but the limitations of his resources must be considered.

A PBY could cruise at 100 knots. Search aircraft flew no further than twenty miles apart. At sunset, Saturday night, December 6, the Kido Butai was about five hundred fifty miles out. Considering the fourteen-hour range of the PBY, seven out and seven back, eleven of those hours would have been spent out of the search area. At twenty miles apart in the search area at maximum distance, it would have required forty-five aircraft to cover just one hundred eighty degrees or half a circle from Oahu. The numbers speak for themselves. How long would it be before all the PBYs were down for one-hundred-hour inspections or complete overhaul, with no spare parts, to say nothing of the wear and tear on the crews?

Considering downtime for the aircraft, as well as those that were being used only to supply spare parts, Kimmel had fewer than seventy PBYs to work with. To provide the necessary, continuous reconnaissance, he would have needed two hundred fifty aircraft to do the job. All along, he had been requesting Washington to send more, and Washington had promised he would get them. But instead, two hundred fifty PBYs were sent to Britain at the direction of Harry Hopkins, a man who had absolutely no naval or military experience whatsoever. But he had Roosevelt's approval.

General Martin had the six B-17s being used for crew training, and the obsolete B-18 bombers at Hickam; the old P-26s and P36s at Wheeler; and a number of noncombat aircraft of the Eighty-Sixth Observation Squadron based at Bellows. So his main fighting strength was in his ninety-nine P-40s at Wheeler Field bordering Schofield Barracks in the middle of the island, of which sixty-six would be in commission the morning of December 7.[41] In response to the sabotage warnings from Washington, the island was at Alert No. 1. The aircraft were parked wingtip to wingtip, and with the fuel tanks mostly empty, the estimate was four hours to get them all gassed, armed, and into the air. The only dispersion of P-40s consisted of a few at Bellows used for target practice and a few at Haleiwa on the north shore used for takeoff and landing training.

The Consolidated PBY patrol bomber that was in such short supply.

Boeing P-26s (left) and Douglas B-18s at Hickam Field, 1940.

The first of the two B-24s to be used in the photoreconnaissance mission to the Marshall Islands arrived at Hickam on Friday. It, too, would be caught on the ground on Sunday.

Along with consulates around the world, the Japanese in Honolulu were following suit and burning or destroying anything that could be of value to the Americans. Admiral Bloch's Fourteenth Naval District received word of this activity on Friday. If there was anything ominous involved, Washington would surely have advised. Both he and Kimmel agreed that Washington should be notified, or perhaps they had the answer. Bloch sent this off on Saturday: "Believe local consul has destroyed all but one system although presumably not included in your eighteen double five of third [although the Honolulu consulate was presumably not included in the Japanese orders, which had been conveyed to Kimmel in the message referred to]."[42]

For some time Roosevelt had been considering a direct appeal to the emperor, and the time had come. Against the advice of the State Department (Hull and Stimson), but with their reluctant help, a borderline plea was composed by the president on Saturday. With time running out, it would be very similar to the request that Prince Konoye had sent to him in August that FDR had rejected, while there had still been time to save the situation. This one would be void of the demands that he had made of Konoye. By about 8:00 p.m., the pilot message went off to Ambassador Grew in Tokyo to expect the communiqué that he would have to deliver: "An important telegram is now being encoded to you containing … text of message from the President to the emperor."[43] Within the hour, the message itself was on the way:

> Almost a century ago the President of the United States addressed to the Emperor of Japan a message extending an offer of friendship…. That offer was accepted, and in the long period of unbroken peace and friendship which has followed, our respective nations, through the virtues of their peoples and the wisdom of their rulers, have prospered and have substantially helped humanity….
>
> Developments are occurring in the Pacific area which threaten to deprive each of our nations and all humanity of the beneficial influence of the long peace between our two countries….
>
> Both Japan and the United States should agree to eliminate any form of military threat….
>
> During the past few weeks it has become clear to the world that Japanese military, naval and air forces have been sent to Southern Indo-China in such large numbers as to create a reasonable doubt on the part of other nations that this continuing concentration in Indochina is not defensive in its character….
>
> I am sure that Your Majesty will understand that the fear of all these peoples [of the Southwest Pacific] is a legitimate fear…. I am sure that Your Majesty will understand why the people of the United States in such large numbers look askance at the establishment of … bases manned and equipped so greatly as to constitute armed forces capable of measures of offense.
>
> It is clear that a continuance of such a situation is unthinkable. None of the peoples whom I have spoken of above can sit either indefinitely or permanently on a keg of dynamite.
>
> There is absolutely no thought on the part of the United States of invading Indo-China if every Japanese soldier or sailor were to be withdrawn therefrom….
>
> I address myself to Your Majesty at this moment in the fervent hope that Your Majesty may, as I am doing, give thought in this definite emergency to ways of dispelling the dark clouds. I am confident that both of us, for the sake of the peoples not only of our own great countries but for the sake of humanity in neighboring territories, have a sacred duty to restore traditional amity and prevent further death and destruction in the world.[44]

Because Grew had to go through the protocol of contacting the prime minister for his appointment with the emperor, this was Prime Minister Tojo's perfect opportunity to drag things out. It would be important to make sure that the emperor did not see the president's message until it was too late. And he did not.

Chapter 9

Air Raid Pearl Harbor,
This Is No Drill

On Saturday night, Mrs. Roosevelt hosted a party at the White House. But by 9:00 p.m., the president had retired to his second-floor study, where he was conversing with Harry Hopkins, when one of the White House ushers entered, followed by a navy courier. The officer carried with him a locked briefcase, which he opened, and he handed the contents to the president. The dispatch consisted of a number of pages that had just come from Navy Decoding Headquarters down the street. After FDR had read them all, he handed them to Hopkins with the statement, "This means war."[1] After a ten-day wait, was this the answer to the November 26 Ten Point Note? After Hopkins completed his study of the papers, he handed them back to the courier, who relocked them in the pouch and left.

By procedure, on even days of the month, the Army Signal Intelligence Service translated intercepts and delivered them to Secretaries Hull and Stimson, General Marshall, and other authorized readers of Magic. The Navy Communications Intelligence Unit handled the same task on the odd days and delivered the messages to the president, Secretary Knox, CNO Stark, and their authorized officers. On Saturday, it was the army's turn.

Earlier that day, around noon, Magic started to decode what was apparently going to be the answer to the Ten Point Note in a message from Foreign Minister Togo to Ambassador Nomura. In essence, negotiations would be broken off by Japan, but the ambassadors in Washington were to continue as if nothing had changed:

1. The Government has deliberated deeply on the American proposal of the 26th of November and as a result we have drawn up a memorandum for the United States contained in my separate message #902.
2. This separate message is a long one. I will send it in fourteen parts and I imagine you will receive it tomorrow. However, I am not sure. The situation is extremely delicate, and when you receive it I want you please keep it secret for the time being.
3. Concerning the time for presenting this memorandum to the United States, I will wire you in a separate message. However, I want you in the meantime to put it in nicely drafted form and make every preparation to present it to the Americans just as soon as you receive instructions.[2]

The receipt of the fourteen-part message is considered proof by many that Washington allowed Pearl Harbor to happen. The pilot message itself alerted that a message was coming that was considered so secret that its contents were to remain confidential until the time for presentation. Extra diligence had to be taken to make sure that it was decoded and ready for delivery at a time to be announced in a separate message, and the time for presentation would be critical to the entire effort. It is known that this pilot message, while only raising eyebrows, was in the hands of the State Department by 3:00 p.m. on the afternoon of December 6, and it warned all authorized readers that something big was coming. The navy translators had replaced the army at 1:00 p.m. and were about to close down at 4:30 p.m. for the weekend when Part 8 appeared, signaling that all parts were not necessarily in a sequential order. Everyone stayed on.

Sometime after dinner, thirteen parts were in their possession, translated and about ready for distribution. The late-afternoon workload had been such that, upon request, the army personnel had returned to duty. As there was still no sign of the fourteenth part, Lieutenant Commander Alvin Kramer, the senior officer on duty, decided that there was no reason to hold back the existing parts while waiting for the last one, and shortly after 8:30 p.m., as per custom, he was on the phone calling the authorized recipients that highly classified intelligence was on its way. Of the utmost curiosity was the fact that the message had been sent in English. Unknown to its initial readers, this was done so as to avoid any delays or errors and would eliminate the possibility of Nomura's diminishing or mellowing its meaning. In brief, the thirteen parts consisted of the following points.

Part 1 referred to the fact that Japan's policy had been continuously aimed at stabilization and peace in East Asia, and that China had failed to appreciate Japan's true desire for peace, forcing Japan to join with Germany and Italy to prevent any extension of warlike disturbances.

Part 2 referred to the United States and Great Britain as having resisted all of Japan's efforts in its relationship with France for the joint defense of French Indochina, as having coerced the Netherlands East Indies to join with them to strain economic relations with Japan, and as placing a stranglehold on Japan, thereby endangering the Empire of Japan's existence.

Part 3 raised the issue that in August, Prime Minister Konoye had proposed a meeting with the president, but the Americans had insisted that an agreement should be met before the meeting, putting the cart before the horse, and as such, the United States displayed no interest in negotiations nor in conciliation.

Part 4 reiterated that the Japanese on November 20 had submitted a proposal to arrive at a solution in the Far East, suggesting restoration of commercial relations, restoring trade with the Netherlands East Indies, and dispatching no troops to any region (except in French Indochina) in all of the South Pacific or Southeast Asia. (Japan had promised to remove troops from Indochina in exchange for the United States' help to resolve China.)

Part 5 indicated that the United States made known its intention to continue support for Chiang Kai-shek, and finally, on November 26, had introduced ten harsh demands on Japan, stating that the time was not ripe for peace between Japan and the United States.

Part 6 stated that Japan wanted to include China in trade and even volunteered to remove troops from South Indochina as a signal to that end, but was rebuffed by the United States.

Part 7 asserted that the United States had refused to bend one inch in any discussions, and that world peace was based only on principles favorable to the United States.

Part 8 stated that while the United States discouraged Japan's obligation to the Tripartite Pact, they thought nothing of supporting Great Britain, China, Russia, the Netherlands, and Thailand against the Tripartite nations.

Part 9 stated that while the United States was attempting to secure peace in the Pacific, they continued "in aiding Great Britain and may be preparing to attack, in the name of self-defense, Germany and Italy, two Powers that are striving to establish a new order in Europe."[3]

Part 10 indicated that where the United States objected to settling international issues militarily, they had no objection to such settlements by economic pressure. "The Japanese Government cannot tolerate the perpetuation of such a situation since it directly runs counter to Japan's fundamental policy to enable all nations to enjoy each its proper place in the world."[4]

Part 11 stated that the six nations of Japan, United States, Great Britain, the Netherlands, China, and Thailand should restore trade relations, and at the same time recognize the agreement that Japan currently maintained with France concerning French Indochina.

Part 12 indicated that the United States only recognized the Chungking government without taking the Nanking government into consideration, which demonstrated a lack of willingness to negotiate, and demonstrated clearly the intention of the United States government to obstruct the restoration of normal relations between Japan and China, which would, in turn, restore peace to East Asia.

Part 13 reiterated that Japan had been interested in negotiations all along but the United States' proposal of November 26 indicated that the Americans were neither interested in negotiations nor in the stabilization of the yen to the dollar, in that "the proposal in question ignores Japan's sacrifices in the four years of the China Affair, menaces the Empire's existence itself and disparages its honour and prestige. Therefore, viewed in its entirety, the Japanese Government regrets that it cannot accept the proposal as a basis of negotiation."[5]

There it was. While some authorized to read Magic would claim that it was work for diplomats, parts 2, 9, 10, and 13 were threats indicating military action and were certainly not diplomatic in tone. What could the fourteenth part add that hadn't already been said?

Starting with Commander Kramer's Saturday night deliveries of the thirteen parts, history will record an almost unlimited variety of scenarios, all designed to cover or protect each member of the authorized readers of Magic from any degree of liability in connection with Pearl Harbor. The whereabouts of each officer was key to viewing and acting on the Japanese response to the Americans' November 26 Ten Point Note.

Kramer first called those on the navy list to advise that he would be delivering top secret intelligence for their viewing. He then requested his wife to act as chauffeur. The president was first on the list, but Roosevelt's naval aide, Captain John Beardall, had a dinner engagement at the home of Director of Naval Intelligence Admiral Wilkinson. So Lieutenant Lester Schulz, the temporary communications watch officer reporting to Captain Beardall, was briefed to be on the alert to receive a message for immediate delivery to the president. When Schulz delivered the message to Roosevelt, he heard him respond, "This means war." And yet, what Roosevelt had just read failed to inspire any attempt to contact his top military commanders.

Second on Kramer's list was Navy Secretary Frank Knox. Upon reading the complete dispatch, Knox picked up the phone and arranged a meeting with Hull and Stimson for 10:00 a.m. Sunday, and he ordered Kramer to appear with any updates. While he was phoning those on the list, the call to Admiral Stark revealed that he was at the National Theater attending a performance of *The Student Prince*. There was no attempt to contact him at the theater in the interest of not raising undue public alarm. However, Captain Harold Krick, Stark's flag secretary, would later indicate that upon returning home, Admiral Stark called the president and learned of the message. Another failed call was to War Plans Director Admiral Turner who, later it was revealed, was out walking his dogs.

Next on the list was Admiral Wilkinson. In addition to Captain Beardall, Kramer also found General Miles at Wilkinson's party. According to Kramer, all three read the contents of the pouch, to which there was no conformity of response. Lieutenant Commander Arthur McCollum, an assistant intelligence chief, was in his office Saturday afternoon and was sure Wilkinson, Stark, and Turner had seen it then. Wilkinson would testify at the Hewitt Inquiry in June 1945 that he had seen it, but to the congressional investigation of 1945–46, he reversed his claim and testified that he had not. When Kramer had delivered the message to Wilkinson's party, the general consensus from those in attendance was to wait for the fourteenth part to come in. Wilkinson then told Kramer to go home and to make the balance of the deliveries Sunday morning.

Kramer recalled that after reading the message, General Miles apparently made no effort to call General Marshall or Secretary Hull. A call to the White House by Beardall to make sure that the president had seen it further reduced the urgency of the situation. Kramer returned his documents to the Navy Department on Saturday night and went home.

Colonel Rufus Bratton, Kramer's equivalent delivering for the army, phoned his recipients, informed them of the pilot message, and advised that he would make deliveries as the parts came in. All knew that it would be the answer to the Ten Point Note. He made the delivery to Hull, but as a result of the phone call to Miles, Bratton was ordered to make the balance of the deliveries on Sunday morning. While some would later charge that he failed to deliver, he would not have had the authority to withhold vital security information strictly on his own volition. What looks suspicious from the very top is the fact that not one of the four officers authorized to alert overseas commands—Stark, Turner, Marshall, and Gerow—saw the fourteen parts until Sunday morning. What kind of odds would Las Vegas make of that?

Almost unbelievably, on the most important day of their lives, neither Marshall nor Stark could later recall where they were or what they were doing. Marshall was later reminded by his wife that he was at home because she was recovering from broken ribs. But according to Kimmel's intelligence officer, Captain Layton, Marshall left his office early on Saturday with specific instructions to Colonel Bratton that he did not want to be disturbed, while he was highly aware of the explosive situation in the Pacific, and that he was retiring to his quarters at Fort Myer. That night, however, he attended a reunion of World War I veterans in downtown D.C. It was just too suspicious that everyone of importance should not be disturbed.

In that connection, it is equally unbelievable that the intelligence chiefs of both services, Turner and Gerow, would pass instructions not to deliver until Sunday top-secret intelligence to those authorized to warn overseas commands. They knew that these officers had not seen it. Had they themselves been under specific orders, or were they simply following the do-not-disturb order?

To build up aircraft requirements in the Philippines, Washington had authorized sixteen B-17s to be transferred there in November 1941.[6] The Thirty-Eighth Reconnaissance Squadron from Albuquerque, New Mexico, led by Major Truman Landon, would supply eight aircraft, and the Eighty-Eighth Reconnaissance Squadron from Fort Douglas, Utah, led by Captain Richard Carmichael, would supply the other eight. Landon's B-17s would be piloted by Captain Raymond Swenson, and First Lieutenants Karl Barthelmess, Bruce Allen, Earl Cooper, Harold Hastings, Robert Richards, and Boris Zubko. And those piloting Carmichael's B-17s would be First Lieutenants Harold Chaffin, Richard Ezzard, Frank Potter, Robert Thacker, Frank Bostrom, Harry Brandon, and David Rawls.

Top: Unidentified crewmen inspect a B-17C: Note the straight vertical fin. *Bottom:* A Boeing B-17E with an enlarged vertical fin that, from a distance, sometimes led to the plane's being mistaken for a Japanese aircraft.

General Marshall was concerned over the modification delays on installing the long-range tanks and sent General Hap Arnold to Hamilton Field in San Francisco to impress the necessity for speed. Where the greatest distance would be the first leg of the trip to Hawaii, the most dangerous would be from Hawaii on to the Philippines. At Hickam Field, the cosmoline would be removed from the guns and the guns would be armed, and the five-man crews would be increased to ten. Seeing them off, General Arnold warned them not to fly too close together because if the United States found itself at war before they reached the Philippines, they may be attacked.

On Saturday, December 6, at 9:30 p.m. PST, the B-17s took off on their twenty-four-hundred-mile flight to Hawaii. On departure from Hamilton, two of the Thirty-Eighth's aircraft, piloted by Hastings and Zubko, experienced engine problems and did not depart. One of the Eighty-Eighth's aircraft, piloted by Potter, experienced the same and aborted takeoff. And another Eighty-Eighth aircraft, piloted by Ezzard, developed problems in the air and returned to the field, leaving four B-17Cs and eight B-17Es to fly into history.

For the planes' flight across the Pacific, the navy had positioned ships for the B-17s to home in on, and again, KGMB was delivering Hawaiian music as an additional means of navigation. At 0745, Captain Carmichael of the Eighty-Eighth had attempted to contact Hickam Tower, but because of the distance, the transmission was garbled.

At about 5:00 a.m. on Sunday, the graveyard shift at the Navy Department in Washington started to receive what appeared to be the beginning of the fourteenth part from the Magic machine. It had been a full twelve hours since the first thirteen parts were received, and its delay was at once obvious. Part 14 read:

> Obviously is it the intention of the American Government to conspire with Great Britain and other countries to obstruct Japan's efforts toward the establishment of peace through the creation of a New Order in East Asia, and especially to preserve Anglo-American rights and interests by keeping Japan and China at war. This intention has been revealed clearly during the course of the present negotiations. Thus, the earnest hope of the Japanese Government to adjust Japanese-American relations and to preserve and promote the peace of the Pacific through cooperation with the American Government has finally been lost.
>
> The Japanese Government regrets to have to notify hereby the American Government that in view of the attitude of the American Government it cannot but consider that it is impossible to reach an agreement through further negotiations.[7]

Within two hours came two more supplements, the first of which designated the time that the ambassadors were to present Tokyo's response to those in Washington: "Will the Ambassador please submit to the United States Government (if possible to the Secretary of State) our reply to the United States at 1:00 p.m. on the 7th, your time."[8] The second supplement issued final instructions to destroy any remaining intelligence: "After deciphering Part 14 of my #902, and also #907, #908, and #909, please destroy at once the remaining cipher machine and all machine codes. Dispose in like manner all secret documents."[9]

There it was, the fourteenth part, Japan's answer to the Americans' Ten Point Note: a termination of negotiations. But most important was the supplement stating a specific time for presentation of the dispatch. Even to the most uninformed, it was obvious that something was going to happen somewhere at the stated time.

Ever since the November war warning, Admiral Kimmel had been concerned that he be totally prepared if war should start in the Pacific. He was busy assembling a checklist-type document that he titled *Steps to Be Taken in Case of American-Japanese War Within 24 Hours.*

It covered notification to subordinate commands, air patrols, and other necessary personnel. He spent Saturday morning in briefing with his second in command, Admiral William Pye. Pye was one of those convinced that if war came, a strike would not be directed at the Americans but rather at the British or the Dutch.

Fort Shafter was the scene of the usual Saturday morning staff meeting. General Short's G-2, Colonel Fielder, who worked closely with the Japanese-American community toward army recruitment, was not one to coordinate with his navy counterpart. But his assistant, Lieutenant Colonel George Bicknell, had friends not only in naval intelligence but also in the local FBI. Bicknell maintained the opposite view of Fielder's, supporting the internment of Japanese-Americans in the event of war, and as such was keeping a closer eye on things. It was from the navy that he discovered that the local Japanese were burning documents and destroying codes, which he felt indicated that something was about to happen somewhere. Fielder was unimpressed.

That same afternoon, Bicknell received a call from his contact with the Honolulu office of the local FBI. He was asked to come over immediately. Upon arrival, Bicknell was handed a transcript of a monitored phone call from Honolulu to Tokyo. It was a very unusual conversation when one considers the cost of such a call in those days. The subjects ranged from flying weather to seamen roaming the streets, and ended with a discussion of the types of flowers in bloom. The call was just too suspicious, and the FBI was convinced that it should be passed on to the army. Bicknell was alarmed. He automatically called Fielder. He had something of dire importance for Fielder and Short. Again Fielder was not impressed, but in making their dinner engagement, both men read the transcript. The two decided that it was nothing to be alarmed over, and that ended it.

The aircraft on the army and naval installations were secured for the weekend. At many sites, gas tanks were emptied, guns were removed for cleaning, ammo was locked up, guard was doubled in accordance to Alert No. 1, and the weekend passes were issued.

At Hickam, there were approximately fifty-five bombers parked on the half-mile-long ramp, which included the B-18s, the B-17s, and the one B-24 intended for the reconnaissance mission to the Marshals. Bordering Hickam was Pearl Harbor, where sixty-five aircraft, mostly amphibians, were parked, with the PBYs all tethered next to Hangar Six at the south end of Ford Island. At the Kaneohe Naval Air Station on the northeast coast, thirty-seven aircraft, mostly PBYs, were parked on the ramp just out of the water. At Ewa Marine Corps Air Station, there were forty-seven aircraft, consisting of SBDs, F4Fs, and SB2Us. At Wheeler Field in the center of the island, across the road from Schofield Barracks, there was the baker's mix of mostly P-26, P-36, and P-40 fighters, and a variety of single-engine aircraft, totaling about 145. And finally, at Bellows there were approximately twenty planes, which included observation aircraft and the P-40s being used for training.

Within Pearl Harbor itself, the battleships and cruisers were moored to concrete quays at Ford Island in the center of the harbor. On the southeast side was Battleship Row with the *California* in the lead, followed by the oiler USS *Neosho* (AO-23). Then moored in pairs were the *Oklahoma*, the *Maryland*, the *West Virginia*, and the USS *Tennessee* (BB-43). The repair ship, USS *Vestal* (AR-4), and the USS *Arizona* (BB-39) were followed by the USS *Nevada* (BB-36). On the west side of the island were the seaplane tender, USS *Tangier* (AV-8), and two light cruisers, the USS *Raleigh* (CL-7) and USS *Detroit* (CL-8), along with the USS *Utah* (BB-31) moored between the *Tangier* and *Raleigh*. (The *Utah* had been converted from a battleship to a target ship.) With the exception of the USS *Pennsylvania* (BB-38) which was in dry dock, all ships were at Condition 3. This required that one-quarter of their antiaircraft batteries were to be manned and the balance ready for quick response, and all were pointed toward the harbor entrance for a fast exit that would eliminate any maneuvering time.

At Wheeler Field, the main fighter base, 90 percent of army personnel were available for duty, along with perhaps one hundred fighters that could have been brought into the fight with advance warning. Instead they sat parked, out of fuel and ammunition, which would require four hours to get them all airborne. And with the proper alert from Washington, the aircraft that would have warned them, the PBYs, would have been hundreds of miles at sea and not sitting on the ramps undergoing maintenance for wear and tear demands.

Honolulu itself was settling into its usual beautiful, peaceful Saturday night that only that city can offer. In the distance, the black hills met the dark blue sky with a sporadic light here and there in the hills. With the December moon reflecting off the water, one could see the silhouette of Diamond Head where it met the ocean. The streets faced either the mountains or the ocean with the street lights exposing the palm tree–lined boulevards, each view more exotic than the last. The Moana and Royal Hawaiian Hotels were the scenes of dinner parties with the cares of reality far removed. Admiral Kimmel, Admiral Pye, and a few friends attended a dinner party at the Halekulani Hotel, but by 9:30 p.m., Kimmel was on his way back to his quarters at Makalapa Heights at Pearl Harbor. Short and his G-2, Colonel Fielder, had gone to dinner at the Officers' Club at Schofield Barracks, and like Kimmel, Short was back in his quarters on Palm Circle at Fort Shafter by 10:00 p.m.

Back in Washington, no one was in greater anticipation of the fourteenth part of Japan's message than Commander Kramer, who was back in his office by 7:30 a.m. on Sunday. Most resident deliveries would not be necessary. He added the fourteenth part to the folders to be ready for distribution. Admiral Stark had already arrived and was handed his copy on Kramer's way to the White House. From there, Kramer was off to the State Department to deliver to Secretary Knox. They met on the way in, and at that moment, Colonel Bratton arrived to deliver to Secretary Hull. Captain Beardall presented the president's copy in his bedroom. FDR's only comment was, "It looks as though the Japs are going to break off negotiations."[10] Upon Kramer's return to the Navy Department, recipients were all present and hashing over the meaning of the message. Admiral Wilkinson suggested another warning to Admiral Hart in the Philippines. There was no response from Stark.

By 10:30 a.m. in Washington, the two supplements stating the delivery time were in Kramer's hands. This was only one hour away from Nagumo's takeoff time from the Kido Butai. Kramer then made a time check on the wall map to interpret the delivery time of 1:00 p.m. in Washington. He noted that it would correspond to 1:00 a.m. on the Kra Isthmus (Siam) and 3:00 a.m. in the Philippines. No major attack would begin in the dead of night, with most major targets blacked out and with landing forces fumbling around on unfamiliar terrain. This would also rule out Malaya and the Dutch colony. But 1:00 p.m. did equate to early morning on Oahu and to high noon at the Panama Canal, where a task force would have to sail through many hours of daylight in highly traveled commercial sea lanes, eliminating the element of surprise.

Colonel Bratton had reached General Miles and General Gerow and hurried them into their offices in the Munitions Building.

Meanwhile, the navy was having their meeting. One of those meeting with Stark was

Commander McCollum, who headed up Far East Section of the Office of Naval Intelligence. Born and raised in Japan, McCollum was considered an expert on the Japanese, and in his capacity, he was the communications routing officer responsible for providing Roosevelt with Japanese intercepts. McCollum would later become known as the author of the McCollum Memo, which many believe influenced Roosevelt's actions to provoke Japan into war.

The McCollum Memo, which was drafted in October 1940, included eight points, all of which Roosevelt would follow through with by the time Pearl Harbor was attacked. The points specified that the Americans should gain access to British bases in the Pacific, continue aid to the Chinese, deploy ships and submarines to Asian ports, increase U.S. naval strength at Pearl Harbor, instruct the Dutch not to negotiate with the Japanese, and finally, apply trade embargoes on the Japanese. Summarizing these points, McCollum stated, "If by these means Japan could be led to commit an overt act of war, so much the better. At all events we must be fully prepared to accept the threat of war."[11] There is no proof that Roosevelt actually saw this memo, but McCollum did pass it to then Captains Walter Anderson and Dudley Knox, both of whom were close to Roosevelt.

At the gathering in Stark's office, Commander McCollum reiterated that the situation was elementary in that the deadline would be timed to an attack, with the only question being where. Wilkinson suggested that perhaps a call to Kimmel was in order. Stark excused them with the statement that he should call the president first. Kimmel was never called, and for that matter, neither was the president. Stark would later testify that the president's personal line was busy. The disaster at Pearl Harbor was the result of a busy signal. An unofficial statement from a member of the White House staff had the president at his desk working on his stamp collection with the phone off the hook. What would the president's reaction have been at the request for a call to Admiral Kimmel?

Back in the Munitions Building, Miles was in a huddle with Gerow and Bratton. The more conversation they had, the more convinced they were that a new warning including the deadline should be sent to the Hawaiian commanders at once. But General Marshall should concur, and he was nowhere to be found.

The occurrences of Saturday night and Sunday morning can be described with many interpretations. Although the Roberts Commission was designed to not implicate anyone in Washington, the Army and Navy Boards of 1944 would search for the truth. Were the changes in testimony truly the result of lapses of memory? Or were some covering themselves from potential future liability in connection with their participation in the Saturday and Sunday events? Their military careers could hang in the balance. Even Kramer and Bratton would have to change their testimonies to fit that of their superiors, which made them appear incompetent. The disappearance of the key military leaders, and the orders not to disturb them in the most critical hour in American history, leaves little doubt that unusual orders had been issued. The following could illustrate what appears to be the dragging of feet in the final hours to allow the attack on Pearl Harbor to happen.

Just before 9:00 a.m. on Sunday in Washington, Colonel Bratton phoned Marshall at his home at Fort Myer and was told by his orderly that the general was on his usual Sunday morning horseback ride. In so many words, Bratton told the orderly that it was imperative that he track down Marshall at once and get him to a phone. He was instructed to get help if necessary. The call was not returned until 10:25 a.m. With phone security and time in mind, Bratton told Marshall that he was on his way and would be at Fort Myer in twenty minutes with new Magic. Marshall said no, he was on his way to the War Department. Later, he would not even recall talking to Bratton.

At 11:25 a.m., Marshall arrived at his office and methodically started to study the fourteen parts as the clock ticked down. A twenty-minute trip for Bratton was a one-hour trip the other way. And this was on a Sunday morning, years before the thought of traffic jams. It had been a full twenty-three hours since the pilot message announcing the fourteen parts had been received. Miles and Bratton made attempts to brush ahead to the fourteenth part, but Marshall would not be swayed. By 11:30 a.m., they were joined by Gerow, and between the four of them, it became quite apparent that something was about to happen at an American installation in the Pacific in an hour and a half. A call by Marshall to Stark to energize interest in a new warning to Pacific commanders with the time deadline failed. They had already been sent sufficient warning. Marshall started writing out a warning in longhand for MacArthur and Short. The phone rang. It was Stark, who had reconsidered and wanted Marshall's warning passed on to Hart and Kimmel. Marshall wrote: "Japanese are presenting at 1 p.m. eastern standard time today what amounts to an ultimatum [and] also they are under orders to destroy their code machine immediately. Just what significance the hour set may have we do not know but be on the alert accordingly. Inform Naval authorities of this communication. Marshall."[12]

The message was completed and ready for delivery at 11:58 a.m. Marshall then sent Colonel Bratton to the Army Signal Center to forward the message to Hawaii. Upon his return, Marshall inquired how long it would take to deliver. Bratton returned to the center for the answer, which was "about thirty to forty minutes."[13] Marshall had no choice but to be satisfied with that. But this did not include the required time to encipher for delivery and decipher for receiving the message. Whoever took the message would have understood at a glance that time was of the essence. That person appears to have been Colonel Edward French, commanding the Army Signal Center, who learned that heavy static was blackening out the army circuit to Hawaii. So he took it upon himself to send the message in the clear by Western Union to Seattle and then via RCA Commercial Radiogram to Honolulu, where it arrived at 7:33 a.m. Hawaiian time, just twenty-two minutes before the attack.

But because it was not marked "urgent" or "priority," it sat in the out basket in Honolulu and Short never saw it until 2 p.m. Sunday, and Kimmel two hours after that. Had Marshall been aware of this, he may well have elected to call Short on the scrambler phone, which he feared could compromise Magic. Considering the urgency of the situation, it was a total breakdown in communications, one that would later support Roosevelt's claim of a surprise attack.

Outside the entrance of Pearl Harbor, the *Ward*, a World War I four-stacker destroyer, was cruising on patrol, guarding the harbor entrance under the command of its newly appointed skipper, Lieutenant William Outerbridge. This was Outerbridge's first patrol with the *Ward*. The responsibility for guarding what was known as the prohibited area, the two square miles covering the harbor's entrance, was divided with three other old veterans, the USS *Chew* (DD-106), the USS *Schley* (DD-103), and the USS *Allen* (DD-66). And each ship patrolled from Saturday to Saturday.

Their mission was to identify all ships entering this area, which required a monotonous routine of sailing back and forth. Although U.S. submarines entered and left the harbor, they were always surfaced and escorted by a destroyer. But any unidentified vessels entering the area were to be sunk. It was now a standing order from Kimmel that any unidentified sub operating in the prohibited area would be attacked because such a presence could signal the approach of an enemy fleet. This, of course, was contrary to FDR's order that Japan must fire the first shot.

With the approach of such an enemy fleet, Kimmel would promptly dispatch his forces to meet the enemy. But with what? His two carrier task forces were gone and his third carrier was in San Diego.

At 3:42 a.m. in Hawaii and after 9:00 a.m. in Washington, things were starting to stir in the Navy Department, and Colonel Bratton was trying to locate General Marshall. At Pearl Harbor, the minesweeper USS *Condor* (AMC-14) signaled the *Ward* that it had identified the periscope of a submerged submarine fifty yards off its bow, headed for the entrance of the harbor. The periscope was leaving its telltale feather of white water, revealing its direction. The *Ward* immediately went to general quarters, signaling the crew to prepare for battle. The object disappeared and no sound contact was made. At about 5:00 a.m., the submarine net gate at the entrance to Pearl Harbor opened to allow the *Condor* to enter. Following some distance behind was the *Antares*, a stores cargo ship returning from Canton Island. As the *Ward* observed the passage of the *Antares*, both its helmsman and officer of the deck identified the conning tower of a submarine attempting to follow the *Antares* into the harbor. Lieutenant Outerbridge was recalled to the bridge. The crew was still keyed up from the first sighting.

At 6:40, the ship went back to general quarters, and at 6:45, at a distance of one hundred yards, the No. 1 gun fired America's first shot of World War II. It missed. The No. 3 gun, another four-inch rifle, fired the second round that hit dead-on, and the sub disappeared. The sub's two-man crew would be the first official casualties in America's new war. In addition, a PBY that had observed it all dropped depth charges, along with the *Ward*. The *Ward* immediately sent a message to the Fourteenth Naval District: "We have attacked, fired upon, and dropped depth charges upon sub operating in defensive area."[14]

Known for firing the Americans' first shot of World War II, Outerbridge would later experience a very unusual twist of fate, exactly three years from the day of the *Ward* action at Pearl Harbor. Outerbridge was later assigned to command the USS *O'Brien* (DD-975), which assisted with Allied landings at Normandy, and then returned to the Pacific theater to perform the same duties during the Americans' landing in the Leyte Gulf. The *Ward* had also been assigned to Leyte Gulf, and on December 7, 1944, while performing patrol duty, the *Ward* was severely crippled by Japanese kamikazes. Outerbridge, in command of the *O'Brien*, was ordered to sink the *Ward*.

The *Ward* message, moving up the Fourteenth Naval District, eventually reached Captain J.B. Earle. Earle, who had previously commanded Destroyer Squadron Five, was assigned as Admiral Bloch's chief of staff in June 1941. Earle requested confirmation before taking the report any higher. There had been so many reports of sightings in the past few weeks, with most turning out to be whales. But Earle did report the incident by phone to Bloch, and between them, the decision was made to await confirmation. Then came the PBY report of dropping depth charges on a submarine. Still no confirmation was received. In fact, it would remain unconfirmed for over sixty years until August 2002, when the submarine was discovered in twelve hundred feet of water in the exact position reported by the *Ward*.

At 5:30 on December 7, about two hundred fifty miles north of Oahu, two float planes were launched from the Kido Butai cruisers that would scout ahead to confirm the American fleet location in either Pearl Harbor or its alternative, Lahaina anchorage.

The pilots of the strike force were already prepared to launch and were in their cockpits

USS *Ward* #3 gun, currently located at the St. Paul capitol building in Minnesota.

anxiously waiting for their takeoff orders. The first wave would include fifty-one Aichi (Val) dive bombers that carried a two-man crew and five hundred pounds of bombs, with defenses of three 7.7mm machine guns.[15]

Next were forty-three Mitsubishi fighters (Zeros) which carried two 7.7mm machine guns and two 20mm wing cannons.[16] Pilot armor and safety measures were sacrificed to increase their speed and maneuverability, tradeoffs which were certainly liabilities if they were hit.

Next were the Nakajima B5N2 three-place bombers (Kates), forty-nine of which took on the horizontal bombing role, carrying armor-piercing bombs, and forty of which took on the torpedo bombing role.[17] Their torpedoes would have the modified fins designed for Pearl Harbor's shallow harbor of only forty feet. The creation of the modified torpedoes to operate in Pearl Harbor's shallow waters had been an ordnance headache. And this turned out to be elementary compared to the art form needed to drop them with any hope of a hit.

The Kate had a range of over a thousand miles, but its defense consisted of only one flexible 7.7mm Lewis gun in the rear cockpit. Much of its credit was due to its torpedo that could be dropped higher, farther, and faster than U.S. torpedoes, thus requiring less run-in time to the target. And as the war progressed, this scenario would not change. The Kates would sink several U.S. carriers, the *Lexington* in the Battle of the Coral Sea in May 1942, the *Yorktown* in Battle of Midway in June, and later in October, the USS *Hornet* (CV-8) at the Battle of Santa Cruz. As the tide of the war later changed, however, the Kates would be relegated to kamikazes.

At 6:00, the procession started from all six Japanese carriers until all 183 aircraft were in the air. When all were airborne, they headed south. Only one aircraft, a Zero, aborted its takeoff and crashed off its ship's bow.

As the planes departed for Pearl Harbor, thirty-nine stayed behind to protect the fleet. It took only fifteen minutes to launch all 183 aircraft of the first wave. One departure from U.S. policy is that none of the Japanese pilots wore parachutes.

At 7:00, the routine started again with the second wave, consisting of seventy-eight Val dive bombers, thirty-five Zero fighters, and fifty-four Kates in the horizontal bomber role.[18] Again, after forming, they too headed south.

Situated some twenty-five miles north of Honolulu and two hundred thirty feet above sea level was a mobile radar unit on Opana Point, an ideal position to command the view of the ocean north of Oahu. The SCR-270, also known as the Pearl Harbor Radar, had a range of one hundred fifty miles with distance accuracy of one hundred thirty miles. The first of the sets had been operational since mid–November.

The road leading to the Opana Point Radar Station as it looks today.

Private George Elliott had actually helped install the unit, and on Saturday, December 6, he and Private Joseph Lockard were assigned duty at the site, which included orders to operate the radar unit from 4:00 to 7:00 on Sunday morning. Camping out in a tent for the night, they arose at about 3:45 to power up the equipment. Lockard, who was more experienced than Elliott, manned the scope while Elliott worked the plotting table. When their shift came to an end at 7:00, they were just about to close down the radar set, but their transportation back to civilization and breakfast chow had not arrived yet. Elliott, the trainee, suggested keeping the set on until their transportation arrived so that he could have more training. He was fascinated by its whole concept and capability. With Lockard as instructor, Elliott changed places with him and was seated at the oscilloscope.

Almost immediately, the revolving line revealed a blip at the top of the scope, a blip so bright that Lockard wondered if the set was out of calibration. He replaced Elliott at the controls and checklisted everything. It all checked out perfectly. But there it was, a blip brighter than they had ever seen, indicating that there was something out there larger than they could imagine. They zeroed it in at three degrees north, 137 miles out, at about the maximum range of their set. Private Elliott was convinced that they should call the sighting in to the information center as good work on their part. Lockard was of the opinion that their shift was over, but he would continue to plot if Elliott wanted to call it in. There were two mobile phones at the site, a tactical line and an administrative line, both hooked to the information center.

Elliott rang up on the tactical line with no answer, not a good sign. He then tried the administrative line, which was answered by Private Joseph McDonald, the switchboard operator. McDonald told Elliott that the plotters working at the information center had already gone to breakfast because the shift was over. Elliott explained what he had seen and insisted on passing it up the ladder. Would McDonald find someone who would call back? While Elliott was talking with McDonald, the connection was broken.

After consulting with Lieutenant Kermit Tyler, explaining Private Elliott's call from Opana Point, McDonald tried to reach Opana Point, and this time Private Lockard was on the phone. McDonald explained to Lockard that Lieutenant Tyler was not concerned, and Lockard asked to speak with the lieutenant directly. When Tyler got on the phone, he explained to Lockard that whenever a flight of aircraft was due in from the mainland, Station KMGB would remain on all night for the planes to home in on. As he had just listened to the Hawaiian music on his way to Fort Shafter to pull his four-to-eight shift, Tyler told Lockard that he and Elliott must have spotted the B-17s that were due in at 8:00 from San Francisco. His response to Lockard was, "Well, don't worry about it."[19] Private McDonald, who was worried about it, thought Tyler was inexperienced and considered calling Wheeler Field himself, but was afraid he could be court-martialed for going over the lieutenant's head. No disciplinary action was ever taken against Lieutenant Tyler precisely for that reason, lack of training and no supervision.

The irony of the incident was that the Opana radar may well have actually had the B-17s in their scope. Both the B-17s and the Japanese were homing in on Radio Honolulu, and being just a few miles apart, their formations were closing in on one another. Unknown to Tyler, the B-17s, over the twenty-four-hundred-mile trip, were now no longer in formation, and some had wandered slightly north of course. The lead navigator, a young second lieutenant, no more experienced than the others on this trip, found that as he approached Oahu, he was about one hundred miles north of course. As he made his course correction, they found themselves slightly behind and to the left of the first wave of Japanese aircraft. As Elliott and Lockard watched, and the images on the scope came within twenty miles of the island and then started to fade out as the formations turned left or right and were lost behind the hills. The station was shut down at 7:45, as the truck had arrived.

Within minutes of the *Ward*'s message of the sinking of the submarine, there was another distraction. A large white sampan, similar to those used by the local Japanese fishing community, was lying well within the prohibited area, just off the harbor entrance. Suddenly, as if aware that it had been spotted, the sampan got under way as if trying to outrun the *Ward* or escape. But when the *Ward* gained closure, its master appeared on deck waiving a white flag. Outerbridge considered this strange behavior for a fishing master in peacetime.

Meanwhile, the two Japanese reconnaissance planes reported back to the Kido Butai. One reported no ships at the Lahaina anchorage, while the other identified nine battleships and a number of cruisers at the Pearl Harbor anchorage.

Commander Mitsuo Fuchida, responsible for the entire aerial attack, was flying in a three-place Kate torpedo bomber. While formations were still together north of the island, the plan in coordinating the attack was to fire an in-flight flare to inform the squadrons that surprise had been achieved. This would put the immediate emphasis of the attack at Pearl Harbor at the south end of the island. Two flares would indicate that the Americans had been warned, which would divert many to attack the airfields so American fighters could not meet the attack. After firing the surprise flare, Fuchida was convinced that not all had seen it. After he fired a second flare, the squadrons banked right down the west coast of the island. As Fuchida's plane rounded Barbers Point on the southwest corner of the island, his radio operator sent the message "Tora, Tora, Tora"[20] back to the fleet, indicating that surprise had been achieved and that they were attacking.

It was 7:55 when the first Japanese aircraft, a Val dive bomber, approached Ford Island from the south and, followed by the others, released the first bomb on the navy hangars at the south end of the island.

At 7:35, Kimmel's duty officer called with the report from the *Ward*. Minutes later, Patwing 2 called with the report from the PBY that had dropped depth charges on the sub. Kimmel justified the request for confirmation because of all the false alarms involving whales and blackfish. But while Admiral Bloch was awaiting confirmation, Kimmel would tend to the matter personally instead of arousing all of the various staffs. At 7:55, he was on the phone with Commander Vincent Murphy, receiving word that the *Ward* had sunk the sub. He also received another call from his duty officer that the *Ward* had also stopped a sampan prowling quite suspiciously near the entrance of the harbor. It was seconds before 8:00 when suddenly Kimmel's yeoman burst in and announced a message from the signal tower: "Air raid Pearl Harbor, this is no drill."[21] He informed his headquarters at the submarine base that he was on his way. He skipped breakfast and quickly shaved, and as he went out of his front door, high on the hill overlooking the harbor, still buttoning his coat, he could see the aircraft flying over Ford Island and the smoke starting to rise.

The Roberts Commission would unjustly blame Kimmel for the failure of the Outerbridge message to cause alarm. But the *Ward* report was sent to the Fourteenth Naval District, which was for Admiral Bloch, not Kimmel, and while Bloch waited for confirmation, Kimmel prepared for duty. Having been CINCPAC himself, Bloch was certainly aware of the need for information from subordinate commanders in order to make concise and heavy decisions.

Yet today, strangely, Admiral Bloch is memorialized in at least three locations in Pearl Harbor. There are no memorials at Pearl Harbor for Admiral Kimmel or General Short.

At 7:40, Commander Fuchida's first attack wave had arrived at Kahuku Point, where Opana is located, and banked right, following the Waianae Mountain Range coastline. Upon reaching Kolekole Pass, easily identified by a huge white cross mounted on the side of the slope, they split into two groups.

On a side note, the wooden cross at Kolekole Pass dated back to 1920 as a symbol of Christianity at Schofield. In 1946, it was replaced by a steel, twenty-five-foot cross. But in 1997, the American Civil Liberties Union threatened to sue the army, claiming the necessity for separation of church and state. In anticipation of losing the fight, the army ordered that the cross, one of the most historic symbols of the attack on Pearl Harbor, be dismantled. Today, only a plaque remains.

The main thrust of the attack force, including all the torpedo bombers, would continue toward Pearl Harbor. The balance banked left into the pass to deal with the airfield. Upon emerging on the east side of the mountains, Schofield Barracks lay dead ahead and Wheeler Army Airfield was just to the right. Their mission: to eliminate American fighter opposition.

Within ten minutes, all five airfields—Wheeler, Hickam, Ford Island, Kaneohe, and the

The cross at Kolekole Pass; it had been the signpost to Wheeler Field.

Marine base at Ewa—were put out of action, virtually paralyzing any air retaliation. Amazingly, a handful of army fighters did get into the air and, when compiling all their handicaps, performed far above expectations. The only airfield the Japanese missed was Haleiwa, an auxiliary field on the northwest coast, from which two fighters took to the air. Although Schofield Barracks was not formally attacked, being across the road from Wheeler Field, it received much carry-over strafing. Along with a few pilots from Wheeler who were able to get off the ground, these represented most of the U.S. aerial defense of the Pearl Harbor attack.

Within the first fifteen minutes, the Japanese also accomplished most of their main mission, the destruction of the fleet.

At Pearl Harbor itself, about forty Kate torpedo bombers suddenly appeared from the direction of the submarine base, east of Ford Island, which offered a long, low approach, leaving the port sides of the *California*, *Oklahoma*, *West Virginia*, and *Arizona* fully exposed. Hits were made on all. Then the horizontal and dive bombers made coordinated attacks on the inner ships, the *Maryland* and *Tennessee*. Within minutes of the start of hostilities, the radio message was flashed from the headquarters building on Ford Island, "Air raid Pearl Harbor, this is no drill."

The first ship to sink was the former battleship *Utah*, which was located on the west side of the island. Because it had been converted to a target ship, it may have appeared to be a carrier with its heavy deck planking. Early on, the comment was made that anyone who would mistake a battleship for an aircraft carrier shouldn't have been on the raid. The *Utah* took two torpedoes and rolled over. A plaque near the site where the ship remains today notes that there are still fifty-eight crewmen aboard.

Amidst all of this, the B-17s arrived from San Francisco. The Thirty-Eighth's pilots spotted a group of fighters coming out to meet them and felt honored to have an escort in. But suddenly the friendly aircraft started shooting at them. After a fourteen-hour trip, with their fuel tanks almost exhausted and being unable to protect themselves, they were desperate to get on the ground. Each pilot was on his own, taking whatever evasive action he could and looking for what might afford the safest place to land. Some planes were saved, some were total wrecks.

Two of the aircraft were destroyed and a third headed back out to sea and then returned for a downwind landing at Bellows. Lieutenant Richards of the Thirty-Eighth overshot the runway and stopped in a ditch at the end while the Japanese continued to strafe the plane. (Initially, maintenance personnel thought the plane was salvageable, but in the end, it was only good for spare parts.)

Captain Swenson, also of the Thirty-Eighth, actually got on the ground at Hickam, but Japanese strafing hit a flare storage box in the middle of the fuselage, burning out the center of the aircraft and killing a flight surgeon. But the four engines in the front were salvaged.

Four other B-17s actually landed at Hickam with varying degrees of damage. Captain Carmichael and Lieutenant Chaffin, both of the Eighty-Eighth, settled for a twelve-hundred-foot auxiliary strip on the north shore at Haleiwa. Lieutenant Bostrom, also of the Eighty-Eighth, gave up on Hickam and Barbers Point, and finally settled for the Kahuku Golf Course. Unbelievably, the plane was repaired, and within a week was flown to Hickam. Two other B-17s from the Eighty-Eighth eventually landed between the attacks. Given the fact that some of the U.S. fighter pilots had initially mistaken the arriving B-17Es, with enlarged vertical fins which seemed strange to them for Japanese, it's a wonder that any survived their arrival. With

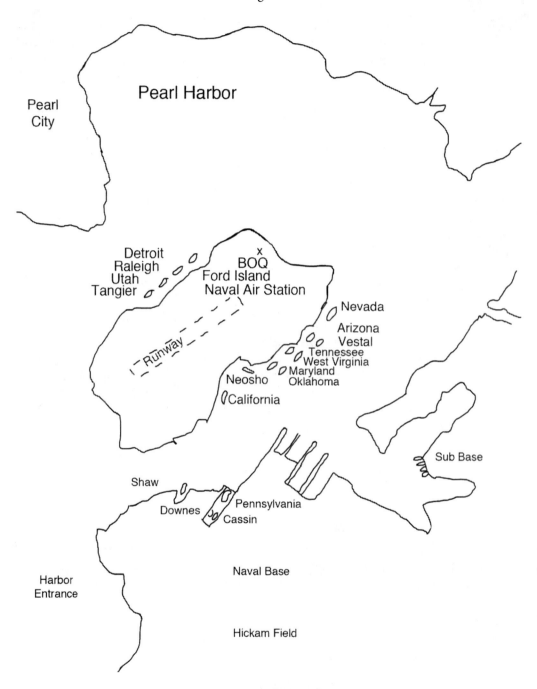

Ford Island (at center)

the exception of the B-17C that landed at Bellows (not repairable) and a B-17C destroyed on the ground at Hickam, as well as the B-17E from the golf course, the nine others landed at Hickam and were saved. There are several eyewitness accounts that one of the B-17s actually landed at Wheeler, then immediately took off for Hickam. Actually, with nineteen bombers on the field that were put out of action, there were twenty-two that endured without a scratch.

Within minutes, the harbor was a patchwork of white torpedo wakes all aimed at predetermined ships, and soon most of Ford Island was ringed with black smoke billowing up from ships in their death throes. By 8:15, it was over. The bases had just started to take inventory of themselves and count their losses when, just as suddenly, the second wave struck at 8:40.

The second wave followed down the eastern shore of Oahu, attacked Kaneohe and Bellows for a second time, and then continued on to Hickam, where they inflicted most of the damage to the general base. Many of the planes attacked the brand-new consolidated barracks, known today as the PACAF Building, and many principal buildings some distance from the flight line. The balance of the planes continued on to Pearl Harbor. (Today, much of the damage to PACAF remains as a shrine to those who died there.)

Interestingly, just before the first attack started, the destroyer USS *Monagham* (DD-354) had been ordered out of the harbor to assist the *Ward*. En route to the entrance, she identified one of the Japanese midget subs that had successfully gotten into the harbor, where she rammed and sank it. This was the only midget sub proven to have actually made it into the harbor.

The author viewing some of the strafing at the two-thousand-man barracks, which is now the Pacific Air Force Headquarters building at Hickam Air Force Base.

The first attack wave had inflicted such extensive damage that the second wave just finished destroying anything that the first one didn't. At the lead of the battleships, the *California* had taken three torpedoes and a number of bomb hits. To make things worse, its watertight hatches were all open for inspection, which helped to ensure its sinking. She was about to capsize when a young lieutenant saved the day by ordering counterflooding. But because of the torpedo hits, she sank in three days anyway.

Behind the *California* was the *Oklahoma*, which took nine torpedoes. She started to list to port, and within thirty minutes rolled over. Inboard, the *Maryland* took bomb strikes, but survived. Behind outboard was the *West Virginia*, which took nine torpedoes. Also struck with many bomb hits, it just sank in place, pinning the *Tennessee*. Eventually, sixty-seven bodies were found on the *West Virginia*, along with a calendar indicating that some of the crew had survived until December 23.[22] Sixteen days on trapped air and canned food.

The *Tennessee* took bomb hits, but she too would survive. The repair ship *Vestal* had saved the *Arizona* from the torpedoes. But with five thousand cans of powder and thousands of rounds of ammunition in her hold,[23] the *Arizona* sank from one well-placed bomb hit among others, taking 1,177 men down with her, the greatest loss of all the ships.[24] The *Vestal*, too, settled to the bottom.

To the rear of Battleship Row was the *Nevada*. Although her captain was ashore, she got underway. But recognizing that if she sunk she would block the harbor entrance, her temporary captain opted to beach her at Hospital Point, after which she took one torpedo and five bomb hits. At 1010 Dock, south of Battleship Row, the light cruiser USS *Helena* (CL-50) took one torpedo that actually passed under the outboard ship, the mine layer USS *Oglala* (CM-4). While the *Helena* did not actually sink, the *Oglala* blew apart from the concussion. The other cruisers were relatively secure from torpedo attacks, being moored in concrete slips.

The battleship *Pennsylvania*, which was in dry dock, took only one bomb hit. But the two destroyers ahead of her in the same dry dock, the USS *Cassin* (DD-372) and the USS *Downes* (DD-375), both took bomb hits and were severely damaged. Most of the other destroyers were anchored in groups out in the middle of East Loch, the largest water area in Pearl Harbor, except for the USS *Shaw* (DD-373). Located in a floating dock west of the *Pennsylvania*, the *Shaw* took three bomb hits, one of which, similar to the *Arizona*, hit the forward magazine and destroyed the ship from the bridge forward.

As the ships exploded, men were blown into the water, which was covered with thick black oil escaping the ships' tanks. Those not catapulted into the water had to jump into the massive oil slick, much of which ignited into a sea of flames. And through this, sailors had to try to swim ashore to Ford Island. As men emerged from the water in every state of dress, their entire bodies were black except for the whites of their eyes.

Admiral Bellinger's yard at his quarters near Battleship Row was a lawn filled with wounded and dying. There were eyewitness accounts of men emerging from the burning water, climbing up the small bank to the grass, and just lying down and dying. On everyone's minds, both military and civilian, was the question: do they try to take care of themselves, or do they prepare for the next round from the Japanese?

The new Bachelor Officers' Quarters, just completed on Ford Island, today's Navy Lodge, became a combination of supply depot, hospital, and morgue. And for days after the attack, boats would continue to patrol the harbor, just looking for more bodies.

In the coming days and weeks, families all around America would receive the dreaded telegram listing their family members as missing in action or confirmed dead. The telegrams would be followed by Purple Heart citations, and that was it. As for military security, they were very brief. Here today, gone tomorrow.

On the airfields, aircraft losses were not restricted to just those planes sitting on the ground, and the heroic attempts by some of the American pilots were dauntless.

The first two confirmed takeoffs of American pilots to get into the air were Second Lieutenants George Welch and Kenneth Taylor, both of the Forty-Seventh Pursuit Squadron, who sped by automobile from Wheeler Field north to the auxiliary strip at Haleiwa. Ground crews had their P-40s armed, gassed, and ready to go by about 8:30. Being directed south toward the marine base at Ewa, each of the pilots claimed two victories.

Both Welch and Taylor returned to Wheeler Field to gas up and re-arm. Welch was in the air first, and as Taylor was about to start down the runway, the field experienced another Japanese attack. During takeoff, Taylor came under attack, but Welch, already in the air, saw what was happening and came to the rescue, claiming his third victory. Welch then headed back to Ewa, where he claimed his fourth.

Two of the fighters were lost at Bellows when Second Lieutenants George Whiteman and Samuel Bishop attempted takeoffs. Whiteman was killed just as he got airborne at the end of the runway. From Sedalia, Missouri, Whiteman would become the first American aviator killed in World War II, for which he would be posthumously awarded the Silver Star. In 1955, with the reactivation of Sedalia Air Force Base in Missouri, it was renamed Whiteman Air Force Base. Bishop actually got into the air but was jumped by a number of Zeroes and crashed into the ocean, where his aircraft remains today, several hundred feet offshore. Though he was wounded, Bishop managed to swim ashore.

Amidst all the chaos and strafing at Wheeler Field, Second Lieutenant Phil Rasmussen, who had been on his way to the bathroom, climbed into a Curtiss P-36 and took off, still clad in his pajamas. Over Kaneohe Bay, where all the action was, he was charging his guns, which started firing prematurely. Unbelievably, while he was trying to get things under control, a Japanese Val passed right in front of him and exploded.

Rasmussen casually told this author that both his wings were raked with machine gun and cannon fire. His tail wheel was shot off, severing his rudder cables, and with his canopy blown off, he returned to Wheeler, where he started receiving ground fire from Schofield. With no directional control, he made what must have been a spectacular landing. And with over five hundred holes in his aircraft, it was junked. He has since been referred to as the "Pajama Pilot."

Second Lieutenant Gordon Sterling of the Forty-Sixth Pursuit Squadron was on the flight line looking for an aircraft so he could get into the fight. He spotted a P-36 that another pilot had temporarily abandoned to run for a parachute. Sterling jumped in and handed his wristwatch to a mechanic, hollering above the engine noise, "See that my mother gets this. I won't be coming back."[25] Then, over Kaneohe Bay, another pilot witnessed a Zero diving down in flames with Sterling, in flames, following it, with another Zero in flames following Sterling. All three crashed into the bay.

First Lieutenant Lewis Sanders, of the Forty-Sixth Pursuit Squadron, led a flight of four P-36s off Wheeler in the middle of the fight. Heading east toward Bellows, he spotted Japanese air activity just north of Kaneohe, from where he led the four into the fight, shooting down one enemy aircraft.

Charles Lindbergh in a Curtiss P-36 at Camp Ripley in Minnesota, 1939.

Second Lieutenant Harry Brown of the Forty-Seventh Pursuit Squadron got into the air from Wheeler and headed north toward Kaena Point, from where the Japanese were making their organized withdrawal. It was over the point where future air ace Lieutenant Brown shot down a Kate.

Lieutenant John Dains of the Forty-Sixth Pursuit Squadron flew two missions that morning in a P-40. After running out of ammunition the second time, he switched to a P-36, but by now, the Japanese aircraft had departed. So he returned to Wheeler. While in pattern to land, he was shot down by friendly fire from Schofield Barracks, which adjoined Wheeler, and he crashed onto the golf course.

Of the 145 aircraft on the field at Wheeler alone, forty-two were destroyed, and another fifty-six were put out of action.

To the surprise of the Japanese airmen, the ships' crews responded with their antiaircraft guns, amazingly within the first five minutes of the attack. Destroyer crews did the same, and for all practical purposes, the destroyers remained relatively untouched. At the army bases, the few three-inch antiaircraft weapons were quick to return fire, followed by a hail of bullets from weapons all the way down to machine guns, rifles, and pistols.

By 9:30, the last planes of the second wave had disappeared. Commander Fuchida, who had been assessing damage and observing the second wave, waited until the second attack

Dependents load onto U.S. Army transport *U.S. Grant* after it delivers troops (1942). The ship departed Manila as quickly as possible.

was completed and then returned to the aircraft carriers. To the Americans' credit, the Japanese had lost five Kate torpedo bombers, fifteen Val dive bombers, and nine Zero fighters,[26] plus all five midget submarines and one full-size sub still unreported today. And although they made it back to their carriers, another sixty-one Japanese aircraft suffered such severe damage that they were total write-offs.[27]

In addition to the attack, there had been another close brush with disaster involving the *Enterprise*, still two hundred miles west of Pearl Harbor on the return trip from Wake. Foul weather had delayed refueling at sea, which had saved the day because the carrier had originally been scheduled to return to Pearl Harbor at 7:30 on December 7. At dawn, Admiral Halsey had flown off eighteen of his SBD two-man dive bombers, to patrol ahead and land at Ewa. Flying into the middle of the attack before they realized what was happening, six were shot down by the Japanese, and at least one more was shot down by American ground fire.

Amongst the military personnel all across the island, the realization started to set in that they had just departed one age and were entering a new one, an age of war, whether for six months or six years. Life would never be the same. The new beginning would start by picking up the pieces and taking stock of what was gone and what was left. Where navy losses were mainly in ship and Ford Island damage, the base repair section, along with the overhaul and assembly sections of the engine repair department at Hickam Field, were completely destroyed. Over half of the Hawaiian Air Depot property stock was destroyed, along with all test equipment. Hickam's administrative files and 75 percent of the aero repair branch were liquidated. These areas at Hickam alone accounted for 163 killed, 43 missing, and 326 wounded.[28]

Of the 2,403 lives lost at Pearl Harbor, it was, as noted, the *Arizona* that suffered the greatest loss for any single ship, claiming 1,177 lives. Eventually, sixteen Medals of Honor would be awarded for actions at Pearl Harbor, eleven of which were awarded posthumously.[29] Oddly, for all the heroism displayed and sacrifices made by the army pilots, no Medals of Honor were awarded them. All went to navy personnel.

Initially, losses released to the press were held to a minimum for reasons of security, but the public was demanding court-martials and execution of the Hawaiian commanders. One paper stated that if Kimmel and Short had any honor, they would commit suicide. Both would have welcomed court-martials because within that legal process, they could have at least presented their sides of the story. But this could compromise national security, so they were denied.

In Admiral Yamamoto's original estimate, the destruction of the U.S. Fleet at Pearl Harbor would essentially put the Americans out of business in the Pacific for about two years. And this may have been quite possible if his pilots had concentrated on the oil storage and shipyards. Japan would continue her conquest of the western Pacific over the next two years, but even with twenty-one U.S. ships sunk or damaged at Pearl Harbor, valuable strategic targets were overlooked.

One such example was the Lualualei Naval Magazine located at the entrance of Kolekole Pass on the west side of the island. Its underground storage held thousands of rounds of ship ordnance, fourteen-inch and sixteen-inch projectiles, along with thousands of bags of powder and a variety of other ammunitions. An admitted oversight of the Japanese attack plan, this facility remained untouched.

One of the memorials at Kaneohe Naval Air Station identifying sites of December 7 action.

Other examples were the fuel storage tanks, containing four to five million barrels of oil. Had they been hit, it could have possibly taken years to replace. Bombs might not have even been needed to destroy them; machine-gun strafing might have done the job.

With the bigger targets so tempting, the Japanese totally overlooked the submarine base and its facilities, enabling American subs to immediately wander the Pacific looking for targets. Considering the Americans' inefficient torpedoes available during the first year or two of the

Fraternization with Orientals was prohibited after December 7. Presumably, this unidentified couple was photographed before that date.

war, however, saving the subs lost some of their combat potential. Even the dock and repair facilities were mostly untouched. Destruction of these would have required any repairs to be conducted all the way back on the U.S. west coast. Another potential but overlooked target was the Joint Army Navy Defense Center, then under construction at Red Hill, where petroleum was stored.

Many Pearl Harbor observers also agree that the Japanese made a huge tactical error in leaving the oil storage tanks alone. But the final, approved Japanese plan called for ship and aircraft targets only, no storage facilities included. The emperor himself had insisted that there should be no civilian casualties. Yamamoto had even suggested the occupation of Hawaii with an accompanying expeditionary force, but his suggestion was refused.

Nagumo's aerial commander, Mitsuo Fuchida, had argued for a third strike to finish the job, but Nagumo disagreed. He believed that the second strike had accomplished the main objective of the overall mission, and he had other concerns as well. Most of the Japanese losses suffered so far had occurred during the second strike, and considering their accomplishment, he didn't want to risk losing more of his aircraft. Not knowing where the American carriers were, he was also concerned that the Americans still had enough air power to bomb his own carriers. Running low on fuel, and unwilling to risk night landings that a third strike would have entailed, he headed back to Japan. Admiral Yamamoto had originally supported Nagumo's decision against a third strike, although soon after, he realized the error of not taking out the dockyards, maintenance facilities, and supply depots as well, which would have hampered U.S. retaliation. Everything that was destroyed could be replaced.

Perhaps the most redeeming factor in the entire attack was that much of the American fleet was caught in port. Had Kimmel been able to rally enough of a task force to get out of port, and had he been caught at sea, this armada, of whatever size, with absolutely no air cover, would have been decimated by the Japanese. With full crews at sea, rather than the partial crews encountered in port, total American losses of 2,403 may have climbed to perhaps twenty thousand killed, drowned, or captured.

In a footnote to the attack, the Dutch ship, *Jagersfontein*, which had sailed from the U.S. west coast, was just about to enter the Honolulu commercial harbor five miles east of Pearl Harbor, when the shooting started. Already at war with Germany, the crew just uncovered their weapons and joined in, the Americans' first official ally in the attack on Pearl Harbor.

By December 7, Colonel Friedman, who headed the Signal Intelligence Service, was in the middle of a nervous breakdown. When told of the successful Japanese attack at Pearl Harbor, he cried out, "But they knew, they knew, they knew."[30] His stay in the hospital was under guard so that he would not say anything to the wrong people.

In Tokyo, Ambassador Grew had learned of the president's last-minute appeal to the emperor by listening to the radio. A station in San Francisco described the message as an effort to maintain peace. The State Department gave a heads-up to Grew that the message was coming, which had been filed Saturday evening in Washington, or 10:00 a.m. Sunday morning in Tokyo. The arrival-time stamp on it was 11:00 that morning, but it was 10:00 Sunday night before it was handed to Grew, another significant delay with communications, this one caused by the Japanese Ministry of Communications Censorship's imposition of delivery delays on incoming and outgoing messages. The complete message was in Grew's hand in another hour.

Without hesitation, he called Prime Minister Tojo for an immediate audience with the emperor. Tojo insisted on reading the message first, and Grew met with him at 12:15 a.m. Monday (Tokyo time). The attack was still two hours away. After studying the message, Grew was dismissed, while Tojo would pass his request to the emperor. Pearl Harbor was in ruins by the time Grew's phone rang at 7:30 a.m. on Monday. Given the excuse that there had been attempts to reach him for two hours, Grew was requested to appear at the foreign minister's office at once. However, his phone hadn't rung.

Upon arrival at the foreign ministry, he was handed what he was told was the emperor's reply, which was nothing but a copy of the fourteen-part note. Returning to his embassy, he heard a newsboy selling extras in the street, announcing that Japan was at war. In another hour, he received his official notification of war, and within minutes, the police arrived to officially close the doors. It would be much later that morning before the emperor would receive the notification of war. He had never seen President Roosevelt's last-minute attempt to delay the inevitable.

News of the attack on Pearl Harbor reached Berlin later that night, and at first, Foreign Minister Von Ribbentrop refused to believe it. Initially, the question was whether or not it would even be necessary to declare war on the United States, now that Germany's Axis partner had already done it.

Secondly, Germany was concerned as to whether or not Japan would attack Russia from the east to take the pressure off the western front. But the Japanese refused to be maneuvered into such a commitment.

At the onset, Hitler was excited to hear about Pearl Harbor because he now had an ally that had not been defeated in three thousand years. But his enthusiasm quickly cooled with the realization that Japan would now be busy in the Pacific. Japan could not consider the risk of relieving German armies at Moscow by diverting Russian divisions to the east that would be guarding from an attack by Japan.

The tide on the Russian front had already started to turn in November due to the dropping temperatures. Germany had not considered a campaign longer than six months to conquer Russia, so no thought had been given to the issue of winter clothing or cold-weather gear.

With much of German armor deployed to southern Russia, it was October 2 before General Field Marshal Fedor Von Bock, commander of Army Group Center, received the order from Hitler to start the drive for Moscow. This caught the Russians by surprise because they had expected an advance during the summer, not in the fall with winter setting in. Although a half million Russian troops had been captured, German commanders were, in the backs of their minds, remembering Napoleon in the winter of 1812, and they were suggesting a halt and dig-in for the winter.

General Field Marshal Gerd Von Rundstedt, commander of Army Group South, agreed. Even General Field Marshal Wilhelm Von Leeb, commander of Army Group North, endorsed the plan. But with just Von Bock siding with Hitler, the offense was reinstated on November 15. The Germans had reached a point only twenty miles from Moscow, but they couldn't move another inch. The winter of 1941–42 was Europe's coldest winter in well over a century. With snow waist deep, temperatures plummeted to forty degrees below zero, which is the same for both Fahrenheit and Celsius.

German propaganda films showed the German Army advancing steadily, but letters home told an entirely different story. German troops were freezing to death or suffering from severe frostbite, and equipment refused to operate. Back in Germany, there was a mass winter clothing drive to do without so the troops at the front could have more. There was even a clothing confiscation drive in Norway, but with some trains being derailed before they even got to the front, the efforts made little difference.

And then Germany suffered even more setbacks. Field Marshal Walther Von Brauchitsch had a heart attack and asked to be relieved of command. The following week, Von Bock also asked to be relieved of command, and further into December, Von Leeb resigned after Hitler had rejected his request to withdraw his forces south of Leningrad. Hitler's solution to these setbacks was to appoint himself overall commander.

At dawn on December 6, the Russian counteroffensive started along a five-hundred-mile Moscow front. Marshal Georgy Zhukov was the architect of the entire Russian counterattack that is unimaginable by today's readers of war, particularly considering the subzero temperatures. The oil in General Guderian's (German) tanks actually froze. No foxholes could be dug because the ground was like steel. Even weapons refused to fire because of their fine tolerances in working parts. In colder conditions, however, Russian tolerances were greater and presented fewer problems.

General Heinz Guderian would eventually fall out of favor with Hitler as well. During the final drive on Moscow, the Russians counterattacked with severe losses to the Germans.

Guderian had requested to withdraw his forces, and when Hitler ordered him to stand fast, Guderian disobeyed the order and ordered withdrawals anyway. By December 26, he, too, was relieved of his command.

Because Germany had underestimated the Russians, the weather played a large part in the defeat of the Germans. Hitler, of course, blamed his generals for misadvising him as to the duration of operations. In the end, Germany would lose two-thirds of her army manpower in Russia to the harsh weather alone.

Returning to events in the Pacific, Japan's attack on Pearl Harbor was to be coordinated with simultaneous attacks on Malaya and the Philippines, which had originally been scheduled for 5:45 at Hawaii. But Admiral Nagumo's pilots feared complications from takeoffs in the dark, so departure was delayed for two hours. Because the forces landing in Malaya never got the word, the Japanese troops landed on schedule in the dark, a full two hours before Pearl Harbor was attacked.

In the Philippines, General MacArthur received the warning sent at noon by Marshall, to which he did not respond. Three hours later, Marshall sent another message ordering MacArthur to initiate war plan Rainbow Five, and to cooperate with British and Dutch forces to the extent that it would not interfere with his primary responsibilities. He didn't answer that message either. Washington now imagined that the reason for no response was that the Philippines were under attack. On Stimson's order, a third message was sent to MacArthur to "reply immediately."[31] Now at Marshall's direction, General Gerow made a direct call to MacArthur, who offered no excuses for not keeping Washington advised, and "No,"[32] he had not been attacked. But he had received word of Pearl Harbor at his hotel at 3:30 that morning from Sutherland, and shortly after from Hart. No attack had come to the Philippines yet because the Japanese were grounded on Formosa by heavy fog.

Admiral Hart's headquarters had monitored the "Air raid Pearl Harbor, this is no drill" alarm, and received a follow-up message from Kimmel informing him, "Japan has started hostilities."[33] And yet MacArthur neglected to respond to three messages from Washington and had to be personally called to confirm he had received them. Now, all Hart's navy could do was wait.

General Brereton had been awakened at 4:00, and by 5:00 was in MacArthur's outer office, asking for permission to go to war by launching his B-17s for a strike on Formosa. Sutherland responded by authorizing him only to prepare for war, but to stay on the ground. At 7:15, Brereton was back in Sutherland's office demanding to see MacArthur, who was actually in and alone. The answer was still, "No."[34] There was not sufficient data on Formosan targets to justify an attack. Any lack of target information was because MacArthur had not authorized reconnaissance flights. Previously, he had authorized flights north only to the International Treaty Line, which would only put them in view of Formosa but accomplish nothing. For now, the Americans could only attack when they themselves were attacked. Somehow, the Japanese strike at Pearl Harbor didn't seem to count, and after all, the Philippines were not the United States. Although Brereton did issue an order for three B-17s to make a photoreconnaissance flight to Formosa, the actual origin of that order is not clear.

It was during the preparation for the reconnaissance mission that Brereton received a call from General Arnold in Washington. The destruction of the American air force in Hawaii had prompted the call, warning Brereton not to get caught on the ground. The only bright spot had been that on Brereton's order the night before, sixteen of his B-17s, in an effort to disperse them, had been ordered to the new airfield at Del Monte on Mindanao. On Monday morning, many of the balance of his remaining bombers were ordered into the air just to get them off the ground, while Brereton waited for MacArthur's order to do something.

Admiral Kimmel would be held in judgment for an attack that he did not know was coming, but the absence of leadership in the Philippines, when it was known that an attack was expected, is incomprehensible. After the war, General MacArthur would insist that Brereton had never recommended an attack on Formosa, which he further insisted would have failed in any account for lack of target intelligence and fighter protection for that distance. But that is why the B-17s were there. They constituted the best and only offensive weapon. There were those in Washington, including the president, who had originally insisted that the B-17s be sent to Britain. If there were no plans for them in the Philippines, it was the duty of the overall commander to insist on one. And MacArthur would later maintain that it was his idea to send some of the aircraft to Del Monte. Yet it was understood that for any offensive action, the B-17s would have to return to Clark for fuel and maintenance. Recognizing that Clark would have to be defended, Brereton had ordered fifty-four of his fighters into the air with thirty-six being held in reserve.[35] They saw nothing.

On Formosan airfields, five hundred miles to the north, over two hundred more Japanese aircraft were waiting, all gassed up and armed, and the pilots prepared with target photos.[36] With engines warm, the planes were just sitting on the ramps waiting for the heavy fog to lift. Their attack on the Philippines and Malaya was supposed to be timed to the Pearl Harbor attack. And what was worse, the weather over their targets was forecast to be beautiful, which most certainly meant that upon hearing of the attack on Pearl Harbor, the American B-17s were at this moment flying toward Formosa to catch them on the ground with full gas tanks. It could have been a Pearl Harbor in reverse, a perfect opportunity for the Americans, but where were they? At any moment, bombs may come whistling down through the overcast, but there was nothing.

As the morning passed, the fog over Formosa lifted, and by 10:15, all aircraft were in the air headed for Luzon, still expecting to encounter the Americans coming from the other way, which would complicate matters.

At about 9:30, the radar station at Iba, west of Clark Field, reported a large formation of enemy aircraft approaching from the north. The U.S. fighters were scrambled to cover both Clark Field and Manila. But the Japanese formation suddenly banked to the left and bombed the Philippine summer capital at Baguio, some distance to the north. There had been no interception, and the Japanese had escaped their first major attack unscathed.

As the American fighters were being recalled, Brereton again called Sutherland. Either the B-17s had to go to war or they would be destroyed on the ground. The reconnaissance mission to Formosa was now authorized. All B-17s were ordered back to Clark to refuel. The phone rang. MacArthur now authorized bombing missions to Formosa. Upon return, the B-17s were gassed up and bombed up for a 2 p.m. departure for Formosa. By now it was almost noon and ten hours since the Oahu attack.

Years later, General Sutherland would insist that all B-17s had been ordered to Del Monte with a plan to bomb Formosa, using Clark as a fuel stop. But it was Brereton who insisted on photos first. Holding the bombers at Clark Field that first day, according to Sutherland, was all Brereton's decision.

At about 11:20, Iba called again and reported the approach of another big attack. The fighters were again scrambled from neighboring fields, but once in the air, they were vectored toward Manila.

It was exactly 12:35 when personnel at Clark Field looked up to the sounds of approaching aircraft. There were two waves. In the first, there were fifty-three medium bombers and thirty-four Zero fighters, followed by fifty-three Zeroes in the second wave.[37] Everyone ran for cover and watched helplessly as the pride of the American air force was reduced to skeletons. It ended as fast as it had started, with MacArthur's heavy, long-range punch suffering total defeat in its first encounter.

As with the attack on Pearl Harbor, the Japanese controlled the sky, destroying 50 percent of American bomber and fighter strength. From the start, any intended offensive of American missions against Japanese shipping wound up to be more defensive in nature.

Typical of the odds was the example of just one B-17 on just one mission in an attempt to slow down the Japanese landings at Legaspi, southeast of Manila. While over the target area, First Lieutenant Hewitt Wheless was attacked by eighteen Japanese fighters. One of his crew members was killed, and two were wounded. A gear-up crash landing was imminent to try to save the lives of the wounded aboard. Wheless made a night belly landing on unfamiliar terrain on a field scattered with obstacles to prevent Japanese landings. On inspection, the aircraft had over a thousand bullet holes, and Wheless was awarded the Distinguished Service Cross for this action.

Japan's attack on the Philippines provided Lieutenant Buzz Wagner of the Seventeenth Squadron the distinction of becoming the Americans' first flying ace of World War II. By December 18, and flying a P-40, which is less agile than a Zero, he would bring down his fifth enemy fighter while destroying many more Japanese planes on the ground, earning himself the Distinguished Service Cross as well.

Six hours had passed since the Japanese had attacked the Philippines, and Washington still had not been informed of the disaster. General Marshall, totally unaware of what had occurred, sent another message to MacArthur: "Request report on operations and results."[38] This was followed by a message from General Arnold: "Reports of Japanese attacks all show that numbers of our planes [referring to Pearl Harbor] have been destroyed on the ground. Take all possible steps at once to avoid such losses in your area including dispersion to maximum possible extent, construction of parapets and prompt takeoff on warning."[39]

Then finally to Marshall, MacArthur reported his interpretation: "Experienced heavy attack by fifty-two, two-engine bombers at high altitude coordinated with forty dive bombers. Damage heavy and casualties reported at about twenty-three dead, two hundred wounded. Our air losses heavy and enemy air losses medium. Now have available seventeen heavy bombers, fifty to fifty-five P-forty and fifteen P-thirty fives. Am launching a heavy bombardment counter attack tomorrow morning on enemy airdromes in southern Formosa."[40]

And to Arnold, it would take MacArthur two days to respond. It took time to compose an alibi for getting caught on the ground, ten hours after the attack on Oahu, especially with all of the warnings. But he insisted that he had exercised every precaution considering the limited time and reserves that were available. His aviators had "fought from fields not yet developed and under improvised conditions ... and under the severest handicaps."[41] Although he defended his pilots, he was not able to answer the most important question: when on full alert with ten hours to prepare, and being notified in advance of the approach of an enemy formation, how had he gotten caught with all those aircraft on the ground?

General Claire Chennault, legendary leader of the Flying Tigers, who had gone to the aid of Chiang Kai-shek in 1941, later wrote: "If I had been caught with my planes on the ground, I could never have looked my fellow officers in the eye. The lightness of which this cardinal sin was excused by the American High Command has always seemed to me one of the shocking defects of the war."[42]

The air force that Washington had pinned its hopes on to save the Philippines had vanished within thirty minutes. Yet MacArthur was later promoted to four stars in December, and Sutherland was promoted to two stars. In the interest of saving the remaining American aircraft in the Philippines to fight another day, fourteen B-17s took off from Del Monte and relocated to Australia.

If MacArthur was not being taken to task, General Brereton would be. On December 11, Brereton received an irate call from General Arnold in Washington. Even by then, Washington had not been fully informed of what had happened, and clearly, Arnold thought it was Brereton's fault that so many planes had been destroyed. "How in the hell could an experienced airman like you get caught with your planes on the ground?"[43] After all, the reason they had sent Brereton to the Philippines was to avoid that very situation. Brereton asked Arnold to withhold his judgment until he received the final report, confirming to him that he had "done everything in our power to get authority to attack Formosa on 8 December but had been relegated to a 'strictly defensive attitude' by higher authority."[44]

After the call, Brereton met with MacArthur, asking him to call Hap Arnold to set the record straight. What actually transpired in that phone call is not known. In Brereton's final meeting with MacArthur, however, before leaving for Australia on December 24, MacArthur's parting words to him were, "I hope you will tell the people outside what we have done and protect my reputation as a fighter."[45] Whether or not Brereton held any animosity toward MacArthur for the catastrophe in the Philippines, he responded, "General, your reputation will never need any protection."[46] A good response, considering that Brereton, too, could have been scapegoated for the disaster in the Philippines, as Kimmel and Short would be for the disaster at Hawaii.

Brereton would later attribute the downfall of the Philippines to lack of security and mobility, adding that had the war plans to reinforce the Philippines not been delayed, additional air bases would have allowed for plane dispersion, and concluding that even a few months' delay would have entirely upset the Japanese attack schedule. "So long as we held the Philippines and had a heavy bomber force intact, it would have been extremely hazardous for the Japs to by-pass them, leaving an air force remaining on their flank and rear."[47]

The question of MacArthur's defense plan for the Philippines may never be resolved. President Quezon reportedly told Dwight Eisenhower in 1942 that it was MacArthur who had hoped that the Philippines could remain neutral. Yet MacArthur himself stated that there was no question that the Philippines would be attacked. If this is true, why was no offensive action taken against the Japanese during their bombing raids prior to the invasion?

Reflecting on the blunder in the Philippines, it is important to look at MacArthur's defense strategy. He had rejected the defensive nature of War Plan Orange-3 and Rainbow 5, which focused on defensive measures for Central Luzon only, with the ultimate goal to hold Manila Bay and delay any Japanese landings. Defense plans for the Philippines were in existence long before MacArthur returned to the islands. The most updated revision of War Plan Orange-3 (WPO-3) of April 1941 was the ideal plan for what was available.

The plan required American troops to defend Central Luzon in the Manila Bay area, preventing enemy landings. Failing to do this, the troops were to defeat the enemy troops that had landed. And failing to do this, they were to fight a delaying action while withdrawing to the Bataan Peninsula, still controlling Manila Bay. Of importance, this plan did not contemplate the use of the Philippine Army from any of the Philippine Islands.

The success of the plan required the withdrawal of massive supplies from the Manila warehouses for transport to Bataan to feed thirty-one thousand men for six months.[48] It would be up to the native Filipino-American defenders to fight a delaying action and to protect the long roads, keeping them open for the supply transports.

There was no stipulation as to what would happen after the defenders were defeated. It was just assumed that in that time, the U.S. Pacific Fleet would have fought its way through to the rescue and would drive the enemy into the sea. And yet no one in authority ever thought that this would happen, because the estimate was two years for the U.S. Navy just to fight its way across the Pacific. There was no plan to relieve Bataan, since the assumption was that it would just go down in defeat.

MacArthur had the answer: transform the WPO-3 defeatist plan into a victory plan. Being an optimist or a dreamer, he convinced his subordinate commanders and the War Department in Washington that the Philippines could resist an enemy attack. From his date of recall to active duty in the U.S. Army, he thought only of replacing WPO-3 with his own plan.

The Philippine Army had one regular division and ten reserve divisions. Because WPO-3 depended on troops already there, MacArthur told Washington that a two-hundred-thousand-man Philippine army was just around the corner in inscription and training.[49] The numbers and the degree of training were greatly exaggerated.

With Washington approval presumed, he organized Luzon into two forces: the north Luzon force, under the leadership of Major General Jonathan Wainwright; and the southern force, under the leadership of Major General George Parker, Jr. Similar to Wainwright's fate, Parker would also be taken prisoner after the fall of Bataan. Surviving his internments in Formosa and Manchuria, he was released in August 1945 and retired shortly after his return to the United States.

MacArthur's plan was to defeat the enemy on the invasion beaches. There would be no withdrawal to Bataan. His generals were to hold the beach areas at all costs. And when the invasion started, artillery and light tanks were rushed to the one-hundred-twenty-mile Lingayen coastline to defend against General Homma's Fourteenth Army. The trained Philippine Army that MacArthur had boasted to Washington about, broke and ran at the first appearance of the Japanese.

MacArthur's reported estimate of enemy strength was seventy to eighty troop transports discharging eighty to one hundred thousand troops, and yet he reported that his defense only consisted of forty thousand troops.[50] Later, when all the facts were available, the Japanese at Lingayen only numbered about forty thousand, while MacArthur had considerably more troops than what he reported. There were twelve thousand, Philippine scouts and seven native army reserve divisions that had been inducted into U.S. service. Strategists and intelligence experts have numbered MacArthur's troop level at an estimated sixty-five to seventy thousand.[51]

As the situation continued to worsen, MacArthur was finally forced to abandon his own plan and revert to the original Orange Plan. This called for the organized retreat to the Bataan

Peninsula. This situation was the result of his having put too much confidence in the Philippine Army and its reserve. Their performance was poor from the beginning, but MacArthur had always refused to admit that.

On December 23, the April 1941 version of WPO-3 was put back into effect. Now the big problem involved the supplies. Under the Orange Plan, supplies were to start moving to Bataan from the Manila warehouses when the first shot was fired. But under MacArthur's plan, supplies were moving all over to meet each situation. Now with MacArthur and President Quezon moving to Corregidor, Brigadier General Charles Drake, the Manila quartermaster, was ordered to first send supplies for ten thousand troops to last six months to Corregidor before sending anything to Bataan.[52]

Now MacArthur violated his own chain of command when he failed to inform Admiral Hart immediately of the change in the war plan actually in effect. Manila would be declared an open city, and Hart had submarines moored in Manila Bay that had to move fast.

Although MacArthur and Hart had been friends for several decades, their relationship became severely strained during their service in the Philippines. Technically, Hart outranked MacArthur with his four stars to MacArthur's three, and it was thought by some that MacArthur resented this. In any event, he failed to communicate any of the army's activities to Hart, violating the Joint Coastal Frontier Defense Plan that the Hawaiian commanders had drafted. And in spite of Hart's efforts to work with MacArthur, there was no coordination of defense efforts between the army and the navy in the Philippines. By the time Hart learned on December 24 that Manila would be declared an open city, he had a mere twenty-four hours to prepare for evacuation himself, and was forced to leave behind many supplies and ordnance.

MacArthur did inform General Brereton that he (Brereton) would evacuate to Australia by navy PBY. By now, his air force had been destroyed with only a few fighters remaining on Bataan. Brereton offered to stay, but was told he would be of more value in Australia. For Bataan, the rest is history.

War Plan Orange was based, however, on a situation that never came to pass. It was conceived of a war between the United States and Japan alone. Neither side would have allies or attack territory of a third power. It would be a naval war. The plan had been adopted in 1924, when the Americans saw Japan as their most likely enemy.

Toward the late 1930s, Japan had joined Germany and Italy in the Anti-Comintern Pact. Great Britain and France, still suffering from the depression of the early 1930s, both considered appeasement as an alternative to armed conflict. It was February 18, 1938, before the American strategic planners even considered the possibility of the necessity of fighting on two fronts. But an offensive war against Japan would take priority to defend American interests in the Pacific, primarily a naval war.

The Naval War Plans Division in December 1937 sent then Captain Royal Ingersoll to London to discuss potential arrangements of American-British naval cooperation. Concerns about Germany and Italy would require Britain to retain the bulk of her naval forces in the Mediterranean and Atlantic with little or nothing to protect her possessions in the Pacific. The United States would concentrate the bulk of her naval forces in the Pacific with a lightened load in the Atlantic. This would become the basis of the Anglo-American relationship of cooperation during World War II.

In the event of a two-ocean threat, the United States would go on the defensive in the Pacific and prioritize defense of vital positions between the Americas, the Panama Canal, and the Caribbean area. This would be easy if Britain and France were united in the eastern Atlantic, but if they were not, a much larger force would be required to defend American access to either ocean. And who would the American allies be?

All in all, the Joint Army and Navy Board of the war planning division arrived at five possibilities, or five Rainbow Plans, each plan dealing with a different situation. The only commonality in the plans was that the United States would face a coalition of nations and not just one. Rainbow 5 was the plan whereby, if not attacked by Japan, the United States would declare war on Japan to protect Malaya, Singapore, and the Dutch East Indies, to protect rubber and oil resources. It called for aggressive moves against the Marshall and Caroline Islands and Truk. The purpose was to get into Britain's war with Germany.

Nonetheless, MacArthur was determined to keep the Japanese out of the Philippines altogether. But in spite of his accurate prophecy of where the Japanese would land, and with two days' advance intelligence that they were coming, as well as nine hours' notice of Pearl Harbor, he still wasn't prepared when the Japanese did arrive. For the Japanese, the only difficulty was rough seas.

Because Washington's WPO-3 plan had been built around American withdrawal to the Bataan Peninsula, it was essential to get supplies there as soon as the Japanese initially attacked. But because MacArthur had convinced Washington to allow changes to WPO-3 to meet his grandiose plans, many of the supplies had been diverted to the beachheads, supplies that were badly needed in the Battle of Bataan in the early months of 1942.

General MacArthur's plan to defend all of the Philippines officially fell apart on December 22, when he finally realized that he was not even going to be able to defend Luzon. This was something Washington had understood since they drew up WPO-3 in 1938.

So on December 22, the Quezon government was alerted to prepare for a move to Corregidor by the next evening, and MacArthur notified his field commanders that the original WPO-3 was now in effect. This only allowed two days to get all the remaining supplies out of the Manila warehouses that should have already been safely on Bataan. They should have been moved prior to declaring Manila an open city, which, with the Japanese at the edge of town, was an attempt to save Philippine lives.

Another instance of MacArthur's questionable leadership occurred when Colonel Harold George, General Clagett's chief of staff, ordered planes out on a mission without the authorization from MacArthur, who was very upset about things happening on the initiative of his subordinate commanders. He raised hell until he was informed of the damage inflicted on the Japanese. Just to get back at his subordinates, he composed a dispatch describing the raid, giving himself credit for its planning and its execution by Philippine pilots, who had long since run out of airplanes. MacArthur had full authority over junior commanders in the field, which actually encumbered or restricted operations, while his dramatic and fictitious press releases from his public relations personnel painted the picture that he alone was carrying the load for Japanese failure for a quick victory. The participation of the U.S. Army was incidental.

Nor was MacArthur above misleading his commanders in Washington. On January 26, he gave Washington the impression that he himself was on Bataan rather than at his house on Corregidor, as evidenced by this message: "In Luzon: Under cover of darkness I broke contact with the enemy and without the loss of a man or an ounce of materiel am now firmly established on my main battle position."[53]

By February 1942, the situation on Bataan had deteriorated significantly. Up to 80 percent of the defenders were suffering from malaria, respiratory infections, and malnutrition. Quinine was now just a memory. Bandages and gauze were washed out and used over again. And toward the end, it was common not to eat for a week. If wounded, it was just as dangerous to be admitted to the field hospitals, as they were the primary targets of the Japanese.

One field hospital with only four hundred fifty beds found itself overwhelmed in just a few days with fifteen hundred patients, all lying out in the sun. Yet the valiant army nurses worked around the clock, themselves with little food or sleep. They were considered among the real heroes.

In addition to fighting the enemy, the Quartermaster Corps was fighting the food shortage. Behind the lines, they threshed and milled rice, slaughtered the remaining animals, snared what fish they could, and distilled water for its salt. The worst part of meat was cut off and the balance cooked. But eventually they ran out of everything, and the troops were worn down to living skeletons. In the States, all would have been hospitalized, but on Bataan, they were considered fit for duty if they were strong enough to pull the trigger. By comparison, the Japanese were tested, rested, and under orders to finish the job.

General MacArthur would later recommend unit citations for all army units on Bataan and Corregidor, but none for the Marines. His only comment was that the Marines had gotten their share of glory in World War I and weren't going to get any in this one. Ironically, they were the only ones with combat experience, having arrived from Shanghai just days before Pearl Harbor. MacArthur never authorized any visits to Marine units on Bataan, nor did he visit their beach positions on Corregidor.

With such a bleak outlook for Bataan, President Roosevelt ordered MacArthur in February to get out of the Philippines and over to Australia. On March 11, MacArthur left Corregidor's north dock, leaving behind thousands of Philippine and American troops to fight the Japanese. In less than one month, approximately ninety thousand troops on Bataan would surrender, making it one of the largest capitulations in American military history.[54]

It had just been assumed that MacArthur's existing staff would continue the defense of Bataan under General Wainwright. But MacArthur took thirteen army officers with him, and after his departure, in the eleventh hour, it was necessary to scramble to come up with an entirely new command staff. Secretary of War Henry Stimson would later write, "MacArthur, in a pretty complete disregard of everything except his own personal interests, had taken his entire staff away with him from Bataan, leaving Wainwright with the job of building up a new staff."[55]

In spite of the deteriorating and virtually unlivable conditions, MacArthur's last order to Wainwright was to hold on until he (MacArthur) would return with an army. The only ones thrilled at his departure were the Marines. And as far as the rest of those on Bataan were concerned, the captain had left the sinking ship with the only lifeboat available.

To add insult to injury, Wainwright's selection of the new staff didn't sit well with MacArthur, who complained to General Marshall in Washington, an effort that resolved nothing in MacArthur's favor. He had had only himself to blame. American newspapers were now referring to Bataan as the new Alamo.

Another issue inherited by Wainwright was in the neighborhood of three thousand pieces of paperwork left by MacArthur on Corregidor, all of which required action of one sort or another. Much of the paperwork concerned promotions that badly needed attention for morale purposes. It required a special task force to expedite it all.

Shortly after MacArthur's departure, Wainwright approached the staff on Corregidor for rations to ease the pain of starvation in the fighting men on Bataan. He was informed by General Lewis Beebe on March 15 that MacArthur had left specific instructions that no rations be sent to Bataan in the interest of Corregidor's holding out as long as possible.

MacArthur's press corps even made his Philippines departure appear to be a great military victory, though it essentially helped to doom those left behind. In his departure, he was authorized to take only his wife, his son, and his chief of staff, General Sutherland. He was not authorized to take the top thirteen army officers, who were personal friends, along with two naval officers (and one enlisted man), leaving behind the huge void of top leadership at a time when it was needed most.

MacArthur's egoism would play out not only in his departure from Corregidor, when he loaded unauthorized personnel into four PT boats for evacuation to Mindanao, but also with his flight to Australia. Four B-17s had left Australia for the trip to rescue Mac and his staff on Mindanao. Two had returned with mechanical problems and a third had crash landed en route. The fourth actually arrived with an inoperative supercharger and no brakes. And to MacArthur's further disappointment, the plane was piloted by a lieutenant who was not a field grade officer worthy of Mac's grade. Mac took one look at the plane's youthful pilot and

The view from the North Malinta tunnel entrance on Corregidor. Bataan can be seen across the channel.

An early 1960s photograph of the north dock from which MacArthur departed Corregidor by PT boat in early 1942.

announced "that he wouldn't risk his family in 'that broken down crate with a boy at the controls.'"[56] This "boy at the controls" departed that night for Australia with sixteen people packed into his B-17, none of whom were from MacArthur's group. Similar to his brakeless landing on Mindanao, they all arrived safely in Australia. This twenty-four-year-old, Harl Pease, Jr., would just five months later earn the Medal of Honor for heroism in the Battle of Rabaul.

MacArthur was now livid and sent a message to General Marshall in Washington to insist that the Australia command send three of their very best B-17s to pick up Mac and his staff. He further stated that he couldn't bear the thought of losing any of his key personnel to inadequate air transportation. In turn, Marshall notified General George Brett in Melbourne to help meet MacArthur's demands. Brett, who had previously served as acting chief of the air corps under Hap Arnold, was now in command of the U.S. Army's forces in Australia. Marshall ordered Brett to select the three best B-17s and to dispatch them to Mindinao for MacArthur's rescue, an order which was reluctantly agreed to. Of the three, one had to turn back because of an oil leak.

The two remaining aircraft were now being flown by captains, and on arrival on Mindinao, the decision was made that if all the baggage was left behind, everyone could squeeze into the two planes, but not before a couple of mattresses were made available in the navigator's compartment for Mac and his family. With everyone packed in, the two bombers took off and headed for Australia. On approach, they found that their destination at Darwin was under attack, requiring them to reroute to an alternate airfield. Upon landing, both the general and Mrs. MacArthur commented to the effect that they were in no hurry to fly again.

After the December 8 attack on the Philippines, Japan's next move had been to remove the British battle fleet at Singapore, as this was the last potential threat to Japanese expansion in the western Pacific. On December 8, Admiral Phillips departed Singapore with the *Prince of Wales* and the *Repulse* to thwart reported Japanese landings at Kota Bharu on the northeastern Malay Peninsula. As soon as he was spotted by the Japanese, Phillips realized the element of surprise was gone, and the operation was canceled. On the return trip to Singapore, and with no air support, the inevitable happened. At 11:40 on December 10, the ships were attacked by almost one hundred level, dive, and torpedo bombers launched from Saigon. Although valiantly defending themselves, both ships were eventually overwhelmed, and after an hour and a half, they went under. The friendly air support of British Buffalo fighters arrived just in time to witness the loss of over eight hundred British seamen along with their commander, Admiral Sir Tom Phillips.

Virtually overnight, Japan had removed all of the obstacles that could prevent her conquest of the western Pacific. Rarely has history witnessed such devastating success over such a large geographic area in such a short amount of time: the American battleships at Pearl Harbor, the U.S. offensive air power in the Philippines, and the British sea power in Malaya. The Japanese success, however, would prove to be her downfall in the strategic decision to expand on her lightning achievements. Japan attempted to broaden the Japanese Empire to include Midway, the Aleutians, India, and Australia as buffers for her dominion, but her enemies would not allow the conquest to continue, and the tides of the Pacific war would start to turn.

On December 8, 1941, FDR asked Congress for a declaration of war on Japan only. Unbelievably, Hitler postponed declaring war on the United States until December 11 because he wanted it to coincide with a speech he was going to deliver to the Reichstag, where he would hurl accusations and insults at FDR personally, blaming him for virtually everything that had taken place so far in the war. Hitler declared that Roosevelt, backed by the millionaires and the Jews, was a man of no conscience. He told members of the Reichstag that the Japanese had been trying to negotiate with this man for years and had finally given up.

Following Hitler's notification of war with the United States, Congress responded with a declaration of war with Germany on December 12, 1941.

In the not-too-distant future, the Battle of Midway would be a disaster difficult for the Japanese to comprehend. Within just six months of the Pearl Harbor attack, four of the six Japanese carriers employed in the attack, the *Akagi*, the *Kaga*, the *Soryu*, and the *Hiryu*, would go to the bottom of the ocean during their attack on Midway. Along with those pilots lost, many more would be lost in the defense of the Solomons. And with little or no reserves, this meant the end of Japanese sea power. The military manpower that remained lacked the needed combat skills, and they would become easy pickings for American air and sea power.

Through correspondence with Japanese veterans, the author learned that by the 1980s, of the 765 Japanese airmen in the sky over Oahu, only eighteen were still alive. By comparison, of the sixty-one American airmen to get airborne over Oahu that Sunday morning, forty were still alive.

There is no doubt that December 7, 1941, provided for Americans the incentive to produce planes, ships, tanks, and guns on a scale unimaginable just two years before. Pearl Harbor had galvanized the will and determination of the nation to ensure American victory under the slogan, "Remember Pearl Harbor."

Kimmel and Short, however, would be left with the image of failure in their Hawaiian commands. General Short would pass away in 1949 and Admiral Kimmel in 1968, while both were still carrying the burden of Pearl Harbor on their shoulders.

Chapter 10

Aftermath and Investigations

Within forty-eight hours of the attack on Pearl Harbor, Navy Secretary Frank Knox suggested to the president that Knox himself should go to Hawaii to see for himself what had happened and to determine who was responsible for the unpreparedness of the Hawaiian forces. Now that the country was officially at war, the administration hoped to head off any congressional investigation that could be embarrassing. By December 10, he was on his way, accompanied by his aide and two staff members. When their PB2Y Coronado departed North Island, San Diego, it was loaded down with medical supplies for Hawaii.

While they were en route, Guam had also fallen to the Japanese, and Kimmel was convinced that Wake Island would be next unless he could get his planned relief expedition launched immediately. With a distance of two thousand miles, there was no time to lose.

Upon landing in Kaneohe Bay, Knox was taken by all of the devastation. Kimmel assured Knox that it wouldn't have happened if he had had any warning and that presently, there was still danger of another attack. Knox retorted, "Did you get Saturday night the dispatch the navy department sent out?"[1] Kimmel responded that he had received nothing since the November 27 alert. Knox replied, "Well, we sent you one."[2] The same question was asked individually to Kimmel's staff members, all of whom knew only of the Marshall warning on Sunday afternoon that had arrived too late. Knox had apparently assumed that the president's statement, "This means war," would have been followed with a war warning, an assumption he made after attending the war council meeting late Saturday night on December 6.

In just thirty-two hours that included meetings with General Short and the Hawaiian territorial governor, Joseph Poindexter, Knox felt that he had gathered enough to report back to the president. (It was Governor Poindexter who, after the attack on Pearl Harbor, declared martial law, allowing the U.S. military to take over.) While in Hawaii, Knox had approved Kimmel's Wake Island operation and understood that a premature removal of Kimmel would sacrifice the mission. The first Japanese attack on Wake, just hours after the attack on Pearl Harbor, had failed, and they were reorganizing for the main thrust. Japan would now have to mount a much larger force to be able to finish the job. On a daily basis, Americans read of the island's heroic resistance. This would certainly vindicate Kimmel's plan to strengthen the island. No other commander could launch an expedition in time. Saving Wake Island could also save Kimmel's prestige and inspire a reputation as an aggressive commander.

In his report to the president, Knox was of the opinion that any blame for the success of the attack had to be shared equally between Kimmel and Short. The bulk of the blame, however, laid in the denial of U.S. Magic intelligence, as well as the lack of patrol aircraft and antiaircraft guns. He acknowledged that there had been "a lack of a state of readiness against such an air attack"[3] but also that neither of the Hawaiian commanders "had been privy to the Magic intercepts."[4] In his conclusion, Knox stated that "several factors were beyond the responsibility of the two commanders: Japanese fifth columnists and inadequate fighter planes and anti-aircraft guns."[5] This meant that Washington had failed. Knox realized that Kimmel would have to be relieved because his name was now associated with the disaster, but not before the Wake Island operation. Knox also recommended the creation of an official board of inquiry to investigate the attack. Next, he proposed realignment within the navy, creating the position of commander in chief of the U.S. Fleet, to be filled by Admiral King, currently the Atlantic Fleet commander, thus reducing the authority of Admiral Stark's role as chief of naval operations.

President Roosevelt, on December 16, made the arguable decision to replace Kimmel, Short, and General Frederick Martin, effective immediately, rather than allowing them to continue with their wartime leadership roles while they were the subjects of an investigation. Was Roosevelt assuming guilt before the facts were even in?

At a press conference convened to answer America's demand to know what had happened at Pearl Harbor, Knox assured the American people, "In the Navy's greatest hour of peril, the officers and men of the fleet exhibited magnificent courage and resourcefulness."[6] Then came the blow that "the services were not on the alert against surprise attack."[7] He continued that the president was going to commence a complete investigation, and that no action would be taken against the Hawaiian commanders until "the facts and recommendations made by this investigating board,"[8] meaning the Roberts Commission, were in. Didn't the fact that the commanders were immediately relieved of their duties automatically imply their guilt to the American people?

The president's choice would be the investigative board consisting of two army officers and two navy officers, presided over by Justice Owen Roberts, an associate justice of the Supreme Court. How could a justice of the Supreme Court preside over a kangaroo court that would predetermine guilt before the investigation had even opened?

Justice Owen Roberts had established his reputation during the 1920s when he was appointed by the U.S. Attorney General's office to investigate the bribery that had taken place during the Teapot Dome Scandal. President Herbert Hoover was so impressed with his work that he later appointed Roberts to the Supreme Court in 1930. Although Roberts was the only Republican serving on the court during World War II, he believed in broader government powers, and as an interventionist, he became one of Roosevelt's strongest supporters in the aid to Britain and U.S. involvement in the war. As journalist and political commentator John Flynn would write in 1945, even though Justice Roberts was a Republican, Roosevelt's appointment of Roberts to head the investigation "was a master stroke. What the public overlooked was that Roberts had been one of the most clamorous among those screaming for an open declaration of war."[9] And because of this, Flynn said that Roberts could be counted on not to "cast any stain upon it in its infancy."[10]

The four members of the commission constituted a stacked deck: Major General Frank McCoy, a trusted aide of General Marshall; Brigadier General Joseph McNarney of the Army Air Corps, ambitious and desperate for promotion, who was also recommended by Marshall; Admiral William Standley, a former chief of naval operations; and Rear Admiral Joseph

Reeves, who had left retirement to preside over the navy's involvement with Lend-Lease. With the exception of Standley, the others all owed favors to the administration.

Sitting on the sidelines with the rest of America was former President Hoover, who had been a good friend of General McCoy's. When McCoy was appointed to the Roberts Commission, Hoover dropped him a note to congratulate him. And at the same time, he asked McCoy if the State Department had adequately warned the Hawaiian commanders of the potential repercussions of the Hull Note. Hoover added, "Now the only reason why I write this is the feeling that some Admiral or some General in the Pacific may be made a goat for action or lack of action higher up, and thus a great injustice done."[11]

The provost marshal of the Roberts Commission, a Marine colonel, had little legal experience, and the court recorder had no experience of any sort. Secretaries Knox and Stimson held an initial meeting with the members of the Roberts Commission to predetermine their mission and to set the guidelines for the investigation. Specifically, no fault could be found with Washington. As Roberts would later testify during the joint congressional investigation of 1945–46, his role was not to question the president or his cabinet members, but to limit the investigation to the army and navy only.

The investigation convened before all members of the commission were even present. Admiral Standley had been delayed en route to Washington, and interviewing had commenced in his absence even before determining the guidelines. Three days were devoted to interviews in Washington, which were meaningless as no guilt was to be cast on those at the Capitol.

The commission then moved to Hawaii, where they installed themselves at the Royal Hawaiian Hotel. Anyone was invited to testify. The atmosphere was anything but that of a legal environment. Principles of justice were totally disregarded, and unbelievably, Admiral Kimmel and General Short were denied the benefit of counsel. Nor were they allowed to hear the testimony of other witnesses. They not only could not cross-examine any witnesses, but they had absolutely no idea of what the evidence was.

Rear Admiral Theobald was permitted to assist because Kimmel was not allowed counsel. He would later write that not only were the defendants unable to defend themselves, the hired recorder staff was so inept that when Kimmel's testimony was shown to him for verification, it was full of errors, and in some cases, passages were unintelligible. Kimmel's documentation was not identified, and significant sections of his testimony had even been omitted. Questions and their respective answers made absolutely no sense. How could a commission with these standards be placed in a position with the authority to judge?

Kimmel and Theobald spent two days trying to restore some degree of accuracy to Kimmel's testimony, and when they were finished, they submitted it to the recorder, who advised them that no changes would be authorized. Attempts to explain that these were not changes, but corrections to clarify the record, a record that was inaccurate and incomprehensible, fell on deaf ears. They now submitted the corrections to Admiral Standley, who told them, again, that no changes could be made. But Standley relented to the point of allowing notations of the errors to be placed in an appendix. It was stressed to no avail that it would be far more difficult for a reader to reconstruct Kimmel's testimony if he had to continually refer to an appendix, but there would be no reconsideration.

Standley insisted that nothing could be done, as Justice Roberts would not alter his decision. Admiral Theobald reiterated that all Kimmel was looking for was that he be treated in the same manner as he would be in a military court. What was the purpose of the commission if its four members couldn't overrule the chairman's decision? It was clear that Justice Roberts was calling all the shots. Admiral Standley's answer to Theobald's concerns was surprisingly blunt: "Admiral Kimmel and you are under no illusions about what is going to happen to him as a result of this investigation, are you?"[12] Theobald acquiesced that the verdict was in before the jury had even deliberated.

When Admiral Kimmel and General Short were charged with failing to consult with one another on the November 27 war warning and for not changing the existing plans to meet the impending attack, Theobald stressed that these charges were unfounded because they did not specifically indicate what the "orders, warnings [and] plans"[13] were. As Kimmel would later explain:

> The conflicting and confusing orders sent to General Short and to me is best illustrated by the indictments in the findings of the Commission which states that General Short and I did not consult as to the meaning of the warning messages received. Aside from the fact that we did confer both before and after the receipt of the message, it is a strange doctrine that would require the admiral commanding the Pacific Fleet to consult with the commanding general at Hawaii to determine the meaning of a message from the Chief of Naval Operations and equally ridiculous to require the commanding general at Hawaii to consult with the commander of the Pacific Fleet to determine the meaning of a message sent to him by the Army Chief of Staff. Yet this was the principle indictment used by the Roberts Commission in their attempt to fasten the blame for the Pearl Harbor disaster upon General Short and me. The mere statement that such a consultation was necessary to determine the meaning of an order is an indictment of the agency which originated it.[14]

In addition, Kimmel could not understand how, in Justice Roberts's opinion, Magic intercepts were incidental to the investigation. Justice Roberts would later tell the congressional committee of 1945–46 that had such intercepts been presented, he probably would not have read them. How could a thorough investigation of the attack or an accurate allocation of responsibility be made without an understanding of the Magic intercepts, and equally important, of their distribution prior to the event?

When a copy of a particular Pacific Fleet confidential letter was mentioned for reference, not one man on the five-man commission could find it. When Kimmel ordered an additional five copies for the members, the flag secretary informed him that this would make a total of seventeen copies that he had made, an example of the board's lack of attention to detail. Yet at the same time, while Kimmel and Short were only required to answer questions but not allowed to cross-examine witnesses, they were being assured that they themselves were not on trial, but only serving as witnesses.

At the same time, the commission found no fault in how the secretaries of state and war and the senior military leadership in Washington had fulfilled their duties with respect to Pearl Harbor. Had Washington been included in the one-sided investigation, how could General Marshall and Admiral Stark have avoided charges of denying intelligence to Hawaii and not ordering the activation of the Joint Coastal Frontier Defense Plan, unless they themselves were under orders from their commander in chief, the president?

The interviews and testimony moved from the Royal Hawaiian Hotel to Fort Shafter and eventually back to Washington, where one by one, the brass testified that Hawaii had received as much intelligence as Washington had had prior to the attack, attempting to reduce their involvement and to magnify Hawaii's errors.

Although the existence of Magic was known to the Roberts Commission, it was totally left out of its report to the president. By the end of January, Justice Roberts had completed the investigation and submitted his report to the president who, upon study, was convinced that there was no evidence of responsibility by the army or navy that could cast a shadow on members of his administration.

The commission's attempts to persuade Americans that only Kimmel and Short were responsible did not fly with everyone, namely the press. After the conclusions of the Roberts Commission were published, several newspapers protested that further investigation was required. *The Washington Times-Herald* demanded that Congress "fix due guilt for negligence where it belongs"[15]; the *New York Times* wrote that the Roberts Report "seemed too sweeping in exculpating their superiors in Washington from blame and in too easily finding that each of these 'fulfilled his obligations'"[16]; and the *New York Tribune* alleged, "The want of foresight at Pearl Harbor was paralleled higher up."[17] As Admiral Standley, who had served on the Roberts Commission, would later point out, the report did contain true statements, "but the many sins of omission in the picture were omitted from our findings because the President in his executive order setting up the Commission had specifically limited its jurisdiction."[18]

It is also interesting to note that during the joint congressional investigation of 1945–46, Justice Owen Roberts had been asked why the printed version of the Roberts Report had amounted to only 1,862 pages when the original, oral version had totaled 1,887 pages.[19] He could not justify the discrepancy. Had the American public actually gotten all the facts?

Meanwhile, with the removal of Kimmel, Short, and Martin on December 16, Admiral Pye, Kimmel's second in command, took temporary command of the Pacific Fleet the following day until its permanent commander, Admiral Chester Nimitz, arrived. Kimmel had been assured that he'd get another command. In his December 29 letter to Kimmel, Admiral Stark wrote, "Don't worry about our finding duty for you. I value your services as much as I ever did and more and I say this straight from the heart as well as the head."[20] But the handwriting was on the wall, and Kimmel would be forced into retirement within a month. And along with Short, the two became scapegoats for Washington's failures.

As suspected, Admiral Pye, as temporary commander, was not going to stick his neck out in an attempted reinforcement of Wake Island, which, if it failed, would put him in the same predicament as Kimmel. Reinforcements were to be supplied Wake Island by means of Task Force 11 under the command of Rear Admiral Frank Fletcher. At the center of Fletcher's task force was the *Saratoga*, which had been ordered from San Diego the day Pearl Harbor was attacked. Sailing on December 8, and loaded with Grumman fighters, Douglas dive bombers, Douglas torpedo bombers, and Brewster Buffalo fighters, the *Saratoga* reached Pearl Harbor on December 15. After refueling, it headed for Wake Island on December 16.

Admiral Pye, who was more of an administrative admiral, had served on the staff of the Atlantic Fleet's commander in chief during most of World War I and had never seen any combat action. Because the wheels had already been put in motion to reinforce Wake Island, Pye had no choice but to go along with the plan. But he had his own plan, which was more conservative. In what would become the most hotly debated issue in the defense of Wake Island, Admiral Pye ordered Admiral Fletcher's relief force to refuel at sea when it did not need refueling.

It delayed the help that the island desperately needed in its dying throes. On December 23, the day of Wake Island's surrender to the Japanese, it was still being argued to continue an attack that had already been canceled. Even the seaplane tender *Tangier*, a Pearl Harbor survivor, would attempt an unescorted sortie to Wake to try to rescue survivors, but this effort, too, was canceled. Just before the island formally surrendered, Pye timed his recall of the task force back to Pearl Harbor. If Kimmel had been allowed to retain his command, for even just another ten days, Wake would have been the Americans' first victory in the Pacific, later claimed at the Battle of Midway.

Over a year and a half had passed since the Roberts Commission published their conclusions and Kimmel was more determined than ever to clear himself. Toward the end of 1943, he enlisted the services of a retired navy captain, Robert Lavender. Being a patent attorney, Lavender advised Kimmel that he was not qualified to adequately represent him, but he would assist if he could. And instead, he referred Kimmel to a Boston attorney, Charles Rugg, who had served as assistant attorney general during the early 1930s in the Hoover administration. Around the same time, late 1943, Navy Secretary Frank Knox had given Kimmel the approval to review the navy's records relevant to Pearl Harbor.

Unbeknownst to Kimmel, Captain Safford, who was still with OP-20-G in December 1941, was also doing his homework. Thinking that Kimmel and Short would, at some point, be court-martialed, and thinking he might be called as a witness, he started reviewing the Magic decryption files to refresh his memory. Reviewing the Roberts Commission report as well, he realized what little intelligence had actually been sent to the Pearl Harbor commanders prior to the attack. Understanding now that Kimmel and Short had been scapegoated, he, too, became more determined than ever to set the record straight.

With Knox's authorization, Robert Lavender, who was assisting Rugg, took on the task of going through the navy records. Although Safford had prompted him on what to look for, Lavender was astounded at the "stack of papers two and a half feet high of intercepted messages."[21] Pulling over forty messages he thought relevant to Kimmel's defense, he said he had become "nauseated when I realized what the information in my hands would have meant to Kimmel and the men of the Fleet who died."[22] Lavender shared the information later on with Edward Hanify, another attorney assigned to Kimmel's defense team. Hanify described his disgust, wondering "why the highest leaders of the government of the United States reading the most secret designs of their potential enemy would keep this material from trusting and loyal commanders at the distant, lonely, and inadequately protected bastions of defense with the lives of my fellow citizens in the armed forces at risk."[23]

By February of 1944, the demands of the war were still all-consuming. In the effort to head off any statute of limitations involving court-martials, and to avoid any loss of evidence, Admiral Thomas Hart, former Asiatic Fleet commander now retired, was called by Secretary Knox to gather information to keep the Pearl Harbor issue open until the army and navy could conduct their own inquiries. Hart and his command had experienced the shock waves of Pearl Harbor, and he would make no conclusions or recommendations. As most of Kimmel and Short's immediate staff and subordinate personnel were sent overseas immediately after the attack, where they would not be available for comment or testimony, it would be important to have such a record if need be. It was during the Hart Investigation of 1944 that Admiral Turner, in his testimony, would defend the inactions of Washington, stating that it was the policy of the chief of naval operations "not to nag on matters of that sort,"[24] justifying the few messages sent to Hawaii concerning the Japanese communications.

It would take an act of Congress to ensure that the scapegoating of Kimmel and Short was not buried. While Roosevelt supporters opposed any additional investigations during wartime, let alone during the upcoming election, there were sufficient Republicans and anti–New

Deal Democrats to pass a joint resolution which led to the organization of the Army Pearl Harbor Board and the Navy Court of Inquiry.

The Army Pearl Harbor Board convened from July through mid–October of 1944 with the only limitation of this investigation being that the board was "not authorized to criticize Mr. Roosevelt."[25] The purpose of this board was to determine if the army shared any responsibility for the disaster at Pearl Harbor. There were three general officers on the board, of which Lieutenant General George Grunert was the president. Grunert had previously commanded the Philippine Department, and was currently serving as deputy chief of staff of the Army Service Forces. He had served a long and distinguished career and knew the Far East. Also on the board were Major General Henry Russell and Major General Walter Frank. Russell held a law degree and had been in the army since 1916, when he enlisted in the National Guard. Frank had previously served as an air commander at Headquarters Hawaiian Department at Fort Shafter from 1938 to 1940.

The findings of this board shifted part of the responsibility of the Pearl Harbor attack to Washington, lifting some of the blame from General Short, concluding:

> The Chief of Staff of the Army, General George C. Marshall, failed in his relations with the Hawaiian Department in the following particulars:
>   A. To keep the Commanding General of the Hawaiian Department fully advised of the growing tenseness of the Japanese situation which indicated an increasing necessity for better preparation for war, of which information he had an abundance and Short had little.
>   B. To send additional instructions to the Commanding General of the Hawaiian Department on November 28, 1941, when evidently he failed to realize the import of General Short's reply of November 27th, which indicated clearly that General Short had misunderstood and misconstrued the message of November 27 (472) and had not adequately alerted his command for war.
>   C. To get General Short on the evening of December 6th and the early morning of December 7th, the critical information indicating an almost immediate break with Japan, though there was ample time to have accomplished this.
>   D. To investigate and determine the state of readiness of the Hawaiian Command between November 27 and December 7, 1941, despite the impending threat of war.[26]

But Marshall would not stand alone, and the board would also find:

> The record shows that from informers and other sources the War Department had complete and detailed information of Japanese intentions. Information of the evident Japanese intention to go to war in the very near future was well known to the Secretary of State, the Secretary of War, the Chief of Staff of the Army, the Secretary of the Navy, and the Chief of Naval Operations. It was not a question of fact; it was only a question of time. The next few days would see the end of peace and the beginning of war.
>
> If it be assumed that for any reason the information could not have been given to the Hawaiian Department, then it was the responsibility of the War Department to give orders to Short what to do, and to tell him to go on an all-out alert instead of a sabotage alert.
>
> As elsewhere related in detail, when vital information of December 6th reached G-2 of the War Department, not later than nine o'clock the evening of December 6, it was placed in the locked pouch and delivered to the Secretary of the General Staff, Colonel Bedell Smith, now Lt. General Smith, with a warning from Colonel Bratton, Chief of the Far Eastern Section of G-2, that it contained a vitally important message. In fact, the message implied war and soon. Whatever was the reason of Colonel Bedell Smith for not conveying the message to General Marshall on the night of December 6th it was an unfortunate one. And further, with the top War Department officials fully aware of the critical nature of the situation, standing operating procedure should have required the delivery of this vital information to General Marshall at once. He, himself was responsible for the organization and operation of his own immediate office.
>
> This information could have been sent to Short on the afternoon (Honolulu Time) of December 6.

Additionally, this same information was given to General Gerow's Executive, Colonel Gailey, of the War Plans Division, and there's no evidence of action taken by that Division.

The responsibility of the War Department is clearly defined and plain. Action by it would have been sufficient further to have alerted the Hawaiian Department. It was in possession of the information which was the last clear chance to use the means available to meet an attack. It had the background of the full development of the Japanese preparation for war and its probable date.

Again, the equally important and vital information of December 7th, the day of the attack, was in the possession of the War Department at 0900 on the morning of December 7. Under the circumstances where information has a vital bearing upon actions to be taken by field commanders, and this information cannot be disclosed by the War Department to its field commanders, it is incumbent upon the War Department then to assume the responsibility for specific directions to the theater commanders. This is an exception to the admirable policy of the War Department of decentralized and complete responsibility upon the competent field commanders.

Short got neither form of assistance from the War Department. The disaster of Pearl Harbor would have been eliminated to the extent that its defenses were available on December 7 if alerted in time. The difference between alerting these defenses in time by a directive from the War Department based upon this information and the failure to alert them is a difference for which the War Department is responsible....

The War Department had the information. All they had to do was either to give it to Short or give him directions based upon it.[27]

The board did find that Short had failed to place his command on a higher state of alert; to implement the Joint Coastal Frontier Defense Plan; to stay informed to the extent of the navy's long-range reconnaissance; and finally, to replace inefficient staff officers.

General Short had held a high reputation in the army, and many colleagues felt that his failure to appreciate the situation was, in itself, the obvious proof that he did not have sufficient information.

Although the board was under orders not to directly criticize the president, such findings of his General Staff and the War Department itself would automatically include him. After all, he had continuously been advised of Japanese actions and intentions and had been briefed on all intelligence being sent to Hawaii.

And where the Roberts Commission did not have access to Magic in its deliberations, the Army Board did. By the end of their investigation, this board interviewed 151 witnesses in Washington, Hawaii, and San Francisco.[28]

The Navy Court of Inquiry also convened from July until October 1944 and consisted of three retired admirals: Admirals Orin Murfin, Edward Kalbfus, and Adolphus Andrews. The court's president, Murfin, had commanded the Asiatic Fleet, Fourteenth Naval District, and the Pearl Harbor Naval Yard. Kalbus's commands had mostly been at sea, but he presently presided over the Naval War College. Andrews's commands had been at sea and at Pearl Harbor.

Kimmel's intelligence officer, then Captain Edwin Layton, would later detail how the navy inquiry completely exonerated Admiral Kimmel. The Navy Court of Inquiry determined that Kimmel and Short had adequately consulted with one another, and that each of them was "informed of the measures being undertaken by the other in defense of the Base to a degree sufficient for all useful purposes."[29] Layton emphasized, "Kimmel's plan of defense was held to be 'sound' but it depended on 'advance knowledge that an attack was to be expected.'"[30] And considering the limited amount of intelligence Kimmel had at hand, as well as the few planes he had available, he did conduct the long-distance reconnaissance that fit within these limitations.

It was during the Navy Court of Inquiry that Admiral Turner also admitted that he thought the Japanese attack was a very strong likelihood and that he was fully aware that Kimmel did not have an adequate number of planes to perform the necessary long-distance reconnaissance. When asked if he had discussed these concerns with the chief of naval operations, he sidestepped the question, but admitted that more planes could have lessened the losses.

Now the Navy Court of Inquiry criticized Admiral Stark. He was admonished for sending a war warning that, without additional information, did not even closely resemble the full picture that Washington had of the situation. It was Stark who had "failed to display the sound judgment expected of him in that he did not transmit to Admiral Kimmel … important information which he had regarding the Japanese situation."[31] He was also reprimanded for failing to pass on to Hawaii information that was given him, particularly that which he had on the morning of December 7. The board further concluded that in no way could the attack have been prevented, nor could the timing have been predicted, and as a result, no further actions against other naval officers would be considered.

Certainly the secretaries of both services as well as the chiefs themselves were not elated with the army and navy boards' findings, as the blame for Pearl Harbor had just shifted from Hawaii to Washington. In essence, the inquiry had established two categories for their findings, classifying any material dealing with Magic or general intelligence, and that of non-classified information that could be released to the public.

Admiral Kimmel's attorney, Charles Rugg, immediately wrote to Secretary of the Navy James Forrestal, who had been appointed after the death of Frank Knox in May of 1944:

> I request immediate release of findings of Navy Court of Inquiry as to innocence or guilt of Admiral Kimmel. For nearly three years he has borne public blame for Pearl Harbor disaster. He has requested and been denied court martial. His treatment has been un–American. In your letter to Admiral Murfin released to press on October 20 you intimate that facts, now three years old, found by Naval Court may be withheld as "secret" or "top secret" on ground disclosure would interfere with the war effort. Certainly release of findings of court as to Kimmel's innocence or guilt cannot affect war. Past injustices cannot now be remedied. Simple justice and common decency require immediate public announcement of courts finding as to Kimmel's innocence or guilt.[32]

While Forrestal agreed with Rugg, it was now the chief of naval operations, Admiral King, who had replaced Admiral Stark in March 1942, who interceded. (Admiral Stark had been transferred in April to Britain, where he became commander of the U.S. naval forces of the European theater of operations.) Admiral King demanded that all of the findings be considered classified, presumably on the basis that Magic secrecy must be preserved. And he personally questioned the findings of the inquiry, even though he later admitted that he hadn't read them. This would eliminate any possibility that the public would ever see the findings of the inquiry, not only to preserve the secret of Pearl Harbor, but to also avoid any discredit to the administration just prior to the November 1944 election.

Although the army and navy boards had completed their investigations by the fourth week of October, it was not until November 6 that Navy Secretary Forrestal and War Secretary Stimson got together to discuss what would be released to the press. While Stimson would endorse the Army Board's findings, Forrestal would waver concerning the Navy Court's findings. Roosevelt's response to the Army Board's finding was, "This is wicked,"[33] adding that any steps possible had to be taken to keep the conclusions out of the papers. It would not be until the end of November that Stimson and Forrestal agreed to a watered-down release, approved by Roosevelt, and the findings were finally published on December 1, 1944.

The delays in publishing the reports served Roosevelt's political agenda well, as such a revelation of the board's conclusions would have almost certainly removed him from office. The American public would not know when they went to the polls on November 7 that "the Army Pearl Harbor Board and the Navy Inquiry had just placed the burden of blame for Pearl Harbor, not on Kimmel and Short, but on Washington."[34] And there had been more intrigue in the weeks leading up to the election.

New York Governor Thomas Dewey was running as the Republican candidate for the presidency. Being an attorney, he was attuned to the legal circles in Washington and knew Rugg was defending Kimmel. About a month before the election, a rumor spread through Washington that Dewey would make an announcement about Pearl Harbor that would all but guarantee him the presidency.

Shortly before the intended revelation, and while Dewey was on the campaign trail in Tulsa, Oklahoma, a private meeting was arranged with Colonel Carter Clarke, an army intelligence officer, who introduced himself as a most trusted confidante of General Marshall. (Clarke, at the behest of Secretary Stimson, would conduct his own intelligence investigation of the events surrounding the Pearl Harbor attack.) Obviously, the president, as the opposing candidate, could not have personally arranged this meeting himself, but Dewey was still skeptical. Colonel Clarke produced a letter and handed it to Dewey. The introduction asked him not to read beyond it to the sealed portion unless he swore himself to secrecy to Clarke. After reading this, Dewey replied that he wasn't willing to swear himself to secrecy concerning any information that he might already be privy to. So he returned the letter and sent Clarke on his way.

A couple of nights later, Colonel Clarke reappeared with a new letter. This letter did not ask for a secrecy commitment, and General Marshall reassured Dewey that he had conferred with Admiral King only, who was in total concurrence, and that neither Roosevelt nor Stimson had any knowledge of it. The letter implied that, concerning the revelation Dewey planned to make about what the administration knew before Pearl Harbor, from the factory worker to the GI in the frontline foxhole, Americans could lose faith in their wartime leadership. This was exactly why Dewey wanted to make this unveiling. But to go against the advice of Marshall and King, could he be accused of treason, a presidential candidate?

The letter included rather sensitive details on the contributions of code decryptions relating to both the Pacific and European theaters, ending with Marshall's request that Dewey avoid revealing any information that could change the course of the war. That hit below the belt. Dewey certainly didn't want to change the course of the war. After what must have been hours or days of deep contemplation and reflection, he finally chose to say nothing. Whether it was due to patriotism or partisanship, to right a wrong involved a risk he was not willing to take. Dewey remained silent. And that, in essence, ended his assurance of the White House, and FDR went on to win his fourth term.

A couple of months after the election, Secretary of War Stimson opened yet another investigation, led by Major Henry Clausen, who attempted to turn the Army Pearl Harbor Board's findings upside down. During this investigation, and in an effort to bury the facts of the Pearl Harbor disaster once and for all, Senator Elbert Thomas (D–UT) introduced his bill on March 30, 1945, which would prohibit any "disclosure of any coded matter."[35] Thanks to quick thinking on Kimmel's part, he reached out to Eugene Mayer of the *Washington Post*, who published on April 12, the same day that President Roosevelt died, "a stinging indictment of the Democratic attempt to hide the facts of Pearl Harbor,"[36] making it clear that Americans could no longer count on the Senate to protect the people's liberties from "executive depriva-tion."[37] With all the publicity, Senator Thomas's bill died.

The Clausen Investigation would continue until September of 1945, and would provide some relief for Stimson. During this investigation, both Colonel Bedell Smith and General Leonard Gerow would deny Colonel Bratton's delivery of the Japanese thirteen-part message on Saturday, December 6. Along with other denials by these two, Colonel Rufus Bratton and Colonel Otis Sadtler suddenly developed recollection issues, and each changed his previous testimony.

And then, just weeks after Roosevelt's death, there was the Hewitt Inquiry. Navy Secre-tary James Forrestal met with President Truman to let him know that he would be conducting another Pearl Harbor investigation. He, too, had not been satisfied with the Navy Court of Inquiry's conclusions, and Admiral H. Kent Hewitt was assigned the task of heading up this investigation.

The Hewitt Inquiry focused on the existence of the Japanese "winds execute" intercepted at the navy's Station M on December 3. While this team of investigators was able to persuade Commander Alvin Kramer to back down on the testimony he had given at the Navy Court of Inquiry, Captain Laurence Safford stood fast. In spite of Safford's testimony, Hewitt ulti-mately concluded that the winds execute had never been sent, and while Stark had been somewhat blamed for not raising the alarm to Kimmel in the week prior to the attack, he also concluded that Kimmel had received sufficient warning.

While the Hewitt Inquiry was in process, rumors were circulating that the winds execute, on the orders of General Marshall, had actually been destroyed. To refute this allegation, Marshall enlisted the services of Colonel Clarke, which would lead to the Clarke Investigation. Brought under fire in this inquiry was Colonel John Bissell, who, with or without Marshall's knowledge, had supposedly destroyed the message himself. Not surprisingly, Bissell denied the allegation, and the War Department considered the matter closed.

When the actual army and navy reports were released to the public in August 1945, Stim-son and Forrestal openly condemned Kimmel and Short, which only added more fuel to the fire. The press wasn't buying it, and when President Truman was questioned at a press con-ference shortly thereafter, he responded that he had come to the conclusion the Pearl Harbor disaster had been "the result of the policy which the country itself pursued. The country was not ready for preparedness.... I think the country is as much to blame as any individual in this final situation that developed in Pearl Harbor."[38] Now the entire country was to blame, a viewpoint that was not well accepted.

After President Roosevelt's death in April 1945, and at public demand to settle the issue once and for all, the Seventy-Ninth Congress opened its own Pearl Harbor investigation, entered into Senate records as the "Joint Committee on the Investigation of the Pearl Harbor Attack," commencing on November 15, 1945, and running through May 31, 1946. (For those who believe in the stars, the Hitler-Roosevelt coincidences prove most interesting. Hitler became chancellor on Roosevelt's birthday, January 30, 1933. Then the following March 5, he assumed his legislative powers within twenty-five days of FDR's taking office. Their power lasted twelve years, and they died only weeks apart in April 1945.)

Leading the congressional hearings at the onset would be William D. Mitchell, who had served as President Hoover's attorney general from 1929 to 1933. Being assured that no obstacles would be put in his way to get to the truth, he would later have misgivings about taking on the assignment.

By the middle of December, Mitchell had become so irritated with all the political rants and the crossfire of missing files and allegedly destroyed documents that he resigned. He would continue to lead the hearings only until January of 1946, when Seth Richardson took over. Richardson had also served under President Hoover (1929 to 1933), but as assistant attorney general. And although a Republican, he did not add the influence to the hearings that the minority party may have hoped for. It was believed by some that all the dealings his current law firm had with the government may have curtailed his enthusiasm. Richardson took over as general counsel to the congressional committee on January 15, 1946.

The hearings would ultimately generate over fifteen thousand pages of testimony in seventeen volumes that embodied evidence of the earlier investigations. The joint congressional committee consisted of ten members, five from the House of Representatives and five from the Senate. Because the Democrats controlled both Houses, it was decided that they should control the membership within the committee, representing three of the five from each body, resulting in a Democratic majority of six of the ten members. Similar to the Roberts Commission, it appeared that the verdict was in before the hearings even convened.

Interestingly, pursuant to "Senate Resolution 27, Section 3," it is specifically stated that no one testifying could have his evidence used against him in his military status. This section alone would be the subject of repeated abuse to suit the direction of the committee majority. Testimony that had been precisely recalled in detail in earlier investigations now was changed completely or too vague to be accurately recalled in the interest of the witness protecting himself.

There had only been one man in complete charge, President Roosevelt. And if he were in any way discovered to have ordered the manipulation of intelligence, White House minutes, or records of activities, any such revelation could conceivably put his party in big trouble at the polls. The committee's majority saw that such evidence was never introduced.

As previously mentioned, potential witnesses such as Ralph Briggs and Daryl Wigle, who had actually intercepted the winds code alert and who could provide evidence to counter the aims of the committee, were either not called or ordered not to appear. Because denial of the winds execute "higashi no kazeame" was key to the issue of the lack of advance warning for Pearl Harbor, any reference to it would have to be repudiated.

In the week prior to the Pearl Harbor attack, Captain Laurence Safford, head of OP-20-G, had advised the naval monitoring stations on November 28, 1941, to be on the watch for a winds code alert, broadcast on Japanese radio. It was Ralph Briggs, the radioman on duty at Station M, who had monitored and forwarded the winds execute on December 3 to Safford in Washington, who, in turn, forwarded it up the chain of command. But now in the waning days of 1945, the existence of such a message would prove a liability to the committee. Safford had testified at the 1944 Navy Court of Inquiry, which had accepted and acknowledged how his deposition had fit the known facts. In the absence of any Briggs or Wigle testimony during the congressional hearings, Safford and Kramer, who had actually received the winds execute from Briggs, testified again to seeing it. And they were accused of imagining it all. (While Kramer did not deny the existence of the winds execute, he suffered a lapse in memory, testifying that he thought that it could have been Great Britain rather than the United States that was singled out in the message.)

Anyone with knowledge of the winds execute suddenly came under great pressure to change his story. Secretly, Briggs and Safford had collaborated prior to Safford's statement to the committee. Now Briggs was called before his commander, Captain John Harper, and questioned about his meetings with Safford. Harper then ordered Briggs to have no further contact. Safford had even asked the congressional committee to have Briggs appear because it was Briggs who had actually logged in the winds code alert. This was denied by the majority.

Kramer was even threatened with permanent residency in a mental institution if his testimony did not fit the sequence of events that had been decided upon. It had played heavily on his conscience to give false testimony under oath. Within the committee, one faction was trying to suppress the truth while the other was searching for it. The destruction of the files at Cheltenham containing the Japanese intercepts, including the winds code message, which could now be denied as ever being received, was justified with the logic of avoiding a large accumulation of paper. The question of who actually authorized or ordered the destruction of intelligence was never determined.

Of all those who testified throughout the hearings, and in addition to Kimmel and Short, of course, it was Captain Safford who did not suffer from any memory issues. And if the interrogations of others were grueling, the Democrats were relentless with Safford, trying their best to intimidate him. And yet Safford, fragile but determined, held his ground that the winds execute had been received in Washington; that he was aware that the navy had instructed certain messages to be destroyed after the attack; and that he had previously been encouraged during the Clausen Investigation to change his testimony. He was so committed to telling the truth that on several occasions, his answers brought a round of applause from the audience.

In the search for the answer to the question of whether Kimmel and Short had enough information to have been sufficiently warned by top intelligence officers in Washington, the variety of responses should have raised red flags. Both General Marshall and Admiral Stark testified that intelligence was not sent to Kimmel and Short because the variety of information would have only served to confuse them. Apparently they had never considered forwarding only that which was necessary to properly alert the Hawaiian commanders. General Miles, as the army's intelligence director, stated that Magic was not forwarded for fear of the Japanese breaking the American codes. Admiral Turner, Director of War Plans, who had also been making intelligence decisions, testified that he was under the impression that the Hawaiian commanders were getting Magic. Yet, as the man making the decisions on who received what, he knew, or it was his business to know, who received what. Admiral Leigh Noyes, Naval Communications Director, stated that the Hawaiian commanders did not have the capability to receive and decode messages themselves. Although it had actually been decrypted in early October, they all assured the committee in unison that the bomb plot message requesting ship positions in Pearl Harbor was not decoded until after the fact, thus covering themselves for not passing it on in time.

Admiral Kimmel, in trying to convince the committee that the war warning didn't give him the information mandatory to conduct a defense, testified:

> The statement in the Navy Department dispatch to me to the effect that the negotiations had ceased on November 27 was a pale reflection of actual events; so partial a statement as to be misleading. The parties had not merely stopped talking, they were at sword points. So far as Japan was concerned, the talking that went on after November 26 was play-acting. It was a stratagem to conceal a blow which Japan was

preparing to deliver. The stratagem did not fool the Navy Department. The Navy Department knew the scene. The Pacific Fleet was exposed to this Japanese stratagem because the Navy Department did not pass on its knowledge of the Japanese trick.[39]

At first, Kimmel had supported the idea of an independent committee to examine Pearl Harbor, but soon he came to realize he was still not going to get a fair shot. The administration was really running the show. But at the close of his testimony, it was Representative Bertrand Gearhart (R–CA) who summed it all up: "How could Kimmel be condemned for being caught by surprise when everybody above him, the Commander in Chief ... the Chief of Naval Operations, the Chief of Staff of the Army, all insisted that they were surprised?"[40]

The issue of the December 6, Saturday night deliveries of the first thirteen parts, Japan's response to the Ten Point Note, represented a total turnaround from the army and navy inquiries. While both Marshall and Stark still insisted that they could not recall their whereabouts to cover their not acting, coordinating, nor at least conferring, the weight of it all fell to Colonel Bratton. Bratton's routine during this period was like clockwork in his deliveries of intelligence. To the Army Board, he had testified concerning the importance of deliveries of the thirteen parts to head off a certain surprise Japanese move in the Pacific. But now to the congressional committee (as with the Clausen Investigation) and as if to save himself like Kramer, Bratton completely reversed his testimony, stating that the reason he did not make deliveries to Marshall and Gerow, the two army officers authorized to alert overseas commands, was that it was just routine intelligence.

Bratton's known, keen interpretation of such critical material must have played heavily on making him appear like an idiot by not delivering to officers who did not want to be found. Likewise, it is inconceivable that on the most important day of their lives, the two highest ranking officers of the U.S. military should both have a lapse of memory as to their whereabouts unless they, too, were under higher orders. Adding to the mystery, this deception was passed on to their aides, whose job it was to know the exact locations of their bosses at all times. But, knowing the answerability and the responsibility of their appointments to the nation, what alternative answers could they have offered?

Admiral Turner had seen the first thirteen parts before leaving his office on Saturday, and although he was authorized to alert overseas commands, he stated that he had not been approached to do so by Admiral Ingersoll, Stark's assistant, or by Admiral Wilkinson, Director of Naval Intelligence. He knew that both Ingersoll and Wilkinson had also received deliveries from Kramer, and without hearing from either of them, he took no action.

It was December 20, 1945, during the congressional hearings that William Mitchell asked Turner to explain the purpose of the Vacant Sea Order dated November 25, 1941, which had been sent to Hawaii under the order of Rear Admiral Ingersoll. (After the Pearl Harbor attack, Ingersoll would be promoted to vice admiral and appointed commander in chief of the U.S. Atlantic Fleet.)

Turner's response was, "We were prepared to divert traffic when we believed that war was imminent. We sent the traffic down via Torres Strait, so that the track of the Japanese task force would be clear of any traffic."[41] Of Japan's direct or northerly route choices, Washington knew which one to clear, sending all commercial and Allied military traffic thousands of miles out of their way. Directly, the American government cleared the way for them with the premise that if they thought that they had been observed, they might be tempted to cancel the attack, which in fact had been the order. Strangely, few authors have even touched on the

Vacant Sea Order, which adds further evidence that the attack on Pearl Harbor was no surprise.

The committee's Republican minority fought back on every issue possible, but on each one, they were overruled. Referring to the Magic intercepts provided Roosevelt on Saturday night, and concerning his ultimate responsibility as commander in chief to see that Hawaiian commanders were informed, they charged the president with "failure to take this action Saturday night, December 6, or early Sunday morning, December 7."[42] This was hard to refute, given the testimony of Lieutenant Lester Schulz, who had personally carried the thirteen-part message in to Roosevelt on Saturday night. Having been away from Washington, he was not aware of all the controversy surrounding the joint congressional hearings. So when he testified, he told the truth, including the response from Roosevelt, "This means war."[43] The committee's minority pointed the finger at, besides the president, Secretaries Stimson and Knox, Admiral Stark, and Generals Marshall and Gerow. But again, their demands were only noted.

For years, the United States Navy never admitted that they had broken Japan's JN-25 code. OP-20-G, the navy's intelligence and cryptanalysis group, had been reading it since at least October 1941. Perhaps the reason for their denial is the fact that the Japanese used this code to transmit the final instructions to the Kido Butai to attack Pearl Harbor. The navy wasn't running the navy; the president was. This then raises many more interesting questions. Did Washington know even Japan's last-minute orders? The code was never mentioned in any of the prior investigations. The first reference to it was during the congressional hearings, where it was quickly dropped.

Essentially, and to no surprise, the congressional hearings reversed the army and navy boards' findings and absolved Washington, the president and his cabinet, of negligence relating to the Pearl Harbor attack. They concluded that the attack itself was unprovoked and that U.S. policy would not have justified it. In fact, the president and his cabinet had gone out of their way to avoid war. The disaster was the result of Hawaiian leadership. Washington's warnings were not heeded, which was the result of errors of judgment—not dereliction of duty. However, they conceded that War Plans had failed to advise Short of his misinterpretation of the war warning of November 27. They further conceded that intelligence operations had failed to comprehend the significance of the bomb plot messages, and finally to properly monitor the Sunday, 12:00 (noon) warning to Pearl Harbor to ensure its timely arrival in Hawaii. All of these points were well clear of presidential responsibility.

Their conclusion that the president did nothing to invite war is not borne out by the American stranglehold on the Japanese economy, implementing trade embargos in conjunction with Great Britain and the Netherlands East Indies; nor is the conclusion borne out by the Ten Point Note of November 26 that demanded that Japan surrender China and get out of French Indochina. The committee's conclusions had fulfilled its purpose 100 percent: the absolution of the president and his cabinet. The rallying cry, "Remember Pearl Harbor," would for some take on a new meaning: deception, connivance, conspiracy, manipulation, cover-up, frame, and devise.

Even Justice Owen Roberts would admit in 1946 that he had not been provided all the information that Washington had had in their hands prior to the attack. Without correct evidence, he had been trying to build an incorrect image of actual events. He conceded that the request for him to preside over a committee convened, not to decide a case of law under the

Constitution, but instead over a kangaroo court that involved no attorneys or due process, was a request he should have refused.

Washington's admission of guilt over the mishandling of the bomb plot message, requesting the types of ships and their berthing locations in Pearl Harbor, leaves no room for surprise that Pearl Harbor was targeted. And all of Roosevelt's cabinet members would acknowledge that the Ten Point Note, in lieu of a modus vivendi, was the trigger for attack. And finally, Lieutenant Schulz's testimony alone refutes those who denied delivery of the thirteen-part message to FDR and his staff on Saturday night, removing any sound reasoning for not notifying Hawaii by Sunday morning, when they still had the chance. And yet, the majority of the joint congressional committee refused to assign any responsibility to the White House.

Admiral Harry Yarnell, who had commanded the Pearl Harbor naval base during the late 1930s, summed up the whole Pearl Harbor affair quite accurately:

> The most disgraceful feature of the whole affair was the evident determination on the part of Washington to fasten the blame on the Hawaiian commanders. The incomplete and one-sided Roberts report, the circumstances of the retirements of Kimmel and Short, the attempts of the War and Navy Departments to deny access to the intercepted messages by the Naval Court of Inquiry and the Army Board of Investigation, the appointment of secret one-man boards to continue investigations, and finally, the inability of the Joint Congressional Committee to secure access to pertinent files, constitute a blot on our national history.[44]

To hold Admiral Kimmel and General Short completely accountable for the attack on Pearl Harbor belies the American justice system, not simply because of the evidence that has been uncovered since 1941, but also because of the biased manner in which the numerous investigations were conducted.

Withholding evidence and denying testimonies in today's world would not be tolerated. The injustices that Kimmel and Short were served in most of the investigations, and a review of the facts today, clearly warrant the exonerations that so many Americans believed were due.

What is equally questionable is the treatment afforded another military officer of similar rank, General Douglas MacArthur. Even with sufficient warning of enemy attack, his indecision and miscalculations in the Philippines would send tens of thousands of troops to Japanese POW camps or to their deaths, and nearly his entire air force would be destroyed. Yet it is MacArthur who went on to be awarded the Medal of Honor within a matter of months of his departure from the Philippines, and it is MacArthur who would go down in history as one of the greatest American military leaders. It would fall to the next president, Harry Truman, to finally end MacArthur's military career. In April 1951, Truman fired MacArthur because of the manner in which he was handling the war in Korea.

What would also taint MacArthur's reputation later on was the $500,000 he was paid by President Quezon of the Philippines, supposedly for MacArthur's prewar efforts on Quezon's behalf. President Roosevelt and Secretary Stimson were aware of the payment, but turned a blind eye to it.

General MacArthur died in 1964. And in the late 1970s, it was confirmed that the Chase National Bank of New York had accepted a payment of $500,000 in February of 1942, perhaps $5 million in today's values, which was deposited into the personal account of General MacArthur by President Quezon. The administration in Washington wanted Quezon evacuated after their move to Corregidor, and MacArthur argued that it was too dangerous to try to get him out of the country. Had the payment offered by Quezon changed his mind?

Quezon and his family were evacuated by way of U.S. submarine on February 20, 1942, one day after Chase National Bank confirmed receipt of the funds by MacArthur. And this payment was made at a time when the Philippine economy was being bled for their war effort.

It was historian Carol Petillo, while working toward her doctoral degree in the late 1970s, who uncovered confirmation of the payment among General Richard Sutherland's papers located in the National Archives. Among them was Quezon's "Executive Order No. 1" directing total payments of $640,000 to MacArthur and his staff. In addition to MacArthur's payment, Sutherland received $75,000, and two other payments of $45,000 and $20,000 went to Brigadier General Richard Marshall, Jr., MacArthur's deputy chief of staff, and to Lieutenant Colonel Sidney Huff, MacArthur's personal aide, respectively.[45]

Although the payoffs were against U.S. Army regulation, MacArthur had no reservations about taking the money while the islands were being overrun because of his continuous fumbles. In addition to the $500,000, MacArthur demanded $35,000 in personal expenses, dated December 28, 1941, during the final collapse of Manila.[46] The Roosevelt administration was so desperate for heroes that when Chase notified the War Department in February 1942 of the payments, the response to Chase was to complete the transactions. And among all the medals and honors MacArthur boasted about throughout the rest of his life, he never discussed the Quezon reward.

There are some who believe that Mac was paid off not to respond to the initial Japanese attacks, hopefully to convince the Japanese that the Philippines preferred to remain neutral. It possibly explains his refusal to empty warehouses of food and supplies in Manila for transport to Bataan as required by WPO-3 until it was too late; or his refusal to fire upon Japanese-occupied towns because they might harm civilians; or his personal demand requiring his approval for all actions taken in the field by the lower commanders.

MacArthur's credibility would be questioned by many. One example is provided in the diaries of General Brereton, which were published in 1946. Although Brereton is respectful toward MacArthur, he details the events prior to and during the Philippine attack that depict MacArthur's passive leadership in a time of crisis. The day the book went on sale, MacArthur issued another of his now famous press releases stating that Brereton's diary was all lies. He had never heard of Brereton asking permission to bomb Formosa, which would have failed with no fighter support. Yet on December 9, with half of his air force destroyed on the ground, he had told Washington that he was ordering just such a raid. It was quite apparent that MacArthur had prematurely embarrassed himself by condemning Brereton, who had refused to criticize MacArthur's leadership.

Years later, General Eisenhower, who had been MacArthur's aide for seven long years, and who had turned down money offered by President Quezon, commented that Mac was neither above nor below anything. Quezon had also offered Eisenhower a payment of $60,000, but Eisenhower had the foresight to understand the potential implications of a payoff.

American history has proven over and over again that politics and truth do not go hand in hand. And in the case of Pearl Harbor, it is a disgrace that two dedicated military officers who were only trying to serve their country paid the price with the loss of their reputations and utter humiliation. Considering all the evidence that has come to light over the last seventy years, there was far more going on behind the scenes that Kimmel and Short simply had no control over. Providing Hawaii with the needed aircraft for both defense and reconnaissance, and providing the commanders with the Magic decrypts that would have enabled them to

A 1990s meeting of the Minnesota Pearl Harbor survivors. The author is at far left.

prepare for the impending attack, could have changed the outcome considerably. But those decisions were all being made in Washington, and more specifically, by the administration.

Many Americans hold that Franklin Delano Roosevelt was the greatest president of the twentieth century. For some, it may be difficult to consider that he intentionally provoked the Japanese to attack Pearl Harbor. Historian Robert Stinnett points out that the entire presidency of Franklin Roosevelt should not be judged solely on the disaster at Pearl Harbor. One could agree with that assessment had Roosevelt's decisions been honest mistakes or simply poor judgment. But to understand that his decisions were based clearly on his deception at the risk of so many lives, as well as the reputations of others, casts a pall over his presidency and leadership abilities that, hopefully, history will not forget.

Information uncovered since 1941 points to a truth that was not provided the American people or Congress at the time of the attack, that a much greater plan had been laid down long before December 7, 1941. And after the attack, those in Washington simply needed to distance themselves from the actual events as they occurred. Isn't it time now for Americans to put the responsibility for the attack on Pearl Harbor where it belongs?

Chapter Notes

Introduction

1. Robert B. Stinnett, *Day of Deceit* (New York: Free Press, 2000), 219.
2. John Toland, *Infamy: Pearl Harbor and Its Aftermath* (New York: A Berkley Book, 1983), 133.

Chapter 1

1. Terence McComas, *Pearl Harbor: Fact and Reference Book, Everything to Know About December 7, 1941* (Honolulu: Mutual Publishing, 1991), 52–53.
2. Carl Smith, *Pearl Harbor* (Oxford: Osprey, 2001), 90.
3. *Ibid.*, 91.
4. McComas, *Pearl Harbor: Fact and Reference Book*, 122.
5. Smith, *Pearl Harbor*, 54.
6. Deborah Bachrach, *Pearl Harbor: Great Mysteries, Opposing Viewpoints* (San Diego: Greenhaven Press, 1989), 10.
7. Edwin T. Layton, *And I Was There: Pearl Harbor and Midway—Breaking the Secrets* (New York: William Morrow, 1985), 300.
8. McComas, *Pearl Harbor: Fact and Reference Book*, 121.
9. Robert A. Theobald, *The Final Secret of Pearl Harbor* (New York: Devin-Adair, 1954), 8.
10. Lynne Olson, *Those Angry Days: Roosevelt, Lindbergh, and America's Fight Over World War II* (New York: Random House, 2013), 425.
11. Roberts Commission, *Attack Upon Pearl Harbor By Japanese Armed Forces: Report of the Commission Appointed by the President of the United States to Investigate and Report the Facts Relating to the Attack Made by Japanese Armed Forces Upon Pearl Harbor in the Territory of Hawaii on December 7, 1941* (Washington, D.C.: U.S. Government, 1942), 1.
12. *Ibid.*, 1.
13. *Ibid.*, 2.
14. *Ibid.*, 2.
15. *Ibid.*, 12.
16. *Ibid.*, 14.
17. *Ibid.*, 14.
18. *Ibid.*, 21.
19. *Ibid.*, 21.
20. Kemp Tolley, *Cruise of the Lanikai: Incitement to War* (Annapolis, MD: Naval Institute Press, 1973), 273.

Chapter 2

1. John W. Vandercook, "America's Gibraltar of the Pacific," *Liberty Magazine*, December 27, 1941, para. 7.
2. *Ibid.*, para. 21.
3. *Ibid.*, para. 21.
4. *Ibid.*, para. 23.
5. *Ibid.*, para. 25.
6. Thomas Parrish, ed., *The Simon & Schuster Encyclopedia of World War II* (New York: Simon & Schuster, 1978), 491.
7. Richard Connaughton, *MacArthur and Defeat in the Philippines* (New York: Overlook Press, 2001), 39.
8. *Ibid.*, 44.
9. *Ibid.*, 73.
10. Louis Morton, *The Fall of the Philippines (United States Army in World War II, The War in the Pacific)* (Washington, D.C.: Center of Military History, 1985), 37.
11. Duane Schultz, *Hero of Bataan: The Story of General Jonathan M. Wainwright* (New York: St. Martin's Press, 1981), 48.
12. William Bartsch, *December 8, 1941: MacArthur's Pearl Harbor* (College Station: Texas A&M University Press, 2003), 38.
13. Morton, *The Fall of the Philippines*, 46.
14. Walter D. Edmonds, *They Fought with What They Had: The Story of the Army Air Force in the Southwest Pacific, 1941–1942* (Washington, D.C.: Zenger, 1982), 25.
15. Bartsch, *December 8, 1941*, 59–60.
16. Walter Millis, *This Is Pearl! The United States and Japan—1941* (New York: William Morrow, 1947), 32.
17. *Ibid.*, 32.
18. Brian Cull, *Buffaloes Over Singapore: RAF, RAAF, RNZAF and Dutch Brewster Fighters in Action Over Malaya and the East Indies 1941–42* (London: Grub Street, 2003), 40.
19. James Leasor, *Singapore: The Battle That Changed the World* (Garden City, NY: Doubleday, 1968), 122.

20. W.D. Puleston, *The Armed Forces of the Pacific* (New Haven, CT: Yale University Press, 1941), 129.
21. *Ibid.*, 129–130.
22. McComas, *Pearl Harbor: Fact and Reference Book*, 21.
23. Layton, *And I Was There*, 224.
24. *Ibid.*, 224.

Chapter 3

1. Charles A. Beard, *President Roosevelt and the Coming of the War 1941: A Study in Appearances and Realities* (New Haven, CT: Yale University Press, 1948), 178.
2. Parrish, ed., *The Simon and Schuster Encyclopedia of World War II*, 598.
3. U.S. Department of State, *Peace and War: United States Foreign Policy, 1931–1941* (Washington, D.C.: Government Printing Office, 1943), para. 5.
4. Samuel Eliot Morison, *The Rising Sun in the Pacific, 1931–April 1942: History of United States Naval Operations in World War II*, vol. 3 (Edison, NJ: Castle Books, 2001), 63.
5. Barbara W. Tuchman, *Stilwell and the American Experience in China 1911–45* (New York: Macmillan, 1970), 235.
6. Iris Chang, *The Rape of Nanking: The Forgotten Holocaust of World War II* (New York: BasicBooks, 1997), 148.
7. Conrad Black, *Franklin Delano Roosevelt: Champion of Freedom* (New York: PublicAffairs, 2003), 428.
8. Frank Knox, *Annual Report of the Secretary of the Navy for the Fiscal Year 1941* (Washington, D.C.: U.S. Government Printing Office, 1941), iii.
9. *Ibid.*, 5.
10. Department of the Army, *American Military History 1607–1958* (Washington, D.C.: U.S. Government Printing Office, 1959), 373.
11. Millis, *This Is Pearl!*, 103.
12. Leonard Mosely, *Marshall: Hero for Our Times* (New York: Hearst Books, 1982), 148.
13. Millis, *This Is Pearl!*, 103.
14. Parrish, ed., *The Simon and Schuster Encyclopedia of World War II*, 560.
15. Jim Dan Hill, *The Minute Man in Peace and War: A History of the National Guard* (Harrisburg, PA: Stackpole, 1964), 373.
16. Millis, *This Is Pearl!*, 104.
17. Black, *Franklin Delano Roosevelt*, 281.
18. Department of the Army, *American Military History 1607–1958*, 369.
19. Olson, *Those Angry Days*, 227.
20. Robert H. Jackson, *Opinion on Exchange of Over-Age Destroyers for Naval and Air Bases* (Washington, D.C.: Office of the Attorney General, 1940), para. 19.
21. *Ibid.*, para. 11.
22. Layton, *And I Was There*, 87.

Chapter 4

1. Stinnett, *Day of Deceit*, 34.
2. *Ibid.*, 35.
3. *Ibid.*, 34.
4. *Ibid.*, 36.
5. *Ibid.*, 85.
6. Toland, *Infamy*, 8.
7. Millis, *This Is Pearl!*, 62.
8. Joint Committee on the Investigation of the Pearl Harbor Attack, Congress of the United States, *Investigation of the Pearl Harbor Attack* (Washington, D.C.: United States Government Printing Office, 1946), 983.
9. *Ibid.*, 988.
10. Smith, *Pearl Harbor*, 53, 60.
11. Millis, *This Is Pearl!*, 63.
12. *Ibid.*, 64.
13. Joint Committee on the Investigation of the Pearl Harbor Attack, *Investigation of the Pearl Harbor Attack*, Ex. 13.
14. Andrew Mollo, *The Armed Forces of World War II: Uniforms, Insignia, and Organization* (New York: Military Press, 1987), 2–6.
15. *Ibid.*, 83.
16. *Ibid.*, 252.
17. *Ibid.*, 8–11.
18. *Ibid.*, 259.
19. *Ibid.*, 91.
20. Olson, *Those Angry Days*, 27.
21. Millis, *This Is Pearl!*, 65.
22. *Ibid.*, 38.
23. *Ibid.*, 39.
24. *Ibid.*, 39.
25. Department of Defense, United States of America, *The "Magic" Background of Pearl Harbor*, vol. 1 (Washington, D.C.: U.S. Government Printing Office, 1977), 5.
26. Toland, *Infamy*, 264.
27. Millis, *This Is Pearl!*, 59.
28. *Ibid.*, 59.
29. *Ibid.*, 60.
30. Irving Brinton Holley, Jr., *Buying Aircraft: Materiel Procurement for the Army Air Forces (U.S. Army in World War II, Special Studies)* (Washington, D.C.: Department of the Army, 1964), 520.
31. Millis, *This Is Pearl!*, 133.
32. *Ibid.*, 133.
33. *Ibid.*, 133.
34. Joseph W. Martin, Jr., "The Country Needs a Strong Opposition Party: We Must Preserve the American Way of Consideration" (Columbia Broadcasting System, April 3, 1941), para. 6.
35. *Ibid.*, para. 8.
36. *Ibid.*, para. 8.
37. *Ibid.*, para. 12.
38. *Ibid.*, para. 16.
39. Harry S. Truman, *Memoirs by Harry S. Truman: The Year of Decisions*, vol. 1 (Garden City, NY: Doubleday, 1955), 164.
40. Millis, *This Is Pearl!*, 135.
41. *Ibid.*, 187.
42. Black, *Franklin Delano Roosevelt*, 389.
43. Gordon Prange, *At Dawn We Slept: The Untold Story of Pearl Harbor* (New York: McGraw-Hill, 1981), 410.
44. Holley, *Buying Aircraft: Materiel Procurement for the Army Air Forces*, 77.
45. *Ibid.*, 53.

46. Lewis H. Brereton, *The Brereton Diaries: The War in the Pacific, Middle East and Europe, October 3, 1941 to May 8, 1945* (William Morrow, 1946), 6.

47. *Ibid.*, 12.

48. *Ibid.*, 12.

49. *Ibid.*, 13.

50. *Ibid.*, 19–20.

51. *Ibid.*, 21.

52. *Ibid.*, 22.

53. Morton, *Fall of the Philippines*, 48.

54. Husband E. Kimmel, *Admiral Kimmel's Story* (Chicago: Henry Regnery, 1955), 21.

55. *Ibid.*, 21.

Chapter 5

1. Joseph P. Nye, *Can the United States Be Neutral?—Yes, If It Minds Its Own Business* (76th Congress, 1 sess. CR, 84, pt 14, 1939), Para. 2.

2. *Ibid.*, para. 4.

3. *Ibid.*, para. 4.

4. Franklin Roosevelt, "Arsenal of Democracy" (Washington , D.C.: Fireside Chat, December 29, 1940), para. 18.

5. *Ibid.*, para. 71.

6. *Ibid.*, para. 50.

7. Stinnett, *Day of Deceit*, 17.

8. Roosevelt, *Arsenal of Democracy*, para. 24.

9. *Ibid.*, para. 36.

10. Beard, *President Roosevelt and the Coming of the War 1941*, 3.

11. *Ibid.*, 4.

12. *Ibid.*, 14.

13. *Ibid.*, 15.

14. Black, *Franklin Delano Roosevelt*, 615.

15. Beard, *President Roosevelt and the Coming of the War 1941*, 15.

16. Olson, *Those Angry Days*, 284.

17. Beard, *President Roosevelt and the Coming of the War 1941*, 16.

18. *Ibid.*, 17.

19. *Ibid.*, 17.

20. *Ibid.*, 17–18.

21. Olson, *Those Angry Days*, 62.

22. Beard, *President Roosevelt and the Coming of the War 1941*, 18.

23. Hamilton Fish, "We Should Not Convoy Materials to Europe: Convoys Mean Shooting and Shooting Means War" (Washington, D.C.: American Forum of the Air, March 30, 1941), para. 9.

24. *Ibid.*, para. 11.

25. H.W. Brands, *Traitor to His Class: The Privileged Life and Radical Presidency of Franklin Delano Roosevelt* (New York: Anchor Books, 2008), 455.

26. Beard, *President Roosevelt and the Coming of the War 1941*, 32.

27. *Ibid.*, 32.

28. James P. Duffy, *Lindbergh vs. Roosevelt: The Rivalry That Divided America* (New York: MJF Books, 2010), 16.

29. *Ibid.*, 17.

30. *Ibid.*, 17.

31. Beard, *President Roosevelt and the Coming of the War 1941*, 5.

32. Olson, *Those Angry Days*, 236.

33. A. Scott Berg, *Lindbergh*, 415.

34. Olson, *Those Angry Days*, 280.

35. Charles Lindbergh, "Address to the America First Committee" (New York, April 23, 1941), para. 3.

36. *Ibid.*, para. 6.

37. Beard, *President Roosevelt and the Coming of the War 1941*, 39.

38. *Ibid.*, 39.

39. *Ibid.*, 39.

40. *Ibid.*, 40.

41. *Ibid.*, 40.

42. *Ibid.*, 45.

43. *Ibid.*, 57.

44. *Ibid.*, 57.

45. *Ibid.*, 56.

46. *Ibid.*, 64.

47. Millis, *This Is Pearl!*, 49.

48. Beard, *President Roosevelt and the Coming of the War 1941*, 70.

49. *Ibid.*, 74.

50. *Ibid.*, 79.

51. *Ibid.*, 79.

52. *Ibid.*, 79.

53. *Ibid.*, 80–81.

54. *Ibid.*, 82.

55. *Ibid.*, 84.

56. *Ibid.*, 88–89.

57. *Ibid.*, 84–87.

58. *Ibid.*, 93.

59. *Ibid.*, 97.

60. Franklin Roosevelt, "We Are Not Yielding and We Do Not Propose to Yield" (Washington, D.C.: Address to Congress, June 20, 1941), para. 8.

61. Franklin Roosevelt, "Unlimited National Emergency" (Washington, D.C.: Radio Address, May 27, 1941), para. 63.

62. *Ibid.*, para. 91.

63. Beard, *President Roosevelt and the Coming of the War 1941*, 101.

64. Donald Sommerville, *World War II: Day by Day—An Illustrated Almanac 1939-1945* (Greenwich, CT: Dorset Press, 1991), 87.

65. Beard, *President Roosevelt and the Coming of the War 1941*, 105–106.

66. *Ibid.*, 106.

67. *Ibid.*, 106.

68. *Ibid.*, 13.

69. *Ibid.*, 139.

70. Franklin Roosevelt, "Freedom of the Seas" (Washington, D.C.: Fireside Chat, September 11, 1941), para. 1, 2, 41.

71. *Ibid.*, para. 43, 44.

72. *Ibid.*, para. 49, 54, 55, 56, 58.

73. Beard, *President Roosevelt and the Coming of the War 1941*, 141.

74. Millis, *This Is Pearl!*, 184.

75. *Ibid.*, 187.

76. Franklin Roosevelt, "Navy and Total Defense Day" (Washington, D.C.: Radio Address, October 27, 1941), Para. 1–10.

77. *Ibid.*, para 30–31.
78. *Ibid.*, para. 35.
79. *Ibid.*, para. 51.
80. Beard, *President Roosevelt and the Coming of the War 1941*, 144.
81. *Ibid., President Roosevelt and the Coming of the War 1941*, 147.
82. *Ibid.*, 148.
83. *Ibid.*, 148.
84. Millis, *This Is Pearl!*, 189.
85. Parrish, ed., *The Simon and Schuster Encyclopedia of World War II*, 524.
86. Elizabeth-Anne Wheal et al., *The Meridian Encyclopedia of the Second World War* (New York: Penguin Books, 1992), 33.
87. *Ibid.*, 33.
88. *Ibid.*, 33.
89. *Ibid.*, 34.
90. Parrish, ed., *The Simon and Schuster Encyclopedia of World War II*, 289.
91. Beard, *President Roosevelt and the Coming of the War 1941*, 153.
92. *Ibid.*, 153.
93. Wheal et al., *The Meridian Encyclopedia of the Second World War*, 275.

Chapter 6

1. Parrish, ed., *The Simon and Schuster Encyclopedia of World War II*, 47–48.
2. Wheal et al., *The Meridian Encyclopedia of the Second World War*, 115.
3. *Ibid.*, 116.
4. Millis, *This Is Pearl!*, 74.
5. Wheal et al., *The Meridian Encyclopedia of the Second World War*, 146.
6. Millis, *This Is Pearl!*, 95.
7. *Ibid.*, 94–95.
8. *Ibid.*, 95.
9. *Ibid.*, 95.
10. *Ibid.*, 95.
11. *Ibid.*, 95.
12. *Ibid.*, 96.
13. Mosley, *Marshall*, 143.
14. Millis, *This Is Pearl!*, 97.
15. *Ibid.*, 98.
16. *Ibid.*, 98.
17. *Ibid.*, 96.
18. *Ibid.*, 202.
19. Robert A. Taft, "Bureaucratic Confusion at Washington: Fighting for Democracy Abroad While It Wilts at Home" (Washington, D.C.: Columbia Broadcasting System, May 2, 1941), para. 6.
20. Millis, *This Is Pearl!*, 112.
21. *Ibid.*, 113–114.
22. Sommerville, *World War II: Day by Day*, 90.
23. Millis, *This Is Pearl!*, 113.
24. Parrish, ed., *The Simon and Schuster Encyclopedia of World War II*, 560.
25. *Ibid.*, 560.
26. Mosley, *Marshall*, 147.
27. Parrish, ed., *The Simon and Schuster Encyclopedia of World War II*, 16.

28. Wheal et al., *The Meridian Encyclopedia of the Second World War*, 91.
29. Costello, *Days of Infamy*, 10.
30. Toland, *Infamy*, 269.
31. *Ibid.*, 350.
32. *Ibid.*, 350.
33. *Ibid.*, 325.
34. *Ibid.*, 272.
35. Millis, *This Is Pearl!*, 123.

Chapter 7

1. Wheal et al., *The Meridian Encyclopedia of the Second World War*, 146.
2. Millis, *This Is Pearl!*, 142.
3. Department of Defense, *The "Magic" Background of Pearl Harbor*, vol. 3, Appendix (Washington, D.C.: U.S. Government Printing Office, 1977), A-65.
4. Millis, *This Is Pearl!*, 151.
5. *Ibid.*, 154.
6. *Ibid.*, 166.
7. *Ibid.*, 183.
8. *Ibid.*, 184.
9. *Ibid.*, 176.
10. Theobald, *The Final Secret of Pearl Harbor*, 43–44.
11. Department of Defense, *The "Magic" Background of Pearl Harbor*, vol. 4, Appendix (Washington, D.C.: U.S. Government Printing Office, 1977), A-147.
12. Millis, *This Is Pearl!*, 311.
13. McComas, *Pearl Harbor: Fact and Reference Book*, 121.
14. Joint Committee on the Investigation of the Pearl Harbor Attack, *Investigation of the Pearl Harbor Attack*, 518.
15. *Ibid.*, 519.
16. *Ibid.*, 519.
17. *Ibid.*, 519.
18. Millis, *This Is Pearl!*, 215.
19. Department of Defense, *The "Magic" Background of Pearl Harbor*, vol. 4, Appendix, A-21.
20. *Ibid.*, A-22.
21. *Ibid.*, A-39.
22. Berg, *Lindbergh*, 430.
23. Millis, *This Is Pearl!*, 218.
24. *Ibid.*, 218.
25. Department of Defense, *The "Magic" Background of Pearl Harbor*, vol. 4, Appendix, A-57.
26. *Ibid.*, A-58.
27. Millis, *This Is Pearl!*, 219.
28. Department of Defense, *The "Magic" Background of Pearl Harbor*, vol. 4 (Washington, D.C.: U.S. Government Printing Office, 1977), 57.
29. *Ibid.*, 57.
30. Millis, *This Is Pearl!*, 220.
31. *Ibid.*, 220.
32. *Ibid.*, 222.
33. *Ibid.*, 223.
34. *Ibid.*, 223.
35. Department of Defense, *The "Magic" Background of Pearl Harbor*, vol. 4, Appendix, A-16.
36. Millis, *This Is Pearl!*, 225–226.
37. Beard, *President Roosevelt and the Coming of the War 1941*, 511.

38. Millis, *This Is Pearl!*, 227.
39. *Ibid.*, 226.
40. Department of Defense, *The "Magic" Background of Pearl Harbor*, vol. 4, Appendix, A-89.
41. Millis, *This Is Pearl!*, 231.
42. *Ibid.*, 234.
43. *Ibid.*, 234.
44. *Ibid.*, 235.
45. Stinnett, *Day of Deceit*, 144.
46. Theobald, *The Final Secret of Pearl Harbor*, 75–76.
47. *Ibid.*, 76.
48. Millis, *This Is Pearl!*, 240.
49. *Ibid.*, 241.
50. Douglas, Gregory, *The Interrogation of Heinrich Muller*, vol. 1 (San Jose, CA: James Bender Publishing, 1999), 44.
51. Layton, *And I Was There*, 197.
52. Department of Defense, *The "Magic" Background of Pearl Harbor*, vol. 4, Appendix, A-93.
53. *Ibid.*, A-93.
54. *Ibid.*, A-93.
55. Millis, *This Is Pearl!*, 242.
56. Kent Roberts Greenfield, ed., *Command Decisions* (Washington, D.C.: Center of Military History, 2000), 126.
57. Vandercook, "America's Gibraltar of the Pacific," para. 25.
58. Department of Defense, *The "Magic" Background of Pearl Harbor*, vol. 4, Appendix, A-98, A-99, A-100.
59. Millis, *This Is Pearl!*, 244.
60. Department of Defense, *The "Magic" Background of Pearl Harbor*, vol. 4, Appendix, A-103.
61. Beard, *President Roosevelt and the Coming of the War 1941*, 516.
62. *Ibid.*, 516.
63. Millis, *This Is Pearl!*, 245.
64. *Ibid.*, 246.
65. *Ibid.*, 247.
66. *Ibid.*, 248.
67. *Ibid.*, 249.
68. *Ibid.*, 249.
69. Brereton, *The Brereton Diaries*, 34.
70. Tolley, *Cruise of the Lanikai*, 51.
71. John Costello, *Days of Infamy: MacArthur, Roosevelt, Churchill—The Shocking Truth Revealed* (New York: Pocket Books, 1994), 150.
72. Theobald, *The Final Secret of Pearl Harbor*, 81.
73. Department of Defense, *The "Magic" Background of Pearl Harbor*, vol. 4, Appendix, A-118.
74. *Ibid.*, A-81.
75. Department of Defense, *The "Magic" Background of Pearl Harbor*, vol. 5 (Washington, D.C.: U.S. Government Printing Office, 1977), 51.
76. Department of Defense, *The "Magic" Background of Pearl Harbor*, vol. 4, Appendix, A-384–A-385.
77. *Ibid.*, A-120.
78. Millis, *This Is Pearl!*, 286.

Chapter 8

1. Layton, *And I Was There*, 209.
2. Prange, *At Dawn We Slept*, 401.

3. *Ibid.*, 400.
4. *Ibid.*, 400.
5. *Ibid.*, 401.
6. *Ibid.*
7. *Ibid.*
8. *Ibid.*
9. *Ibid.*
10. Millis, *This Is Pearl!*, 269.
11. Robert J. Cressman and J. Michael Wenger, *Steady Nerves and Stout Hearts: The Enterprise (CV6) Air Group and Pearl Harbor, 7 December 1941* (Missoula, MT: Pictorial Histories, 1990), 1.
12. Millis, *This Is Pearl!*, 275.
13. *Ibid.*, 274–275.
14. Layton, *And I Was There*, 222.
15. *Ibid.*, 282.
16. *Ibid.*, 282.
17. *Ibid.*, 283.
18. *Ibid.*, 283–284.
19. *Ibid.*, 281.
20. *Ibid.*, 290.
21. Brereton, *The Brereton Diaries*, 22.
22. Layton, *And I Was There*, 291.
23. *Ibid.*, 293.
24. *Ibid.*, 18.
25. *Ibid.*, 18.
26. Millis, *This Is Pearl!*, 298.
27. *Ibid.*, 299.
28. Department of Defense, *The "Magic" Background of Pearl Harbor*, vol. 4, Appendix, A-215.
29. Millis, *This Is Pearl!*, 300.
30. Brereton, *The Brereton Diaries*, 22.
31. *Ibid.*, 35.
32. Tolley, *The Cruise of the Lanikai*, 51.
33. *Ibid.*, 51.
34. *Ibid.*, 42.
35. Toland, *Infamy*, 304.
36. Millis, *This Is Pearl!*, 307.
37. Department of Defense, *The "Magic" Background of Pearl Harbor*, vol. 4, Appendix, A-126.
38. Millis, *This Is Pearl!*, 309.
39. Department of Defense, *The "Magic" Background of Pearl Harbor*, vol. 4, Appendix, A-150.
40. Millis, *This Is Pearl!*, 311.
41. Smith, *Pearl Harbor*, 60.
42. Millis, *This Is Pearl!*, 316.
43. *Ibid.*, 320.
44. *Ibid.*, 320–321.

Chapter 9

1. Millis, *This Is Pearl!*, 326.
2. Department of Defense, *The "Magic" Background of Pearl Harbor*, vol. 4, Appendix, A-129.
3. *Ibid.*, A-132.
4. *Ibid.*, A-133.
5. *Ibid.*, A-133.
6. Leatrice R. Arakaki and John R. Kuborn, *7 December 1941: The Air Force Story* (Washington, D.C.: U.S. Government Printing Office, 1991), 72.
7. Department of Defense, *The "Magic" Background of Pearl Harbor*, vol. 4, Appendix, A-134.

8. *Ibid.*, A-129.

9. *Ibid.*, A-135.

10. Millis, *This Is Pearl!*, 337.

11. Layton, *And I Was There*, 265.

12. Millis, *This Is Pearl!*, 341.

13. Layton, *And I Was There*, 306.

14. *Ibid.*, 307.

15. Smith, *Pearl Harbor*, 40.

16. *Ibid.*, 40.

17. *Ibid.*, 40.

18. *Ibid.*, 40.

19. Prange, *At Dawn We Slept*, 501.

20. *Ibid.*, 504.

21. *Ibid.*, 507.

22. McComas, *Pearl Harbor: Fact and Reference Book*, 75.

23. *Ibid.*, 70.

24. Joy Waldron Jasper, James P. Delgado, and Jim Adams, *The USS* Arizona: *the Ship, the Men, the Pearl Harbor Attack, and the Symbol That Aroused America* (New York: St. Martin's Press, 2001), 209.

25. John W. Lambert, *The Long Campaign: The History of the 15th Fighter Group in World War II* (Manhattan, KS: Sunflower University Press, 1982), 20.

26. Prange, *At Dawn We Slept*, 544.

27. McComas, *Pearl Harbor: Fact and Reference Book*, 87.

28. *Flying Magazine* 44(1) (January 1949): 58.

29. *Ibid.*, 123.

30. Toland, *Infamy*, 15.

31. Bartsch, *December 8, 1941*, 260.

32. *Ibid.*, 260.

33. Edmonds, *They Fought With What They Had*, 75.

34. Connaughton, *MacArthur and the Defeat in the Philippines*, 166.

35. Brereton, *The Brereton Diaries*, 40.

36. Morton, *The Fall of the Philippines*, 84.

37. Bartsch, *December 8, 1941*, 262.

38. *Ibid.*, 262.

39. *Ibid.*, 262.

40. *Ibid.*, 263.

41. *Ibid.*, 263.

42. Connaughton, *MacArthur and the Defeat in the Philippines*, 178.

43. Brereton, *The Brereton Diaries*, 50.

44. *Ibid.*, 50.

45. *Ibid.*, 62.

46. *Ibid.*, 62.

47. *Ibid.*, 62.

48. Greenfield, ed., *Command Decisions*, 154.

49. *Ibid.*, 156.

50. *Ibid.*, 163.

51. *Ibid.*, 163–164.

52. *Ibid.*, 167.

53. Schultz, *Hero of Bataan*, 150.

54. *Ibid.*, 226.

55. *Ibid.*, 213.

56. George W. Smith, *MacArthur's Escape: John "Wild Man" Bulkeley and the Rescue of an American Hero* (St. Paul, MN: MBI Publishing, 2005), 206.

Chapter 10

1. Layton, *And I Was There*, 331.

2. *Ibid.*, 331.

3. Toland, *Infamy*, 23.

4. *Ibid.*, 23.

5. *Ibid.*, 23.

6. *Ibid.*, 336.

7. *Ibid.*, 336.

8. *Ibid.*, 336.

9. John Flynn, *The Final Secret of Pearl Harbor* (Published privately, 1945), para. 32.

10. *Ibid.*, para. 32.

11. Toland, *Infamy*, 30.

12. Theobald, *The Final Secret of Pearl Harbor*, 155.

13. *Ibid.*, 156.

14. Kimmel, *Admiral Kimmel's Story*, 149–150.

15. Toland, *Infamy*, 42.

16. *Ibid.*, 42.

17. *Ibid.*, 42.

18. *Ibid.*, 38.

19. *Ibid.*, 199.

20. Layton, *And I Was There*, 339.

21. Toland, *Infamy*, 85.

22. *Ibid.*, 85.

23. *Ibid.*, 85–86.

24. *Ibid.*, 75.

25. Kimmel, *Admiral Kimmel's Story*, 164.

26. *Ibid.*, 162–163.

27. *Ibid.*, 163–164.

28. Joint Committee on the Investigation of the Pearl Harbor Attack, *Investigation of the Pearl Harbor Attack*, Part 39, 24.

29. Layton, *And I Was There*, 514.

30. *Ibid.*, 514.

31. Toland, *Infamy*, 111.

32. *Ibid.*, 113–114.

33. *Ibid.*, 133.

34. *Ibid.*, 129.

35. *Ibid.*, 139.

36. *Ibid.*, 140.

37. *Ibid.*, 140.

38. *Ibid.*, 153.

39. Kimmel, *Admiral Kimmel's Story*, 56–57.

40. Toland, *Infamy*, 193–194.

41. Joint Committee on the Investigation of the Pearl Harbor Attack, *Investigation of the Pearl Harbor Attack*, 1942.

42. *Ibid.*, 570.

43. Toland, *Infamy*, 244.

44. *Ibid.*, 254.

45. Jim Warren, "$500,000 From Philippine Leader May Have Influenced MacArthur" (*The Ledger*, January 30, 1980), 12-A.

46. Connaughton, *MacArthur and Defeat in the Philippines*, 218.

Bibliography

Books

Arakaki, Leatrice R., and John R. Kuborn. *7 December 1941: The Air Force Story.* Washington, D.C.: U.S. Government Printing Office, 1991.

Bachrach, Deborah. *Pearl Harbor: Great Mysteries, Opposing Viewpoints.* San Diego: Greenhaven Press, 1989.

Bartsch, William. *December 8, 1941: MacArthur's Pearl Harbor.* College Station: Texas A&M University Press, 2003.

Beard, Charles A. *President Roosevelt and the Coming of the War 1941: A Study in Appearances and Realities.* New Haven, CT: Yale University Press, 1948.

Berg, A. Scott. *Lindbergh.* New York: Berkley, 1999.

Black, Conrad. *Franklin Delano Roosevelt: Champion of Freedom.* New York: PublicAffairs, 2003.

Brands, H.W. *Traitor to His Class: The Privileged Life and Radical Presidency of Franklin Delano Roosevelt.* New York: Anchor Books, 2008.

Brereton, Lewis H. *The Brereton Diaries: The War in the Pacific, Middle East and Europe, October 3, 1941 to May 8, 1945.* New York: William Morrow, 1946.

Chang, Iris. *The Rape of Nanking: The Forgotten Holocaust of World War II.* New York: Basic Books, 1997.

Connaughton, Richard. *MacArthur and Defeat in the Philippines.* New York: Overlook Press, 2001.

Costello, John. *Days of Infamy: MacArthur, Roosevelt, Churchill—The Shocking Truth Revealed.* New York: Pocket Books, 1994.

Cressman, Robert J., and J. Michael Wenger. *Steady Nerves and Stout Hearts: The Enterprise (CV6) Air Group and Pearl Harbor, 7 December 1941.* Missoula, MT: Pictorial Histories, 1990.

Cull, Brian. *Buffaloes Over Singapore: RAF, RAAF, RNZAF and Dutch Brewster Fighters in Action Over Malaya and the East Indies 1941–42.* London: Grub Street, 2003.

Department of Defense, United States of America. *The "Magic" Background of Pearl Harbor,* vols. 1, 3, 4, 5, and vol. 4 Appendix. Washington, D.C.: U.S. Government Printing Office, 1977.

Department of the Army. *American Military History 1607–1958.* Washington, D.C.: U.S. Government Printing Office, 1959.

Douglas, Gregory. *The Interrogation of Heinrich Muller,* vol. 1. San Jose, California: James Bender, 1999.

Duffy, James P. *Lindbergh vs. Roosevelt: The Rivalry That Divided America.* New York: MJF Books, 2010.

Edmonds, Walter D. *They Fought with What They Had: The Story of the Army Air Force in the Southwest Pacific, 1941–1942.* Washington, D.C.: Zenger, 1982.

Flynn, John. *The Final Secret of Pearl Harbor.* Published privately, 1945.

Greenfield, Kent Roberts, ed. *Command Decisions.* Washington, D.C.: Center of Military History, 2000.

Hill, Jim Dan. *The Minute Man in Peace and War: A History of the National Guard.* Harrisburg, PA: Stackpole, 1964.

Holley, Irving Brinton, Jr. *Buying Aircraft: Materiel Procurement for the Army Air Forces (U.S. Army in World War II, Special Studies).* Washington, D.C.: Department of the Army, 1964.

Jasper, Joy Waldron, James P. Delgado, and Jim Adams. *The USS Arizona: The Ship, the Men, the Pearl Harbor Attack, and the Symbol That Aroused America.* New York: St. Martin's Press, 2001.

Kimmel, Husband E. *Admiral Kimmel's Story.* Chicago: Henry Regnery, 1955.

Lambert, John W. *The Long Campaign: The History of the 15th Fighter Group in World War II.* Manhattan, KS: Sunflower University Press, 1982.

Layton, Edwin T. *And I Was There: Pearl Harbor and Midway—Breaking the Secrets*. New York: William Morrow, 1985.

Leasor, James. *Singapore: The Battle That Changed the World*. Garden City, NY: Doubleday, 1968.

McComas, Terence. *Pearl Harbor: Fact and Reference Book, Everything to Know About December 7, 1941*. Honolulu: Mutual Publishing, 1991.

Millis, Walter. *This Is Pearl! The United States and Japan—1941*. New York: William Morrow, 1947.

Mollo, Andrew. *The Armed Forces of World War II: Uniforms, Insignia, and Organization*. New York: Military Press, 1987.

Morison, Samuel Eliot. *The Rising Sun in the Pacific, 1931–April 1942: History of United States Naval Operations in World War II*, vol. 3. Edison, NJ: Castle Books, 2001.

Morton, Louis. *The Fall of the Philippines (United States Army in World War II, The War in the Pacific)*. Washington, D.C.: Center of Military History, 1985.

Mosley, Leonard. *Marshall: Hero for Our Times*. New York: Hearst Books, 1982.

Olson, Lynne. *Those Angry Days: Roosevelt, Lindbergh, and America's Fight Over World War II*. New York: Random House, 2013.

Parrish, Thomas, ed. *The Simon and Schuster Encyclopedia of World War II*. New York: Simon & Schuster, 1978.

Prange, Gordon. *At Dawn We Slept: The Untold Story of Pearl Harbor*. New York: McGraw-Hill, 1981.

Puleston, W.D. *The Armed Forces of the Pacific*. New Haven, CT: Yale University Press, 1941.

Schultz, Duane. *Hero of Bataan: The Story of General Jonathan M. Wainwright*. New York: St. Martin's Press, 1981.

Smith, Carl. *Pearl Harbor*. Oxford: Osprey, 2001.

Smith, George W. *MacArthur's Escape: John "Wild Man" Bulkeley and the Rescue of an American Hero*. St. Paul, Minnesota: MBI, 2005.

Sommerville, Donald. *World War II: Day by Day—An Illustrated Almanac 1939–1945*. Greenwich, CT: Dorset Press, 1991.

Stinnett, Robert B. *Day of Deceit*. New York: Free Press, 2000.

Theobald, Robert A. *The Final Secret of Pearl Harbor*. New York: Devin-Adair, 1954.

Toland, John. *Infamy: Pearl Harbor and Its Aftermath*. New York: Berkley, 1983.

Tolley, Kemp. *The Cruise of the* Lanikai: *Incitement to War*. Annapolis, Maryland: Naval Institute Press, 1973.

Truman, Harry S. *Memoirs by Harry S. Truman: Year of Decisions*, vol. 1. Garden City, NY: Doubleday, 1955.

Tuchman, Barbara W. *Stilwell and the American Experience in China, 1911–45*. New York: Macmillan, 1970.

Wheal, Elizabeth-Anne, Stephen Pope, and James Taylor. *The Meridian Encyclopedia of the Second World War*. New York: Penguin Books USA Inc., 1992.

Government Documents

Dorn, Edwin. *Advancement of Rear Admiral Kimmel and Major General Short on the Retired List*. Washington, D.C.: Undersecretary of Defense, 1995.

Jackson, Robert H. *Opinion on Exchange of Over-Age Destroyers for Naval and Air Bases*. Washington, D.C.: Office of the Attorney General, 1940.

Joint Committee on the Investigation of the Pearl Harbor Attack, Congress of the United States. *Investigation of the Pearl Harbor Attack*. Washington, D.C.: United States Government Printing Office, 1946.

Knox, Frank. *Annual Report of the Secretary of the Navy for the Fiscal Year 1941*. Washington, D.C.: U.S. Government Printing Office, 1941.

Nye, Joseph P. *Can the United States Be Neutral?—Yes; If It Minds Its Own Business*. 76th Cong., 1 sess. CR, 84, pt. 14 (18 July 1939): Apex. 3327–3328.

Roberts Commission. *Attack Upon Pearl Harbor by Japanese Armed Forces*. Washington, D.C.: United States Senate, 1942.

United States Department of State, Publication 1983. *Peace and War: United States Foreign Policy, 1931–1941*. Washington, D.C.: U.S. Government Printing Office, 1943.

Articles

"The Library." *Flying Magazine* 44, vol. 1 (January 1949): p. 58.

"Roll of Honor." *Life Magazine* 12, vol. 16 (1942): p. 79.

Vandercook, John W. "America's Gibraltar of the Pacific." *Liberty Magazine* (December 27, 1941): pp. 10–11, 57.

Warren, Jim. "$500,000 From Philippine Leader May Have Influenced MacArthur." *The Ledger*, January 30, 1980, p. 12A.

Speeches

Fish, Hamilton. "We Should Not Convoy Materials to Europe: Convoys Mean Shooting and Shooting Means War." Washington, D.C.: American Forum of the Air, March 30, 1941.

Lindbergh, Charles. "Address to the America First Committee." New York City, April 23, 1941.

Martin, Joseph W., Jr. "The Country Needs a Strong Opposition Party: We Must Preserve the American Way of Consideration." Columbia Broadcasting System, April 3, 1941.

Roosevelt, Franklin Delano. "Arsenal of Democracy." Washington, D.C., Fireside Chat, December 29, 1940.

_____. "Freedom of the Seas." Washington, D.C., Fireside Chat, September 11, 1941.

_____. "Navy and Total Defense Day." Washington, D.C., Radio Address, October 27, 1941.

_____. "Unlimited National Emergency." Washington, D.C., Radio Address, May 27, 1941.

_____. "We Are Not Yielding and We Do Not Propose to Yield." Address to Congress, June 20, 1941.

Taft, Robert A. "Bureaucratic Confusion at Washington: Fighting for Democracy Abroad While It Wilts at Home." Washington, D.C.: Columbia Broadcasting System, May 2, 1941.

Suggested Reading

Bartsch, William H. *Doomed at the Start: American Pursuit Pilots in the Philippines 1941–1942*. College Station: Texas A&M University Press, 1992.

Beach, Edward L., Jr. *Scapegoats: A Defense of Kimmel and Short at Pearl Harbor*. Annapolis, MD: Naval Institute Press, 1995.

Cannon, M. Hamlin. *United States Army in World War II, The War in the Pacific, Leyte: The Return to the Philippines*. Washington, D.C.: Office of the Chief of Military History, 1954.

Casey, William. *The Secret War Against Hitler*. New York: Regnery Gateway, 1988.

Devlin, Gerard M. *Silent Wings: The Saga of the U.S. Army and Marine Combat Glider Pilots During World War II*. New York: St. Martin's Press, 1985.

Gannon, Michael. *Pearl Harbor Betrayed: The True Story of a Man and a Nation Under Attack*. New York: Henry Holt, 2001.

Michno, Gregory F. *Death on the Hellships: Prisoners at Sea in the Pacific War*. Annapolis, MD: Naval Institute Press, 2000.

Morison, Samuel Eliot. *The Battle of the Atlantic, September 1939–1943: History of United States Naval Operations in World War II*, vol. 1. Edison, NJ: Castle Books, 1948.

_____. *The Two-Ocean War: A Short History of the United States Navy in the Second World War*. Boston: Little, Brown, 1963.

Richardson, David. C. "Pearl Harbor: What Really Happened." *American Heritage* (July–August 2001): 50–57.

Rusbridger, James, and Eric Nave. *Betrayal at Pearl Harbor: How Churchill Lured Roosevelt into World War II*. New York: Summit Books, 1991.

Tillman, Barrett. "Pearl Harbor: The Sleeping Giant Awakens." *Flight* (June 2001): 36–43.

Index

A6M, Mitsubishi Zero fighter 10, 154
ABCD powers 108–9, 131, 136
ABDA Command 26
Abwehr Dienst 94–95
Acheson, Dean 91
Air Mail Scandal 67
Air War Plans Division 22
Akagi, carrier 9, 104, 109, 180
Alamo 177
Alaska 36, 39
Albania 85
alert system, Pearl Harbor 12–14, 57–58, 118–19, 140, 149, 183, 188–89
Aleutians 180
USS *Allen*, destroyer 152
Allen, Bruce 146
Alley, Norman 33
ambassadors, Japanese 106–9, 111, 114–16, 118, 121, 123, 132–34, 138, 143, 148; *see also* Kurusu, Saburo; Nomura, Kichisaburo
America First Committee 36, 67–68, 72, 81, 105, 130
American Civil Liberties Union 158
American Federation of Labor 56
American Red Cross 90
Anderson, Walter Stratton 41, 45–47, 151
Andrews, Adolphus 189
USS *Antares*, cargo ship 10, 14, 153
Anti-Comintern Pact 31, 88, 106, 175
USS *Arizona*, battleship 46, 149, 159, 162, 166
HMS *Ark Royal*, carrier 135
army intelligence 13, 41, 96, 103, 191; *see also* Army Signal Intelligence Service; G-2; Military Intelligence Division
Army Pearl Harbor Board 48,

188–91, 197; *see also* investigations
Army Signal Intelligence Service 40–41, 137, 143, 152, 168; *see also* army intelligence; G-2; Military Intelligence Division
Arnold, Henry "Hap" 11, 50, 58, 117, 128–29, 148, 170, 172–73, 179
Associated Press 74
Atlantic Charter 93, 98; conference 93
Atlantic Fleet 47, 61, 77, 80, 183, 186, 195
Atlantis, cruiser 43
Attack Upon Pearl Harbor by Japanese Armed Forces 12
Australia 26, 42, 58, 110, 131, 173, 175, 177–80
Austria 90
SS *Automedon*, passenger and cargo steamer 43–44
Azores 77, 93

B5N, Nakajima Kate torpedo bomber 10, 154–55, 157, 159, 164–65
B-10, Martin bomber 22–23
B-17, Boeing heavy bomber 10, 27, 29, 50–51, 57, 60, 93, 98, 119, 123, 125, 127, 131–32, 134–35, 140, 146–49, 156, 159–60, 170–73, 178–79
B-18, Douglas bomber 23–24, 49, 52, 57, 60, 140–41, 149
B-24, Consolidated heavy bomber 54, 117, 141, 149
Baguio 171
Bahamas 40
Baltic 34, 86
Bandoeng 137
Bangkok 130, 138–39
Barbers Point 157, 159
Barkley, Alben 66, 72–73
barrage balloons 51, 55, 128

Barthelmess, Karl 146
Bataan 8, 21, 174–78, 198; Battle of 176
Batavia 89–90, 134, 137
Battle of Bataan 176
Battle of Britain 25, 43, 51, 62
Battle of Coral Sea 12, 154
Battle of Midway 12, 113, 155, 180, 187
Battle of Rabaul 179
Battle of Rennell Island 102
Battle of Santa Cruz 155
Battleship Row 149, 162
Beardall, John 145–46, 150
Beebe, Lewis 178
Belgium 30, 62, 104
Bellinger, Patrick 29, 46, 48–49, 57, 59, 61, 139, 162
Bellows Airfield 10, 14, 119, 139–40, 149, 159–61, 163
USS *Benham*, destroyer 72
Bergquist, Kenneth 128
Berlin 37, 43, 79, 88–89, 94, 96, 106, 122, 130, 168; *see also* Germany; Hitler, Adolf
Bermuda 40
Bicknell, George 149
Bishop, Max 53
Bishop, Samuel 163
Bishop Point Relay Station 10
Bissell, John 192
Bletchley Park 41–42
Bloch, Claude C. 48–49, 120, 138, 141, 153, 157–58
Bloom, Sol 74
Bode, Howard 102
bomb plot 101–104, 134, 138–39, 194, 196–97; *see also* intelligence; Magic
Bond, James 95
Bonus March 18, 31
Borneo 26, 120
Bostrom, Frank 146, 159
Boxer Protocol of 1901 116
Brandon, Harry 146

211